Camera Indica:
The Social Life of Indian Photographs

ENVISIONING ASIA

Series Editors: Homi Bhabha, Norman Bryson, Wu Hung

In the same series

Fruitful Sites
Garden Culture in Ming Dynasty China
Craig Clunas

CAMERA INDICA

The Social Life of Indian Photographs

CHRISTOPHER PINNEY

REAKTION BOOKS

To Trudi with love

Published by Reaktion Books Ltd
11 Rathbone Place, London WIP IDE, UK

First published in 1997

Designed by Ron Costley
Printed and bound by BAS Printers Ltd
Over Wallop, Hants

British Library Cataloguing in Publication Data:
Pinney, Christopher
Camera Indica : the social life of Indian photographs. —
(Envisioning Asia)
1.Photography – India 2.Photography – India – History
3.India – Social conditions – Pictorial works
I.Title
770.9′54
ISBN 1 86189 006 0

Contents

Acknowledgements

I have many debts in Bhatisuda and Nagda. For sharing their photographs and thoughts about photographs I must thank Vijay Vyas, Suresh Panjabi, Nanda Kishor Joshi, Babulal Bohra, Manoj and Dinesh Khandelwal, Manoj Jha, Kailash, Pukhraj and Pritibala, Bihari, Ramlal, Lakshman, Kanvarlal, Govardhanlal, Manoharlal, Prakash, Ishvar, Pannalal, Ramchandra and many others. Other individuals in India who have helped in a variety of generous ways include R.P. Gupta, E. Alkazi, Foy Nissen, Satish Sharma, Vinay Srivastava, Ashis Nandy, Patricia Uberoi, Annandalalji Narottam and Ravi Agrawal.

More general debts include those to Roslyn Poignant and David Mac-Dougall for making me see that photographs were worthy objects of anthropological inquiry; to the late Alfred Gell for encouraging me to wander from the straight and narrow; to Barney Cohn and John Falconer for their inspiring work on early Indian anthropology and photography; to Rachel Dwyer for sharing her remarkable knowledge of South Asia; to Simeran Man Singh Gell, Bhaskar Mukhopadhyay, and Chris Wright for inspiration and advice; to McKim Marriott for insights I hope to address next time; to Homi Bhabha for suggesting in the first place that I write a book like this and for his continuous encouragement to think about a new kind of anthropology.

My research on nineteenth-century photography was made possible by a Smuts Research Fellowship at the Centre of South Asian Studies, University of Cambridge between 1987 and 1989, and much of my work in Nagda and Bhatisuda has been funded since 1989 by the School of Oriental and African Studies, the British Academy, and the Nuffield Foundation.

Individuals and employees of the following institutions must also be thanked: Manjiri Telang and Meenal Paranjpe, Dr Bhau Daji Lad Museum, Bombay; Ramesh Jamindar, Asiatic Society, Bombay; Y. S. Chaddha, Indian Art Studio, Bombay; Mr Yogendra Sahai, Sawai Man Singh II Museum, City Palace, Jaipur; Suresh Chabria, National Film Archive of India, Pune; Mr Sharma and A. K. Avasthi, Photographic Section, Nehru Memorial Library, Delhi; Indore State Museum; Prabas Chand of Ami Chand and Sons, Secunderabad; Salar Jang Museum, Hyderabad; National Library, Calcutta; Asiatic Society of Bengal, Calcutta; Chris Wright, Royal Anthropological Institute; staff of the India Office Library and Records, London; staff of the library of the School of Oriental and African Studies, London; Anita Herle, University Museum of Archaeology and Anthropology, Cambridge; Elizabeth Edwards, Pitt Rivers Museum, Oxford; Harry Persaud, Museum of Mankind, London; Terry Barringer, Royal Commonwealth Society; Lionel Carter, Centre of South Asian Studies, Cambridge. For his expert re-photography I must thank Paul Fox.

Note on Transliteration

In the interests of accessibility I have omitted all diacritical marks
and have added an English 's' to make plurals where appropriate.
I apologize to Indian readers. 'Sh' is used for ś and ṣ; and 'chh' for
aspirated 'ch'. I have forsaken consistency where this would
conflict with commonly used forms. The Glossary includes full
transliterations of standard Hindi words.

Preface

My title, *Camera Indica*, is among other things an allusion to *Camera Lucida*, the English-language translation of Roland Barthes's *La Chambre Claire*,[1] which plays an important role in the latter part of this book. However, while acknowledging my debt to a key work on photography, I have also tried to extend Barthes's concerns into an ethnographic realm where what matters is not the personal and private readings of the analyst but photography's impact on the everyday life of a society. This explains my attention to the social practices in which photography is embedded and my attempt to elucidate the perspectives of photographers and their clients on the images reproduced in this book.

Mine is only a partial deference to the canon of writing on photography, though, and there is a twist in the title. At the very moment of genuflection, I also want to move away from the insular security of the Euro-American cultural region – the ground upon which nearly all work on photography has been built. But this twist, created by my hybrid title with its botanical reference to the place that concerns me most, India, runs the risk of being mistaken for an attempt at taxonomy, a closed system of categories wrapped up in the guise of changing practice. This is decidely not my intention, for what I in fact try to chart in the following pages are some aspects of the complex changing ecology of photography.

Two experiences contributed to the line of reasoning pursued in this book and are worth briefly mentioning. When I first started doing fieldwork in 1982 in Bhatisuda, a village in central India, I found myself taking what I perceived to be two different types of photographs: ones for myself and ones for villagers. The photographs I wanted to take at that time were, I thought, candid, revealing, expressive of the people I was living among. I was pursuing the quotidian shadow of what Plutarch once powerfully described as 'the signs of the soul in men'.[2] I recall taking a half-length image of my neighbour Bherulal which seemed to have some of these qualities. We had gone to his fields by his well at around 5 p.m., a good time to capture the effect of the mellowing sun. The print, which I had processed and sent back from the UK, seemed to perfectly capture his mischievous character. There was a twinkle in his eye and the slight shadow that hung on one side of his face gave him an appropriate gravity, for he was an essentially serious, indeed tortured man. His pursed mouth and upright posture also seemed to capture his attempt to impose some order, if only for a moment, as he was always muttering in exasperation. There was a mellowness about the image, a homology between the lengthening shadows at this peaceful time of day and Bherulal's attempt to find tranquillity, that I particularly liked. But it did not appeal to Bherulal, who, when he saw the print, complained about the shadow and the darkness it cast over his face and the absence of the lower half of his body. The image was of no use to him and, slightly shaken, I promised that I would soon take a better, more appropriate, one.

I was to be reminded of Bherulal's irritation at his incomplete capture when, several years later, I listened to professional studio photographers in the nearby town of Nagda joking that village clients would refuse to pay the full fee for anything other than a full-length portrait. 'I will only give you a quarter of the fee,' they would say (or so the photographers claimed), 'because only a quarter of me has come out', or, 'I will only pay half, for half a pose.'

The photographs that villagers wanted me to take were very different from the one I took of Bherulal. These could not be taken quickly since there were lengthy preparations to be made: clothes to be changed, hair to be brushed and oiled (and, in the case of upper-caste women, the application of talcum powder to lighten the skin). These photos had to be full-length and symmetrical, and the passive, expressionless faces and body poses symbolized for me, at that time, the extinguishing of precisely that quality I wished to capture on film.

The second experience was the discovery of a photograph album compiled by my grandfather while a British soldier in India during the Second World War. Amid the depictions of street-traders, ascetics ('acrobat – Calcutta'), army motorbikes and snake-charmers ('snakes alive!') was an image of a ploughman silhouetted against the sinking sun. How evocative of Bhatisuda, I thought. On the reverse, in spidery blue writing and next to a stamp which said 'De Silva's Studio, Jhansi and Lucknow', were the words 'this picture *is* India'. I was struck by the similarities of this image to some of Peter H. Emerson's photographic heroicizations of 1880s East Anglian agriculturalists and pondered on how the essentialization of such images of rural India, filtered from John Ruskin and William Morris by way of George Birdwood, John Lockwood Kipling and Mahatma Gandhi,[3] reflected a similar complex process of cultural coming and going, rather like the Venetian trade beads once exported from Italy to Africa and now, several centuries later, re-exported to Europe and America as signs of an ancient exotic Africa.[4] Although in Bhatisuda I had been asked by several *halis* (ploughmen) to photograph them at work and was later to encounter several locally produced photographs taken during the festival of Divali in which villagers posed with their bulls, Bherulal's complaints about the degree of shadow would have been as nothing compared to the outrage which the radical contrasts of a De Silva's Studio photograph would have provoked. In that image all signs of the individual ploughman were effaced and he was rendered as a simple emblem of noble rustic labour.

This book is an attempt to consider questions such as the relationship between photographic and a wider cultural practice, the different kinds of work that the 'face' and the 'body' are required to do within different photographic traditions, the different ways in which photography comes to be privileged as evidence of internal and external states, and how the particular visual reality associated with particular places comes to be so constituted. These are vast topics and I am able only to skate over many aspects of them. However, by focusing on three 'moments' in the public photographic representation of the face and the body in India I aim to suggest, through the deployment of these various fragments, something of the complex social life of photography.

In the words of Arjun Appadurai, I want to follow the 'concrete historical circulation' of images and trace the 'meanings . . . inscribed in their forms, their uses, their trajectories'.[5] If photographs are indeed usually made into something more than mere 'chemically discoloured paper',[6] what are the forces that construct them into this, rather than that, and how does this change through time, through political position, through 'culture', through class? How do photographs get 'entangled'[7] in different systems?

Prologue

. . . even when the production of the picture is entirely delivered over to the automatism of the camera, the taking of the picture is still a choice involving aesthetic and ethical values: if, in the abstract, the nature and development of photographic technology tend to make everything objectively 'photographable', it is still true that, from among the theoretically infinite number of photographs which are technically possible, each group chooses a finite and well-defined range of subjects, genres and compositions.[1]

The industrial town of Nagda is exactly half-way between Bombay and Delhi. A journey of about twelve hours by Frontier Mail or Dehra Dun Express brings the traveller to this sprawling settlement centred around a vast textile and chemical plant on the banks of the River Chambal. Parallel to the railway line runs Jawahar Marg, the largest commercial street, off which Nagda's main bazaar can be found. Near the railway station are older houses and shops dating from Nagda's pre-industrial existence in the 1950s, and as one walks further east, past vegetable stalls, tea shops and those selling bicycles, irrigation pumps and car parts, one passes various photographers' premises. First is the Venus Studio, outside which stands a woman in a tennis skirt holding a box of Konica film, and further along this same road, on the other side, sandwiched between a stationer's and a *khadi* (homespun textile) retailer, is the small shop front of Suresh Panjabi, the proprietor of Suhag Studio.

Like most of the six main studios in Nagda, Suhag Studio displays a mixture of their own work and publicity shots distributed by local colour-processing studios, which are located in the nearby cities of Ujjain and Indore. By the side of and behind the low white formica desk at the front of the shop advertisements for Midas Color Studio leap at the viewer. The same model appears in two images clutching a *matka* (earthenware water pot) of the sort which is still widely used throughout village India (illus. 1). In both images the model leans against the pot, her hands emphasizing the homology between the curves of the pot and her own form in such a way that eroticism and fecundity are also suggested. But the two elements of the picture are potent signifiers of the rural and of tradition as well. Throughout India's collision with colonialism, woman as a figure has been continually reinvented as a repository of an interior, purer and more

1 Colour publicity photograph issued by Midas Color Studio.

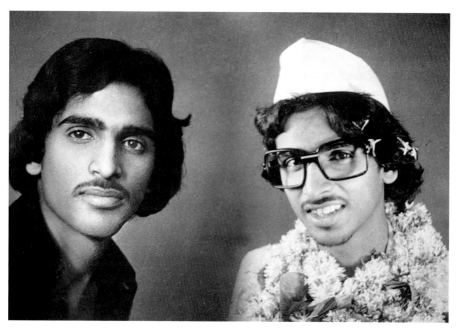

2 Composite print by Suhag Studio, *c.* 1980.

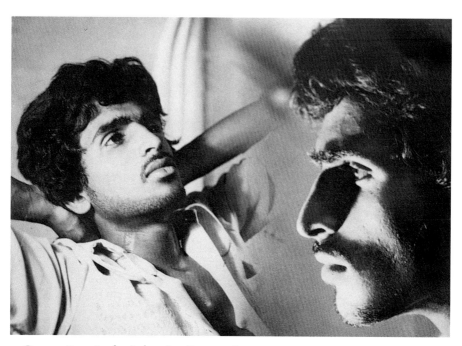

3 Composite print by Suhag Studio, *c.* 1980.

valuable tradition that stood opposed to the moral compromises and degradation of rule by foreigners.[2] During the nationalist struggle, partly through Gandhi's appropriation of the pastoral ideology of Thoreau and Ruskin, the village came to serve as a parallel resource, signifying simplicity and truthfulness. The Midas Color Studio advertisment reflects some of this history but is also informed by the continuing popularity in Hindi film of the erotic village belle who legitimates a normally forbidden sexuality by locating it in the realm of the pure and authentic.

Suresh, an urbane and sensitive man, then pulls from his files some striking images that date from the late 1970s. Many of these are double images produced by masking a section of the print while overprinting with two negatives. In all of these the same faces appear, but with different masks. In one, on the left of the picture, the sitter gazes just to the left of the camera's focus, producing the abstracted and intent look that this photographer always sought in my portraiture sessions with him. On the right of the same image, he adopts the mask of a fêted Congress politician, having donned a *kangressi topi* (a small white hat of the sort popularized by Mahatma Gandhi), glasses (a prop connoting intellectualism) and a garland of marigolds (illus. 2). In other images the doubling is less complex: one depicts the subject in two 'poetic' poses of the sort which Nagdarites would immediately associate with the figure of the poet dramatized – to much popular acclaim – by the leading actor Amitabh Bachchan in the 1975 Hindi film *Kabhi Kabhie* (illus. 3). On the left, a low camera angle empathizes with the sitter's transcendental gaze, and on the right a stark forward light casts a dramatic shadow, giving an urgency and angularity to his deliberations on the state of the world.

Beckoned inside, through a hardboard partition and stepping gingerly over trailing electric light cables, we follow Suresh into his studio. In front of us is a wall covered by a red curtain, to the side of which is a small table on which sit a television and a telephone. Beside this is a wire chair which has been appearing in his photographs (especially those of young children) for the last twenty years. To the left is a wall covered from floor to ceiling with a huge poster image of a garden, whose neo-classical temples are reminiscent of Stourhead in Wiltshire but whose vegetation is most definitely tropical. On the wall facing this is a similar-sized poster depicting an ornate residential dwelling. Constructed of timber and glass and topped with fine terracotta tiles, it stands by a lake in the midst of numerous calla lilies. It is more suggestive of Malaysia than India but is a clear sign of luxury, radically unlike any building in Nagda or any of the surrounding villages. Suresh then pulls back the red curtain revealing the *pièce de résistance* in this chamber of dreams. The great expanse of Dal Lake in Kashmir is laid open, shimmering beneath cascading pine-encrusted mountains, illuminated by efflorescent skies, and all offset by a foreground luxuriating in multicoloured meadow flowers. Dal Lake – for long a perennial location of dance sequences in Hindi movies – will figure again in this account, for many Nagda photographic studios maintain similar painted backdrops. We will also encounter many more images from the magical lenses of Suhag Studio.

This brief introduction to contemporary popular photography will have served, I hope, to establish the vitality and potency of the local space that photography occupies. It is a place where faces can easily become masks and where photography is translated as a complex theatrical idiom capable of representing persons with endlessly diverse exteriors, situated in equally diverse places.

However, if contemporary Nagda photography is predominantly a space of pleasure and of a form of dramatic invention that seeks to push against the limits of the known world, much of the earlier photographic practice in India approached its subjects with an infinitely more troubled and anxious air. It is this period of anxiety which forms the subject of the first chapter.

Des.ᵈ & Lithᵈ by L. Haghe

4 Frontispiece to *A Description of a Singular Aboriginal Race Inhabiting the Summit of the Neilgherry Hills* by Henry Harkness, 1832.

1 'Stern Fidelity' and 'Penetrating Certainty'

Photography as such has no identity. Its status as a technology varies with the power relations which invest it. Its nature as a practice depends on the institutions and agents which define it and set it to work. Its function as a mode of cultural production is tied to definite conditions of existence, and its products are meaningful and legible only within the particular currencies they have. Its history has no unity. It is a flickering across a field of institutional spaces. It is this field we must study, not photography as such.[1]

Photography was first used in India in 1840, a few months after its development had been announced in Europe. As early as January 1840, Thacker, Spink and Co. of Calcutta advertised imported daguerreotype cameras in the daily *Friend of India*.[2] The earliest known image is a daguerreotype of the Sans Souci Theatre in Calcutta and in 1841 the Bengali paper *Sambad Bhaskar* was advertising the willingness of an English resident of Armani Bazaar to make daguerreotype likenesses.[3]

Photography was taken up with alacrity by amateurs, aspirant professionals, individuals with 'scientific' agendas and, within two decades, by the apparatus of the colonial state. This new technology entered a space in which the visual already had a clearly articulated role. Many commentators have noted the pre-eminent role that visuality has assumed within modern disciplinary societies, and colonies were frequently the testing grounds for new techniques of visual control.[4] However, in India specific arguments were made about the particular value of visual signs in a place where other signs were deemed to be unreliable, mysterious and deceptive. In this spirit John William Kaye observed in the preface to the artist William Simpson's portfolio of lithographs, *India, Ancient and Modern* (1862) that:

To represent India by mere word-painting is an almost impossible task. The most graphic writing falls far short of the mark of faithful description. Only a vague, unsatisfactory idea of the objects, represented by the printed page, is left on the reader's mind . . . It is only by the great exponents, form and colour, appealing to the fleshly eye, that truthful impressions can be derived of a country, which differs so essentially from all that is made known to us by the teachings of European experience. The pen may do much to assist the successes of the pencil; but without the pencil the efforts of the pen, when objective description is aimed at, must be feeble and insufficient.[5]

Both before and after photography, however, the 'efforts of the pen' were frequently criticized for their deviation from what they represented. Pre-photographic representations always depended on the trustworthiness of the author/artist and many early volumes of lithographs included assurances of the closeness of fit between the image and the reality. Introducing his *Scenery, Costume and Architecture, Chiefly on the Western Side of India* (1830), Captain Robert Melville Grindlay assured the reader/viewer, 'The author pledges himself to the fidelity of the repesentations.'[6] A few years later a warning was issued in G. F. White's *Views in India, Chiefly Among the Himalaya Mountains* (1836), which included engravings by Turner based on White's sketches, that 'in order to render them valuable as works of art, truth of representation should not be sacrificed to mere embellishment'.

The illustrations to Joseph Dalton Hooker's *Himalayan Journals* (1854) were to be roundly condemned by W. T. Blandford in 1871 because they did 'not convey by any means a correct impression; like most lithographs of foreign scenes printed in England the characteristic features are lost . . . everything is Europeanized'.[7] The same complaint of Europeanization was also levelled at representations of India's peoples. Captain Henry Harkness's 1832 study of the Todas, *A Description of a Singular Aboriginal Race Inhabiting the Summit of the Neilgherry Hills, or the Blue Mountains of Coimbatoor in the Southern Peninsula of India*, was one of the earliest book-length studies of an Indian community with recognizably 'anthropological' concerns. Harkness claimed to have read much in the Todas' faces, for they had 'open and expressive countenances' and 'a large, full and speaking eye'.[8] What was most remarkable about the book perhaps was its striking frontispiece (illus. 4), which, as one much later commentator observed, represented a Toda family in 'a manner suggestive of a Jewish patriarchal family'.[9] The origins of the Todas had been the subject of much speculation from the start of the nineteenth century, with theories advanced of 'God's ancient people' and marooned Roman colonies. Harkness was equally intrigued. The 'efforts of the pen' created a space in which the romantic imagination of the artist could intervene in very direct ways. Clearly intervention continued to be possible during the creation and printing of photographic negatives, but it was intervention of a different order. So, if on these grounds one might wish to dispute William Ivins's claim that the problems associated with the visual syntax ('the lines, flicks and dots that formed the convention for reproduction'[10]) in lithography and engraving disappeared entirely with the advent of photography, Ivins is clearly correct to signal the acuteness of this problem prior to the

THE Saturday Magazine.

N⁰. 629.   APRIL   23ᴿᴰ, 1842.   { PRICE { ONE PENNY.

THE NEILGHERRY HILLS, AND THEIR INHABITANTS. II.

A TUDAR FAMILY IN THE NEILGHERRIES.

WHEN the Tudars of the Neilgherries are spoken of as a tribe possessing characteristics superior to those of the surrounding natives, it must be remarked that this applies to a certain degree of natural intelligence, capable, if well directed, of raising them to a respectable footing in the social scale. Practically speaking, their lives present much that we must lament.

Captain Harkness, after several unsuccessful attempts to discover their religious notions, contrived to gain admission to one of their temples. This temple was in a morrt or family village, at some distance from the inhabited huts; and on opening the door, he found the interior to be divided into two apartments by a partitioned wall. The outer apartment was about ten feet by eight, but only of sufficient height in the centre to stand upright; on two sides were raised benches, a foot and a half from the ground, intended to recline or sleep on; and in the middle a large hearth or fire-place, surrounded by a number of earthen pots, and other utensils. The door-way in the partition-wall being much smaller than the outer one, it could only be entered by a person lying nearly flat on the ground. This apartment was furnished with earthen vessels the same as the outer one; and it became evident to Captain Harkness that these vessels were the same as those used in the dairy, and that no idols or images were in the room. On mentioning his surmises to the Tudars, they frankly told him that theirs was little more than an affectation of a worship resembling that of their neighbours; by which they were enabled to keep on good terms with them. There is, certainly, nothing to regret in the circumstance that these Tudars are *not* Hindoos or Buddhists; but on the other hand there is not the consolation of thinking that they profess a purer faith. The only points which Captain Harkness could at all ascertain were, that they salute the sun at his rising; that they expect to go to a country called Huma-norr after death; and that the dairy, with all its contents, is looked upon as a sacred spot, which the men can only enter after having performed certain ablutions.

We must now direct a little attention to the *Badacars*, the most numerous of the Neilgherry tribes, but of far different character from the Tudars. The latter assert

5   Woodcut in *The Saturday Magazine.*

19

dissemination of photographic reproductions. Lithographic reproductions and engravings tended to increasingly mutate as they were successively copied. Harkness's frontispiece was the basis for a woodcut published in the Society for Promoting Christian Knowledge's *Saturday Magazine* in 1842[11] and the process of copying here involved the imposition of a new 'syntax', a further set of conventionalized constraints (illus. 5).

Photography required no such testimony, for it combined both the privileging of the visual and the indexical yearning[12] for what the Reverend Joseph Mullins, in an address to the Photographic Society of Bengal, described as 'stern fidelity'.[13] This stern fidelity was later theorized by C. S. Peirce in terms of a photograph's 'indexicality'. Peirce identified three types of signs: symbols, icons and indexes. Symbols were arbitrary and conventional – this is how we understand most linguistic signifiers since Saussure. Iconic signs are those that have a relationship of resemblance to their referents (such as painting and, some would claim, onomatopoeic sounds). Those signs are indexical which have some natural relationship of contiguity with their referent. Thus smoke is an index of fire; and photographs, as well as almost always being iconic, are also indexical. They are iconic because they resemble whatever was originally in front of the lens and they are indexical because it is the physical act of light bounced off an object through the lens and on to the filmic emulsion which leaves the trace that becomes the image.

European photographic discourse in India was not able to draw on Peirce's theoretical articulations, but it was precisely photography's indexicality, and its superiority over other more equivocal signs, which gave it such importance in the colonial imagination. One encounters time and time again in administrative and anthropological literature the complaint that in India nothing is as it seems. Dr Norman Chevers, Principal of the Calcutta Medical College, noted the 'uncertainty of general evidence in India'.[14] In India, he claimed, 'the deceit inherent in the character of the lower class of Natives surrounds all judicial investigations with an atmosphere of obscurity', and he cites the case of *Bunwarree Lall* v. *Hetnarain Sing* (*sic*), in which the Privy Council acknowledged the 'general fallibility of native evidence in India'.[15] Much of Chevers's book is given over to the formulation of a systematic medical jurisprudence within which an answer to the question 'What is truth?' (one of his chapter sub-headings) could be found.

The frustration caused by existence in this uncertain world of signs emerges clearly in William J. Herschel's account of the origin of fingerprinting, in which he notes the reassurance that the 'penetrating certainty' of fingerprints permitted after years of distrusting all evidence (which he describes as 'slippery facts') tendered in court.[16] Indeed the indexical certainty of fingerprints (originally experimented with by Herschel in Bengal) can stand as a paradigm for a whole set of efforts to transcend the symbolic vagaries of encounters with India. There is a similar yearning for the index in Denzil Ibbetson's argument in favour of anthropometry, the systematized physical measurement of bodies:

No one who has not made the attempt can well realize how difficult it is to secure a full and accurate statement of custom on any given point by verbal enquiry from Orientals and still more, from semi-savages . . . Cranial measurements on the other hand, are probably almost absolutely free from the personal equation of the observer.[17]

There is perhaps an acknowledgement of the semiotic properties of photography in the pairing – to be found in an early album (*c.* 1860s) of Indian 'types' in the British Museum – of an albumen print inscribed 'Mufsulman' (Muslim) with the dried skeleton of a leaf (illus. 6). Here, parallel indexical traces are laid on the page.[18]

As early as 1856, Chevers, then Secretary to the Medical Board in Calcutta,[19] made remarkable predictions about the utility of photography in his *Manual of Medical Jurisprudence for India*. In the second edition, published in 1870, he recollected these prognostications:

I remarked in the Edition of 1856, that there could scarcely be a doubt that PHOTOGRAPHY would, before many years elapsed, be employed throughout India as a means of identifying bodies, anticipating the disfigurement of rapid decay, and enabling the magistrate and the civil surgeon to examine, in their offices, every detail of a scene of bloodshed, as it appeared when first disclosed to the police, in a place perhaps sixty miles from the [police] station . . .[20]

Chevers noted that already by 1856 the police were using photography 'in the identification of old offenders' and to identify victims. The second edition included a tipped-in albumen print of the 'photograph by means of which the victim of the "Amherst Street Murder" was identified' (illus. 7).

John Tagg, writing chiefly about early photography in Britain, has tried to demonstrate how social practice, rather than any intrinsic semiotic property, placed photography 'within the truth'. The rhetoric of photography's transparency, he suggests, has a history that permits us to 'question the naturalness of portraiture'.[21] He traces both the portrait's role as a commodity and the co-option by an

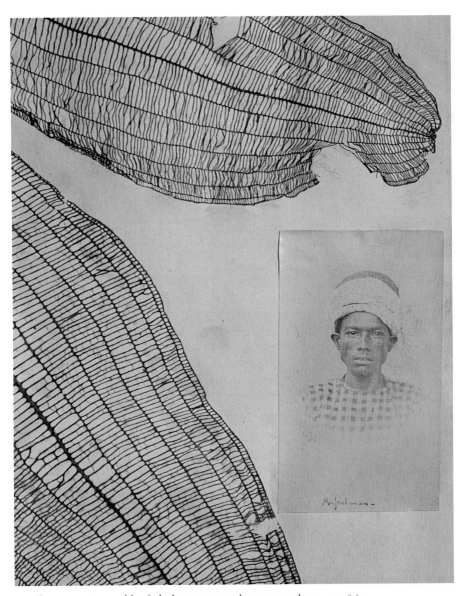

6 Albumen print and leaf skeletons pasted on same sheet. *c.* 1860s.

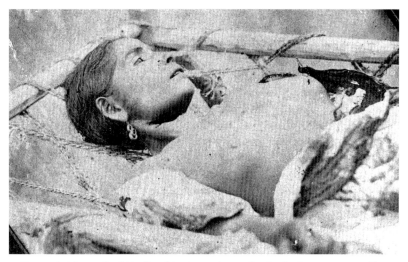

7 From *A Manual of Medical Jurisprudence for India* by Norman Chevers. Tipped-in albumen print.

expanding state of this new technology for the purposes of surveillance in order to show how photography owes its power and meaning to particular 'conventions and institutions'. There was, Tagg claims, a 'rendezvouz' between a new form of the state and a new technology which would allow each to buttress the other's power. The state mobilized photography in its attempt to have knowledge over, and control of, diverse and mobile urban workforces, and the power relations constructed through this process came to invest photography with an authority that could not be reduced to its technical and semiotic properties. The Chevers example is but one of many which demonstrate how photography in India came to be deployed in new spaces of power and knowledge in which photography's 'indexicality' was increasingly stressed and individual faces were largely displaced by generic masks rendered visible to the state. Joseph Mullins of the Photographic Society of Bengal had suggested in 1856 that photographic records of pensioners should be kept to prevent impersonations,[22] and in Lucknow in 1862 there were calls for prostitutes to carry certificates with photographs detailing the presence or absence of venereal disease.[23]

Such uses of photography have become utterly routinized as part of modern experience and are so deeply inserted into social practice that they appear completely 'normal'. But in Chevers's formulation these practices of surveillance were intended as a means not only of procuring evidence but also of effecting power through their very articulation: 'No measure would . . . impress more vividly, even upon the minds of the ignorant and superstitious common people, a conviction of the difficulty of eluding our vigilance.'[24] We can hear a striking echo of this several years later in Samuel Bourne's claim that:

From the earliest days of the calotype, the curious tripod with its mysterious chamber and mouth of brass taught the natives of this country that their conquerors were the inventors of other instruments beside the formidable guns of their artillery, which, though as suspicious perhaps in appearance, attained their objects with less noise and smoke.[25]

Chevers's text also testifies to the powerful effects credited to photography at this time, for he believed it probable that such was the evocative and tangible verisimilitude of such images, particularly in the form of the stereoscope, that reality would return to haunt the perpetrator:

Although many uneducated Natives are scarcely able to comprehend the meaning of ordinary pictures, we have yet to judge the effect which would be produced upon the conscience of a hardened savage, obstinate in the denial of guilt, by placing before him, in the stereoscope, the actual scene of his atrocity – the familiar walls, the charpoy, the ghastly faces – as they last appeared to his reeling vision – the sight which has haunted his brain every hour since the act was done – while he believed to certainty, that its reality could never come before his eyes again.

Such views were typical of an experimental period during which the limits of photographic power were yet to be established and they evoke an echo in 'optograms' produced in Europe in 1868. These were attempts to capture, through photography, the retinal images of murder victims in the hope of capturing a likeness of the murderer, 'as if [at the moment of death] the eye became a veritable camera which for a few hours retained an exact image of the last moment of life'.[26] The utility of photography to the police was also stressed by Joseph Mullins in his talk 'On the Applications of Photography in India', delivered to the Photographic Society of Bengal in October 1856. Additionally he stressed its anthropological value in capturing 'all the minute varieties of Oriental Life; of Oriental Scenery, Oriental nations and Oriental manners'.[27]

In 1861 local governments in India were issued with an instruction to collect photographs of tribes and castes under their jurisdiction. This was reinforced at the end of the year by a further request for 'photographic likenesses of . . . races and classes'[28] to be sent to the Central Committee of the London Exhibition in Calcutta. In response to this, the Revenue Commissioner of Sind replied that he had already directed a Captain W. R. Houghton and Lieutenant H. C. B. Tanner to provide a collection of likenesses. Fifteen copies were made of the photographs that resulted but only one set is known to exist, in the Asiatic Society Library, Bombay.[29] The seventy-three albumen prints show a wide range of individuals and groups, mostly set against plain curtain backdrops with, in some cases, props such as balustrades and tables. In one image, Kadir Buksh Khosa, a Sind landowner, is set against a natural background of rocks through which tree roots coil (illus. 8). This image would be reproduced in the later *The People of India*, an important and ambitious project which is described in more detail below. The letterpress description in this later publication observes that the Khosas were 'insignificant in power' and scattered throughout Sind:

The Subject of the photograph is a landholder with a small estate; a person of no great consequence, but a quiet and respectable member of his tribe. He wears a handsome chintz upper coat, or chogha, and large white turban of muslin, instead of the cap common to Sind.[30]

Such 'environmental portraiture',[31] in which a homology between the sitter and background is invoked, is the exception in this collection but it will emerge as a strong theme in later 'anthropological' images. In the case of Kadir Buksh, the land in the background serves to signify his status and occupation. Many other images introduce material artefacts associated with their occupations. 'Shikarees' ('huntsmen and scavengers') are shown clutching rifles and dead birds; the Mohana or fisherman is shown standing in front of a wooden tripod from which are suspended his nets; two images of embroiderers introduce large pieces of ornately brocaded cloth; and the Amils or Lohanas in government employment are depicted studying ledger books (illus. 9). This latter image was also reproduced in *The People of India*, where the accompanying note observes that 'none wear turbans - [they] have adopted the usual Sindee hat or cap [and] with their dress, they are more like Mohomedans than Hindus'.[32]

  Houghton and Tanner's images reached Calcutta, but not in time to be exhibited as part of the main display. A note in John Forbes Watson's catalogue to the exhibition lists them as part of 'a large collection, embracing portraits from almost the whole of the tribes and classes of India, taken under the auspicies of the Indian Government'. Also in this collection were photographs by the Reverend E. Godfrey and Lieutenant Waterhouse of 'the tribes of Central India', of Bharatpur by Shepherd and Robinson, of Nagpur, Sikhim and Bhutan by Dr Simpson, of the North-Western Provinces by Dr Tressider, of Oudh by

8 'Kadir Buksh.' Albumen print by W. R. Houghton and H. C. B. Tanner, 1861–2.

9 'Amils of Sind.' Albumen print by W. R. Houghton and H. C. B. Tanner, 1861–2.

Captain Fitzmaurice and Lieutenant R. H. De Montmorency and of Hazara by T. T. Davies.[33] The catalogue records that all these images would be published as lithographs, together with detailed descriptive notes, but this appears not to have happened. Seventy-nine of Simpson's 'photographic likenesses of natives of various parts of India' were displayed in the exhibition along with 'portraits of natives' printed at the Madras Industrial School of Arts, and along with many other photographs by Captain Allen N. Scott[34] of a dog, a Brahman priest, an officer of the Irregular Cavalry and a dancing beggar mounted together in one frame. The same section (Class XIV – Photographic Apparatus and Photography) also included stereographs of Trichinopoly, Tanjore and Madurai by Linnaeus Tripe and photographic copies of paintings in the Ajanta caves by Robert Gill.[35]

There were also many enthusiastic amateurs who took ethnology as their subject. The *Indian Amateurs Photographic Album*, which was issued in twenty-four parts between December 1856 and October 1858, contained a section on the Costumes and Characters of Western India. Many of these later appeared against montage landscapes in William Johnson's *The Oriental Races and Tribes, Residents and Visitors of Bombay: A Series of Photographs with Letterpress Descriptions* (two volumes, 1863 and 1866).[36] To a modern eye these images have a surreal quality, but the composite printing was probably precipitated by the 'oversensitivity of collodion to blue light which made it difficult to obtain a single negative that rendered both sky and landscape'.[37] Printing from partially masked negatives surmounted this problem. Johnson's preface to the first volume observed that in Bombay 'faces are to be seen of every variety of hue' and he expressed his hope that the collection would find favour with students of 'Geography and Ethnography, and Lovers of Art'. He gives little insight into the production of the images except to record that 'negatives procured for the present work were made with great labour, and in many instances with no little permission addressed to the scrupulous personages, whose effigies have been successfully delineated by the solar ray'.

Johnson's anthropological quest for difference is made clear in the title he chose for the work. The volumes contained 'numerous representatives of almost all the races and tribes of the Indian Continent and islands' and he signalled that one of his concerns was with systems of identification that included physiognomy and, in the case of Hindus, bodily marks, and, among Parsis and Muslims, costume:

the INDIANS, composed as they really are of different tribes, have great differences in their physiognomy, by which it is not difficult for near observers to recognize them. It is not difficult even for strangers to distinguish them from the people of other tribes, when certain marks which they bear on their persons are attended to. The people who are seen with bedaubments and spots and lines, horizontal and vertical, on their foreheads . . . are all Hindus.

Johnson also provides short notes on how best to recognize Christians, Bene Israel, Chinese, Malays, Arabs, Persians and Africans.

Some of the images, such as Plate 4, 'Vallabhacharya Maharajas' (illus. 10), include the work of other photographers in the composite print: 'We are indebted to Dr Narrain Dajee, a medical practitioner in Bombay, and an accomplished photographer, for the original photograph, or negative, from which our picture is made.'[38] The year before the first volume containing this picture was published the Maharajas, the chief priests of the Pushtimarg, had found notoriety. In Bombay merchant castes such as Bhatias and Lohanas paid religious taxes which enabled the resident Maharajas to acquire extravagant lifestyles. As Amit Ambalal notes, they 'seemed to forget their own true vocation and started spending their lives in indolent ease'. This mismatch between precept and practice was the object of a harsh critique by Karsandas Mulji in the periodical *Satya Prakash* in October 1860. Mulji was then sued for libel by Yadunatha Brijratanju, a Surat Maharaja. The case reached the Bombay High Court in 1862 and, after forty days' examination of numerous witnesses, Mulji was exonerated and his claim that the Maharajas were inclined to 'depraved pleasures, excesses and vices' was upheld.[39]

Vallabhacharyas are devotees of the god Shrinathji and it is thus understandable that a copy of Narrain Dajee's original image should have been found in the Rajasthani pilgrimage town of Nathdvara, the current resting place of the god. The original photograph shows the five priests and devotees seated in front of a plain cloth background (illus. 11). In Johnson's composite image (illus. 10) a new temple backdrop is introduced. The quality of the composite printing is remarkable, with the 'registration'[40] or alignment evident only on the left of the picture.

The illustrations in this work showed exemplars or 'types' and the lengthy letterpresses gave lists of identifying features, which included costume and material artefacts. Particular attention was devoted to markers of difference, to visible signs which could be tabulated against group identities. This quest for difference tended to make the women of a group of more interest, since their costume and material culture were identified as being more resistant to change. Thus costumes of the higher and lower classes of Lowana women are described

10 'Vallabhacharya Maharajas', albumen print from *The Oriental Races and Tribes, Residents and Visitors of Bombay*, 1863.

11 Vallabhacharyas, *c.* 1860.

'as being the most characteristic' since Lowana men are scarcely distinguishable from the men of other castes. Similarly, the Reverend Dr Wilson, the primary author of the letterpress descriptions in the volumes, notes, 'The parties represented in our photographs are fair specimens of their class.' In some cases the critical markers were marginal and required close inspection. Of the Nagar Brahman women (illus. 12), the letterpress noted:

It will be seen on a microscopic examination of the picture that, in addition to the various ornaments already enumerated, the lady on the left is adorned with what we suppose would be termed a toothlet – a gold button screwed to a front tooth, which is bored to receive it. This is a species of ornament peculiar, we are told, to this class of Hindu women. We certainly never remember to have seen it on the person of any other female.

Evidence of the remarkably quick diffusion of photography throughout India can be found in a report on an exhibition in Nagpur in central India in 1865. The comments on Section B (Fine Arts, Class III – Photography) recorded: 'The collection under this class was very large, some thousands of photographs being contributed by Amateur and Professional Photographers from all parts of India.'[41]

Many of the photographs from this early period have become detached from the names of their creators and even in cases where the photographer is known, often almost no information is available about the circumstances in which remarkable images were made. Typical of such cases are four extraordinarily beautiful prints made by G. Western – probably in the mid-1850s – which were deposited in the Haddon Collection in Cambridge University's Museum of Archaeology and Anthropology. Captions to the images inform us that they are of a Sannyasi (illus. 13), a Muslim, a Sikh and a Fakir (illus. 14). All the sitters are photographed against plain backdrops and stand out from the vast archive of colonial Indian photography not only for their beauty but also for their intensity. The vast majority of images in the archive have a certain blankness about them: poses and expressions frequently memorialize indifference and bafflement in the face of the photographers' attempts to visualize categories. Western's images have an intensity and fragility whose absolute atypicality leaps at the viewer. There is nothing casual or unengaged about these images; rather they have an intimacy that seems to spring from some deep knowledge of the sitters, who are clearly equal participants in these portraiture events.

When set against the dominant genre of impersonal and objectified images, Western's photographs share some of the qualities which Tagg suggests were present in the Parisian photographer Nadar's por-

12 'Nagar Brahmin Women.' Albumen print from *The Oriental Races and Tribes, Residents and Visitors of Bombay*, 1863.

13 G. Western, 'a Sannyasi', *c.* 1860, albumen print.

14 G. Western, 'A Fakir', *c.* 1860, albumen print.

traits as compared to his rival Disdéri's 'empty formula[e]'.[42] Whereas Disdéri's routinized procedures were perfectly attuned to the demands of capitalist production, Nadar clung to the more intimate relationship between painter and patron, arguing that although the technique of photography might be mastered in a day it was an infinitely more complex matter to acquire

the moral grasp of the subject – that instant understanding which puts you in touch with the model, helps you to sum him up, guides you to his habits, his ideas and character and enables you to produce not an indifferent reproduction, a matter of routine or accident such as any laboratory assistant could achieve, but a really convincing and sympathetic likeness, an intimate portrait.[43]

In 1857 much of India was convulsed by an insurrection. The motivations of the different groups involved were extremely diverse but widespread violent resistance by the colonized was a great shock both to many of the colonizers and to the British public. As the various regional insurrections were suppressed, Charles John Canning, then Governor-General, was much criticized for what was seen as a weak response, acquiring the derisory title 'Clemency Canning'. He was to become the first Viceroy in 1858, when Company rule ended and the colony came under direct rule by the crown. Canning and his wife (who was patron of the Bengal and Madras Photographic Societies) had developed an interest in photography which was finally to result, several years after his death, in the publication of the eight-volume work *The People of India* (1868–75). The preface to the first volume is worth quoting at length:

During the administration of Lord Canning, the interest which had been created in Europe by the remarkable development of the Photographic Art commended itself to India, and originated the desire to turn it to account in the illustration of the topography, architecture and ethnology of that country.

There were none, perhaps, in whom this interest was awakened more strongly than in Lord and Lady Canning. It was their wish to carry home with them, at the end of their sojourn in India, a collection, obtained by private means, of photographic illustrations, which might recall to their memory the peculiarities of Indian life.

Civilians and army officers were encouraged by Canning to take cameras with them on their travels and deposit copies with him. The collection quickly grew and Canning gave orders to place the project on an official basis. The earliest photographs collected were mainly taken in eastern Bengal but in 1863 Kaye, who was in the Secret and Political Department, saw fit to transform the project into a large publication aiming at national coverage of India's communities.[44] The eight volumes would contain 468 tipped-in albumen prints, and of the 200 sets prepared half were reserved for official use. Fifteen photographers were individually credited in the preface to the series. Of these, De Montmorency, Godfrey, Shepherd and Robinson, Simpson, Waterhouse and Houghton and Tanner had sent images to the 1862 Calcutta Exhibition, of which Forbes Watson had been the director. Other photographers contributing to *The People of India* were J. C. A. Dannenberg, Lieutenant W. W. Hooper, Captain H. C. McDonald, J. Mulheran, Captain Oakes, the Reverend G. Richter, Dr B. W. Switzer and Captain C. C. Taylor.

The recent experience of insurrection and the putative 'official use' lace the text of the volumes with a political contemporaneity. Preoccupations with origins, purity and the prospect of decay which informed so many earlier and later works were swept away by a concern with political loyalty (or its lack) and an ongoing desire to provide practical clues to the identification of groups which had so recently had the opportunity to demonstrate either their fierce hatred of British rule or their acquiescence.[45] Various Nagas are recorded as 'marauding tribes' and consolation is taken from the observation that the 'Afghan Frontier Tribes', though they might wish to launch a jihad against the British, lacked cohesion and this, 'together with the absence of artillery . . . reduces the danger to be apprehended from the tribes *en masse*'.[46] Conversely, the 'Beloch tribes of Sind proper' harboured 'no spirit of fanaticism' likely to overturn 'the present good understanding between the Beloches and the Government of India'.[47]

Early photographic projects in India took form within a much broader museological discourse which created parallel registers of images, artefacts and records of behaviour. *The People of India* is a major contribution to this ongoing project of documentation, but more than any other element it had a pragmatic political edge that attempted to directly relate these registers to the pressing question of the sustainability of British rule in India. The preface notes:

The great convulsion of 1857–58, while it necessarily retarded for a time all scientific and artistic operations, imparted a newer interest to the country which had been the scene, and to the people who had been the actors in these remarkable events. When, therefore, the pacification of India had been accomplished, the officers of the Indian services, who had made themselves acquainted with the principles and practices of photography, encouraged and patronized by the Governor-General, went forth and traversed the land in search of interesting subjects.

The photographs were a mixture of full-face quarter-length portraits, full-length formal portraits with studio paraphernalia and group shots in varying degrees of formality. The classification is extremely erratic and is sometimes by 'caste', sometimes by 'tribe';[48] other captions present groups as 'sects' and images of individuals are also included. These latter tend to be kings or ascetics ('Tun Sookh Doss Bairagi, Hindoo Religious Mendicant, Allahabad' – Plate 103), though there is also a group of named individuals with diverse occupations in Meerut and Aligarh. Some images depict their sitters bearing objects associated with their occupations or caste (a hill porter with a full load and walking stick, a charcoal carrier with a full basket), but many others do not. Such attempts to enhance images with objects, and also the inclusion or exclusion of personal names, reflect very clearly the different approaches of different photographers and forcefully reveal that, although this ambitious project interlocked with many other structures of power in the making, it was very fluid and as yet unstructured by the systematicity that would characterize later interventions.

A more precise sense of the relationship between these political evaluations and the actual photographs can be had through a closer examination of three specific images. Plate 157 from the third volume, a 'Goojur [Gujar] Landholder', is reproduced as illus. 15. The

A ZEMINDAR.

GOOJUR LANDHOLDER.

SAHARUNPOOR.

(157)

15 'Goojur Landholder,' albumen print. From *The People of India*, 1868.

text accompanying another image[49] of individuals of this same caste concedes that they are 'a handsome tribe' with 'powerful figures and fair complexions', but also stresses their political unreliability: 'They are dishonest, untrustworthy, and lawless in a high degree; and require constant and unremitting supervision. They are notorious and successful cattle lifters, pursuing this branch of robbery with determination and skill.'

The text to Plate 157 compounded the opprobrium and located their support of the 1857 insurrection at the core of their stigma:

. . . they are the clans folk of the Goojur who made themselves so notorious at Meerut in 1857 [and] are described as indifferent characters, and for the most part bad cultivators, given to petty thievery and cattle lifting and resorting to indiscriminate plunder in times of disturbance.[50]

The caption casts doubt on this individual's 'zamindar' identity, suggesting that 'he appears from his costume to be an ordinary peasant', despite the fact that he has a thick padded quilt of a type probably not possessed by poorer peasants. Captions to other images of Gujars in *The People of India* complain about the lack of an identifiable Gujar costume, and this perhaps is one of the reasons why it is the items held in the hands of the subject of illus. 15 that especially catch the interest of the writer:

In his right hand is a lathi, or bamboo club, shod at the end with rough iron rings, a most formidable weapon in the hands of a powerful man, as it can be used as a quarter-staff and has a peculiar exercise attached to it, as well of attack as defence, which is taught in village Gymnasia. In his left is a small hooka, the bottom of which is a cocoa-nut; into this a short stem of turned wood is inserted, and the upper plate or chillum, is of pottery . . . Goojurs are much addicted to smoking, particularly ganja, the prepared leaves of hemp or Cannabis Sativa. This has peculiarly exciting and intoxicating qualities . . .

The process of what Edward Said has termed 'textualization', in which the fluid reality of life is converted into volumes collated in libraries, material artefacts in museums and other registers of documentation, is underpinned by a 'citationality', a continual invocation of parallel proofs captured in these other registers.[51] There is an element of this in the relationship between text and image in the above example: the text finds its proof of aggression in the photograph.

But such images also connected to more rigorous structures of complementary classification. Seemingly inconsequential objects, such as hookahs, were collected and hierarchized, and together with countless other objects and texts formed a frame through which India

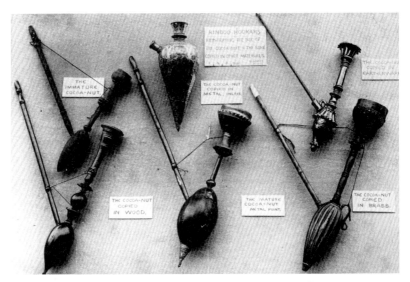

16 'Hindu hookahs', late 19th century albumen print of museum display.

was filtered into Western consciousness.[52] In his Presidential Address to Section H of the British Association for the Advancement of Science in 1913, Richard Temple suggested that:

If any of my hearers will go to the Pitt Rivers Museum in Oxford he will find many small collections recording the historical evolution of various common objects. Among them is a series showing the history of the tobacco pipe, commonly known to . . . Orientalists as the hukka. At one end of the series will be found a hollow coconut with an artificial hole in it, and then every step in evolution between that and elaborate hukka . . . I give this instance as I contributed the series, and I well remember the eagerness of the hunt in the Indian bazaars and the satisfaction on proving every step in the evolution.[53]

The image shown in illus. 16 may well have been this very display, although it could record a similar display in the University of Cambridge's Museum of Archaeology and Anthropology, in whose photographic archive this nineteenth-century print now rests. Labelled 'Hindu hookahs illustrating the use of the cocoa-nut and the same copied in other materials', the display is structured around a hierarchy ('mature', 'immature') and indicates how readily the information in projects such as *The People of India* could be cross-referenced with an infinite range of grids collectively comprising that Orient which was 'suitable for study in the academy, for display in the museum, for reconstruction in the colonial office, for theoretical illustration in

BRINJARA AND WIFE.

ITINERANT GRAIN MERCHANTS.

SAHARUNPOOR.

(161)

17 'Brinjara and Wife', from *The People of India*, 1868.

anthropological . . . theses about mankind'.[54]

The evaluation of Banjaras (illus. 17) in *The People of India* is very different. Many members of this tribal community worked as itinerant suppliers of grain to various armies; they were described as being of great use in the Mahratta War and 'beneficial' in the Sikh campaign. It is ironic, given the praise heaped on them in the 1860s, that they would later be classified as a 'criminal tribe'. In the first place their value stemmed from their aesthetic contribution to the Indian landscape, for both their persons and the encampments they make are described as 'very picturesque'. But it is a political evaluation of their capacity for disorder which soon emerges as the leading theme of the accompanying text:

Brinjarees [Banjaras] are seldom good marksmen, and firearms are always scarce among them, a few rusty matchlocks forming the equipment of a large encampment. Their favourite weapon is a short spear, the staff of which, a stout bamboo, as shown in the Photograph, forms ordinarily a driving pole; but a large sharp spear head is usually carried in the waist band, which can be fitted to it in a moment, and constitutes a truly formidable weapon.

A similar weapon assumed ominous qualities when held by the Gujars. In the hands of the Banjaras its benign potentiality is underwritten by their record of honesty and quiescence:

The men are bold, patient, hardy and venturous; and among all classes of merchants in India have acquired, as is their due, a reputation for perfect honesty. No matter how long, or how arduous the march, or how great the value of their goods they carry, they deliver them according to promise. In marches of hundreds of miles along unfrequented roads, without anyone to overlook them or guard them, the Brinjaree convoys travel patiently and persistently and deliver their invoices correctly. The consignment may be worth tens of thousands of rupees but malversation is unknown.

It is not only the contrasting nuance given to the bamboo staff that differentiates the Banjaras from the Gujar; the Banjaras are also represented as bound by sociality and convention through their depiction as a married couple. The wife sits to the husband's left,[55] and on a lower level, giving a spatial tangibility to her lower status. The image may have evoked Victorian family values in the mind of contemporary viewers, but the text is driven by a sexualized fascination:

. . . the younger women of the Brinjarees are, in many cases, eminently and even remarkably handsome. They are never black, but have a rich ruddy, dark Italian or Spanish colour; and their figures, aided by their picturesque dress, are superb. No one can look upon them without admiration of their spirited and very graceful carriage, and peculiar action in

BUNNEA.

HINDOO TRADESMAN.

DELHI.

(184)

18 'Bunnea', from *The People of India*, 1869.

putting their feet to the ground. No women in India have this light, high-stepping action, as it may be termed, of the Brinjarees, and few their grace and buoyancy of figure.

The case of the third example I will discuss here, the Baniya, or merchant, is more complex, for the Baniyas were seen as dishonest but useful. The text accompanying Plate 184 (illus. 18), depicting a Delhi Baniya weighing goods for a customer, demonstrates the pervasiveness of the museological desire to collect and collate, for it opens with a cascading list of twenty-eight items that a Baniya might sell in his store. Baniyas are useful but not popular, the text continues. The reader is then directed to the photograph, which is adduced almost as a piece of forensic evidence:

he is strongly accused of false weights, or, if the weights be true, of a peculiar and dextrous knack in managing the wooden beam off scales, which have no centre point except a cord fastened to the beam, as shown in the Photograph, by giving it a cant in weighing, which is not detectable even by the sharp-eyed customer.

The Baniya is also a money-lender, the reader is informed, and is expert in the art of usury, usually having 'the population of his village pretty well under his thumb'. But against these unattractive features must be set the colonial power's consciousness of certain concomitant benefits to British rule in India:

... if he has cheating propensities and indulges them to the utmost of his power, the Bunnea is a useful person, and contributes very largely to the furtherance of the general trade of India. In our own terrritory some of them have become millionaires, and the wealth of India, as a class, is with them. They rejoice in the contrast; and are one at least, of the classes of India, who gratefully acknowledge the protection they receive.

The photographic illustration is used here not only as a forensic proof of the claims advanced in the text; it also imposes a distance between the viewer and the subject. At one point the text sets up a dichotomy between the small, self-interested focus of the average Baniya and a much wider frame of global trade to which he unknowingly contributes: 'He little thinks perhaps that his bags of oil seed will go to Marseilles, or his madder, cotton and sugar to Liverpool.' This objectification through the creation of a discourse that speaks from a great distance strikes a new tone, one not present in earlier projects. The intimacy of some earlier 'portrait events',[56] in which the personal encounter of the image-maker impressed a closeness and respect on to the caption or text with which the photograph was sent out into the world, is here lost. The diffraction created as photographs filtered through various sections of the colonial bureaucracy imposes a distance between the voice that speaks about the images and the images themselves. Thus the reader is invited to share in a superior knowledge which is denied to the Baniya himself. In the process, subjects and individuals are transformed into illustrations of a general thesis: they become substitutable elements in a hierarchical structure of categories in which all that matters is to be representative or indicative of some wider group.

The People of India's anonymous 'Bunnea' contrasts strongly with William Johnson's depiction and description of Nansi Parpia (illus. 19), at the centre of a Khoja group in the first volume of *The Oriental Races and Tribes, Residents and Visitors of Bombay* (1863):

The central figure in our group is Nansi Parpia ('Old Nancy' as he is called at times), of shopkeeping celebrity in Bombay, whose kind, accommodat-

19 'Khojas' (including Nansi Parpia), 1863, from *The Oriental Races and Tribes, Residents and Visitors of Bombay*, 1863.

ing disposition is known to many of our British youths in the commencement of their Indian career.[57]

In none of the images in *The People of India* is there any engagement with the face of the sitter. This project is concerned not with individuals but with categories, and in the absence of any plausible theory linking individual faces to social groupings and behaviour, single faces cease to be of interest. Because the work is singularly determined by a desire to classify groups by political allegiance, there is no space to speak of character and individuality. Rather, the concern is almost exclusively with external signs and how these may be read as signifiers of collective behaviour.

My analysis of *The People of India* has attempted to situate a close reading of parts of the text and images in the political context of the aftermath of the 1857 insurrection. Roland Barthes was surely right to suggest that 'a text's unity lies not in its origin but in its destination',[58] but it is famously difficult to find documentation of the reception of the sort of material we are considering here.

However, Bernard Cohn[59] has drawn attention to a remarkable account of one Indian's displeasure at encountering *The People of India*. That individual was Sayyid Ahmad Khan of Delhi, who was later to become a central figure in north Indian Muslim politics, helping found the All-India Muslim Educational Conference in response to the establishment of the Indian National Congress in 1885. In 1869, however, he was a judge in the North-Western Provinces and travelled to London to conduct research for a critique of British histories of Islam. He went, with his two sons, to the India Office Library, which he considered a 'city of books'.[60] The first four volumes of *The People of India* had already been published and the visitors were shown these:

Sayyid Mahmud, younger son of Sayyid Ahmad, turned over the pages looking at photographs of nearly naked men or people in unfamiliar dress. If he had looked further into the later volumes he would have seen portraits of named individuals, some of them acquaintances of his father, Muslims accused of practising 'Hindoo rites in secret', an Aligarh District landholder described as having 'features [that] are peculiarly Mohomedan [which] exemplify in a strong manner the obstinacy, sensuality, ignorance, and bigotry of his class. It is hardly possible, perhaps to conceive features more essentially repulsive.'[61] But before Sayyid Mahmud reached this part he was approached by a young Englishman, perhaps a future Indian Civil Servant, who might have studied the same pictures of scantily dressed hill people and menial labourers that filled the first two volumes of *The People of India*.

'Are you a Hindustani?'

Sayyid Mahmud looked up from the book, blushed, stuttered out a yes, then corrected himself: he was not an 'aborigine', his ancestors had come to India from a foreign country.[62]

Later this disturbing encounter led Sayyid Ahmad Khan to reflect on the impact such representations had on those who were yet to encounter the real India, and allowed him to express the insult and resentment he felt at finding himself the object of such objectifying primitivist discourse:

In the India Office is a book in which the races of all India are depicted both in pictures and in letterpress, giving the manners and customs of each race. Their photographs show that the pictures of the different manners and customs were taken on the spot, and the sight of them shows how savage they are – the equals of animals.

The young Englishmen who . . . come to the India Office preparatory to starting for India, and, desirous of knowing something of the land to which they are going, also look over this work. What can they think, after perusing this book and looking at its pictures, of the power or the honour of the natives of India? . . . Reflect therefore that until Hindustanis remove this blot they shall never be held in honour by any civilized race.[63]

Throughout the nineteenth century, two rather different photographic idioms emerged in India: a 'salvage' paradigm, which was applied to what were perceived to be fragile tribal communities, and a 'detective' paradigm, which was more commonly manifested when faced with a more vital caste society. In the 'salvage' paradigm a scientific and curatorial imperative was dominant – 'fragile' and 'disappearing' cultures and communities had to be recorded ('captured') before their extinction. Two brief examples will demonstrate. In 1874, Forbes Watson had stressed the desirability of 'securing the traces of many tribes now fast disappearing or losing their distinctive characteristics'.[64] Edgar Thurston of the Madras Museum wrote that 'it behoves our museums to waste no time in completing their anthropological collections' of tribal artefacts.

The 'detective' paradigm, by contrast, presumed the continuing vitality of sections of Indian society and stressed the value of anthropological depictions and physiognomic observations as future identificatory guides. India was often singled out as peculiar in this regard – whereas elsewhere native peoples died away before the eyes of the colonizer, in India they flourished. In 1890, Herbert Hope Risley – at the start of his ascendancy over Indian anthropology – told the Anthropological Society of Bombay:

In America, Australia, and Polynesia ancient religious and primitive customs have faded away on contact with the Europeans like the frescoes in

Pompeian villas perish when exposed to the open air. In India alone the native races have held their ground, and we find examples of almost all known stages of primitive culture existing and flourishing side by side with an administration of the most modern type.[65]

It is within the salvage paradigm that an aesthetic of primitivism is most apparent. Official photography was enveloped in a discourse of scienticity and indexicality, but in practice vigorous efforts were often made to construct a different reality for the camera. G. E. Dobson was a zoologist with the Indian Museum, Calcutta, and visited the Andaman Islands in the Bay of Bengal in 1872. In a paper describing this visit, published in the *Journal of the Anthropological Institute* in 1875,[66] he described a group of Andamanese women whose photograph he reproduced (illus. 20). The central figure, he noted, was a resident of the Andamanese Orphan School on Ross Island, and Dobson had seen her almost every day either in the school house or in church 'neatly dressed in white'. However, a photograph depicting her 'destitute of clothes, shaved, and greased with a mixture of olive-coloured mud and fat' was greatly preferable, because what Dobson wanted was not to capture in his negatives the complex contemporary hybrid reality he encountered, but rather to stage a vision of an authentic primitiveness salvaged from imminent extinction. During this period there was a general anthropological concern with salvage, but photographic practice exploited a particular quality of the medium later articulated by Roland Barthes as its 'spatial immediacy and temporal anteriority, the photograph being an illogical conjunction between the here-now and the *there-then*'.[67]

A similar conjunction of photography's temporal anteriority and an 'anthropological' temporal displacement of its object is apparent in a publication that appeared in the same year that Dobson travelled to the Andamans: Edward Tuite Dalton's *Descriptive Ethnology of Bengal*. This work had originally started as a catalogue to accompany an exhibition that Joseph Fayrer had suggested be held in Calcutta. In 1865 he proposed an ethnological display 'with typical examples of the races of the old world' in which exhibits would 'sit each in his own stall, and submit to be photographed, painted, taken off in casts and otherwise reasonably dealt with in the interests of science'.[68] The exhibition was cancelled because of fears about the health of the living specimens who were to be exhibited in the booths. The Commissioner of Assam 'stated his conviction that twenty typical specimens of the hill tribes of his province could not be conveyed to Calcutta and back . . . without casualties that the greatest enthusiast for anthropological research would shrink from encountering'. This he wished to

20 G. E. Dobson, 'Group of five young Anadamanese women', 1872.

avoid because 'it might lead to inconvenient political implications'.[69] The government of Bengal made a grant of 10,000 rupees towards the cost of producing Dalton's work, which focused on tribal groups in Assam and Chota Nagpur.

The book was illustrated with large lithographs based on photographs, the majority of which were by Benjamin Simpson, who had exhibited in the 1862 Calcutta Exhibition. Some of these images were to be used in the book, but he was also commissioned to travel to the Brahmaputra valley 'to add to the collection from that most prolific of ethnological fields'.[70] Photographs were also supplied by a Dr Brown, the Political Agent at Manipur, and Tosco Peppé, who at Dalton's request 'proceeded into wild parts of Singbhum and Keonjhur, and brought his camera to bear on some of the most primitive of human beings, the Juangs, never previously subjected to the process'.[71] One of Peppé's images (illus. 21) depicted two Juang girls, 'wild timid creatures' whom he had 'immense difficulty in inducing . . . to pose before him, and it was not without many a tear, that they resigned themselves to the ordeal'.[72] It is not clear from Dalton's account whether this distress was a result of a fear of the camera or distrust and discomfort at having to act out Peppé's primitivist fantasy, for, as Dalton also notes, 'it was almost their last appearance in leaves'.[73] When the photograph was reproduced in 1908, by Herbert Risley, he was able to report the wearing of leaves as past history, these having been replaced by Manchester saris.[74]

A similar concern with transient communities requiring salvage is explicitly articulated in J. W. Breeks's *An Account of the Primitive Tribes and Monuments of the Nilagiris*, published by the India Museum in 1873. The volume was the Madras government's response to a request from the Trustees of the Indian Museum in Calcutta in 1871 for collections to be made in order to illustrate 'the state of the arts among the aboriginal and other jungle races in India'.[75] The Madras government was in part persuaded by a recommendation by Breeks, the Commissioner of the Nilgiris, who stressed the urgency of the project since 'year by year the Nilagiri tribes . . . are abandoning their distinctive customs'. It was already 'late in the day', he cautioned, for 'a very few years serve to efface all traces of a custom that has been given up'.[76] Breeks proposed that collections of artefacts be made and 'photographs or drawings of each of the tribes and of their houses' be obtained, and to this end, with the assistance of 1,000 rupees from the Madras government, he employed a photographer from the School of Arts at Madras, 'whose performances were by no means satisfactory'.[77] Several of this anonymous photographer's portraits of Todas

48

JUANG GIRLS

21 Tosco Peppé, 'Juang Girls', from Dalton's *Descriptive Ethnology of Bengal*, 1872.

KOTA MAN'S HEAD.

22 From J. W. Breeks, *An Account of the Primitive Tribes and Monuments of the Nilgiris*, 1873.

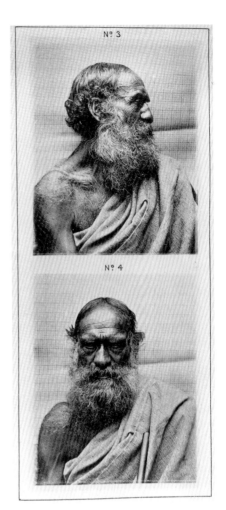

Nº 3

Nº 4

23 From W. E. Marshall, *A Phrenologist Amongst the Todas . . .* 1873.

and Kotas (illus. 22) introduce a measuring stick, the anthropometrist's talisman. Nominally for the purpose of measuring height, these were frequently deployed as mere studio props, rendering little useful information.

It was the idiosyncratic use of such devices and the 'difficulty in questions of comparison' that in 1868 had provoked J. H. Lamprey, the librarian of the Royal Geographical Society to advocate the use of a background grid of 2-inch squares formed by hanging silk thread on a large wooden frame. Perhaps inspired by this, the illustrations in

W. E. Marshall's *A Phrenologist Amongst the Todas* (also published in 1873) deploy a background grid of graph paper in photographs by the Madras studio of Nicholas and Curths (illus. 23). Marshall, like Breeks, was hugely concerned (one is tempted to say anxious) about the accuracy of his observations,[78] but his motivation for using the grid background is not in order to generate reliable comparative anthropometric data, but to assist his phrenological observations. Marshall admitted to 'difficulty in obtaining satisfactory results in investigations amongst very thick tangled hair'[79] and regretted that 'no member of either sex could be induced to having the head shaved':[80] the subject of illus. 23 was chosen because he was one of the baldest men Marshall encountered.

Whereas in a European context phrenology was a technique for diagnosing individuals' dispositions, Marshall attempted to elicit a collective diagnosis of all Todas. Each individual Toda's skull revealed a general truth about Todas as a whole. Marshall gives a very specific reason for this: the English are the 'resultant breed of several distinct races' which have not formed a single type and consequently there is endless variety. In a community like the Todas, however, endogamy (marriage within the group) ensures that they are 'all of the same type' – there is 'an extreme simplicity and uniformity'.[81]

A similar split between individual and collective applications was a contradiction which also lay at the heart of Johann Casper Lavater's science of physiognomy. William Johnson had referred – in his *Oriental Races and Tribes* – to the distinct physiognomy of different groups. Such ideas concerning the readability of physiognomy derived in the short term from the work of Lavater, who between 1774 and 1778 had published *Physiognomische Fragmente*. This book was to cause a sensation in Europe – by 1810 fifty-five editions had been published, twenty in England alone, and it remained a best-seller until 1870.[82] In an important article, Michael Shortland has traced the impact of the Lavaterian stress on the legibility of the body and face in the English novel and other fields.[83]

Lavater suggested that individuals' moral beauty could be judged on the basis of external characteristics, what he called their 'corporeal beauty', and he 'went back to the ancient search for occult analogies between physical characteristics, moral qualities and animal forms, attempting to reduce physiognomics to an exact science'.[84] Certain structural features of the face were codified in a system which permitted the literal and precise 'reading' of character and disposition from external features. 'The countenance is the theatre on which the soul exhibits itself,' he proclaimed, and agreed with Goethe that 'the best text for a commentary on man is his presence, his countenance, his form'.[85] While dissimulation was possible to a limited degree, Lavater's science allowed the examination of 'indubitable marks of internal character':

What man . . . however subtle, would be able to alter the conformation of his bones, according to his pleasure? Can any man give himself, instead of a flat, a bold and arched forehead; or a sharp indented forehead, when nature has given him one arched and round?

. . . where is the art, where the dissimulation, that can make the blue eye brown, the grey one black, or if it be flat, give it rotundity?[86]

Margaret Cowling has stressed the differences between Victorian ideas about physiognomy and its attenuated twentieth-century shadow. She is no doubt correct to stress that in contemporary Britain expression[87] (rather than permanent structural features) is privileged as a signifier of internal qualities, but these changes of emphasis should not obscure the fact that despite its supposedly Cartesian dualist inflection, Western society has consistently demonstrated a reluctance to divorce body and mind, outside and inside.

Lavater stressed that there is a 'national physiognomy',[88] but his analyses show that some national physiognomies are more suspectible to simplistic generalization than others. The Swiss have 'no common physiognomy', Lavater was 'least able to characterize' the French, and most European nationals were so loosely grouped that deviation within certain boundaries permitted only the diagnosis of individual character. Indians, Africans and Mongolians, by contrast, could be easily summarized. Thus did all nations have a common physiognomy but the physiognomy of some was more common than that of others.[89]

Lavater discusses European physiognomies in great detail, discussing many named individuals. Dürer's face, for example, shows him to have 'traits of fortitude' and 'inventive genius'.[90] The three examples of hunters and shamans from the Russian empire, by contrast, have faces that reveal 'indolence and limited sensuality'.[91] Lavater also compares different skulls. That of a German demonstrates that 'the person to whom it belonged was neither stupid, nor a man of genius; but a cold, considerate, industrious character'. An East Indian skull, by contrast, has a pointing arch at the top, a short back and strong jawbones that indicate that it 'is formed for more rude and sensible, and less delicate and spiritual enjoyment than the former'.[92]

This dichotomy between, on the one hand, a complex Europe bearing the marks of an intricate history, giving rise to an individuality of countenance, and, on the other, a non-Western sphere of uniformity, resulting from a lack of history, can also be understood in the context of an emerging Orientalist paradigm in which Europe alone was endowed with agency and historicity.[93] It is also a dichotomy that underpins much photographic portraiture practice in India right through the nineteenth century and beyond. Ray McKenzie has noted that the portraits among the 310 calotypes taken by John McCosh during the Second Burmese War of 1852–3

fall into two very clearly defined sub-groups. British officers and their wives are represented very much as individuals, with the sitter's name and rank or title indicated in almost every case. By contrast, the non-British subjects are identified throughout by a more generalized reference to their nationality or racial background – 'Burmese Beauty', 'Madras Man'. . .[94]

This anonymity, together with the assumption of fixity, was fundamental to notions of 'type' and 'typicality', terms which abound from the 1850s onwards.[95] Two striking examples of the mobilization of this concept occur towards the end of the century. In the 1880s the Calcutta studio of Johnston and Hoffman was commissioned by L. A. Waddell to take portraits of 'types of natives of Nepal, Sikhim and Tibet', probably in a Darjeeling studio. The concern with 'typicality', conformity to a categorical norm, is not confined to the title but pervades the whole of the resulting volume, which comprises sixty full-face and profile images of Himalayan peoples. Many of these images appeared in Waddell's *Among the Himalayas* (1889), in which he observed that the value of photographs was that they have 'all been reproduced by photo-mechanical processes [which bring] vividly before the eyes of the reader truthful pictures of the scenery and people'.[96]

One marker of 'typicality' is costume and some captions comment on the deviation from sartorial norms. The caption to one photograph (illus. 24) reads, 'I(a) Rong – the 'Lepcha' of the Nepalese and Indians and aborigines of Sikhim. Sept, Thar-thing (= 'chief's' clan). (Wearing a Chinese coat, not the usual plaid of striped nettle-fibre home-made cloth.)' The individuals captured in Johnston and Hoffman's images seem reluctant to conform to their types: one Limbu is 'not typical', a Nepalese Amar is 'wearing an European cap' and a Khambu (illus. 25) is, unfortunately, 'not so typical as No. 30'. The negation of a putative identity here emerges as supremely important in this semantic realm in which 'typicality' emerges only through becoming the other of others.

The album of sixty prints records traces of thirty people: each is depicted first in profile and then full-face, reflecting Waddell's desire

194

Rong — the "Lepcha" of the Nepalese & Indians,
& aborigines of Sikhim.
Sept, Thar-thing (= "Chief's" Clan).
(wearing a Chinese coat,
not the usual plaid of striped
Nettle-fibre home-made cloth.)
see No. 13.

Personal names, age &c noted in slip appended at end.

24 'Rong', portrait by Johnston and Hoffman.

252

Khambu or Jimdar of Eastern Nepal
not so typical as No 30.

25 'Khambu or Jimdar', portrait by Johnston and Hoffman.

to capture as much visual evidence as possible. The captions, which suppress individual identity in the quest for collective norms, provide a linguistic doubling of this visual objectification. But these abstract-ed descriptions ('Tamang Bhotiya of Eastern Nepal') are supplement-ed at the end of the volume by notes in Waddell's own hand which list the sitter's personal names (the Rong was named 'Nadup' and the Khambu was 'Bridhan Roy Turuk', aged 24). This list, discreetly tucked away beyond the work of anthropological generalization, sug-gests that Waddell was present when the images were made and had some personal knowledge of the individuals who sat before the cam-era. What is so fascinating, however, is that this information should have been relegated to a mere annexe by the disciplinary austerity of 'typicality'.[97]

Waddell's album found its way, in time, to the Royal Anthropolog-ical Institute Photographic Collection. Clearly it was framed by a set of specific 'academic' concerns and it has remained bound to the insti-tutional structures that created it. By contrast, *Typical Pictures of Indian Natives*, published in 1897, was aimed at a much larger popu-lar market and was indeed to run into many editions. The collection of two dozen coloured studio portraits was intended to enable trav-ellers 'to present to their friends at home a true rendering of the var-ied and picturesque costumes worn by Natives of India'[98] and helped define a genre of popular imagery that within a few years would be globally disseminated in the form of postcards. These popular repre-sentations showed little concern with 'salvage', being much keener to depict a fluid exoticism made more interesting by its visible adapta-tions and hybridity. Thus *Typical Pictures* included an image show-ing a postman standing before a rustic studio backdrop with a letter in his outstretched hand. He is clad in standard-issue clothes, 'a good serviceable blue dungaree unform and a waterproof cape during the monsoon'.[99] Another photograph captured a 'Cabuli' or Afghan horse-dealer, temporarily resident in Bombay, who had faced the camera with great reluctance. The Cabulis' hostility and suspicion simulta-neously reveal their incomprehension of museological forms of knowledge and their fear of the colonial state:

. . . they all enquired the reason of a portrait being needed, and, when informed that it was for the purpose of showing, by the aid of a picture, how an Afghan was dressed, they one and all declared that could not be the truth, as everybody knew that already . . . they eventually came to the conclusion that the photograph was required for the purpose of sending it to Her Majesty, who would, upon receiving it, order the immediate exe-cution of the sitter.[100]

Phototype postcards first appeared in 1899 and were immediately hugely popular. In India many dozens of companies produced images, a large number of which depicted caste and occupational types. Firms such as Bourne and Shepherd in Calcutta and Higginbotham and Co. in Madras became famous for both their postcards and their general photographic work. Other leading postcard producers included Macropolo of Calcutta and Clifton and Co. in Bombay, and Indian studios such as Moorli Dhur & Sons in Ambala, Gobind and Oodey Ram of Jaipur and S. Mahadeo and Sons of Belgaum were also prominent. Many of the cards bearing these companies' imprimaturs depicted occupational groups identified through a set of appropriate material objects: every Bhisti (water carrier) has a goat-skin water bag, every Coolie bears a basket and every Dhobi carries an iron and a bundle of clothes. But there is nothing archaic about these images, all of which situate their subjects in a contemporary time that connects their traditional occupational markers to new colonial artefacts. The Bhisti waters imperial flower-pots, the Dhobi makes his way towards a sahib's bungalow and the sweeper pushes open the door of a modern brick building (illus. 26). All are represented as functionaries of the Raj, symbols not of an imperilled primitivism but rather of a vital and adaptive labour force. Johannes Fabian has drawn attention to the way much anthropological writing invokes its other in a different, earlier time than that of the author and his/her audience.[101] This structural time-lag involves what he terms the 'denial of coevality'. That few of this genre of images attempt this is perhaps due to the presence of a class disjunction which renders temporal disjunctions unnecessary. Several of Higginbotham and Co.'s images make this subservience explicit: 'Our Dhoby, Madras' and 'Our Grass Cutter, Madras' are two of the captions on their postcards which alert us to their function as traces of individuals mediated by class relations within structures of colonial power. This point is also made by a page in an album compiled in 1925–6 which synoptically compresses the experiences of one European (illus. 27). There is a postcard of the boat and the hotel in Bombay that accommodated this traveller, who is also shown at work seated at a desk in the open air. He has included a picture of himself at rest with other Europeans, a clipping for Mellin's baby food citing a letter which his wife may have written much earlier from Lahore (another album in this collection[102] includes images from the Accountant General's Office in Lahore) and a coloured postcard (by Clifton and Co., Bombay) depicting 'a table servant'. All these images are infected by a utility – the means of conveyance, a place to stay, earning a wage and running an ordered household. The page of the album

MEHTAR. (SWEEPER.)

26 'Mehtar (Sweeper)', c. 1910, postcard.

27 Page from photograph album *c.* 1925–6.

is here a prison, fixing the table servant within a parochial set of colonial concerns. The table servants (or Khidmatgars) found employment in a new colonial niche and were not a manifestation of more enduring caste and occupational practices. However, it is clear that much of British colonial society was interested only in the diversity of local populations inasmuch as this provided a service infrastructure of use to themselves.

Within official and academic representations of Indian society, objects associated with traditional caste occupations were used to signify identity and positioning within social hierarchy. These images also echoed the traditions of the medieval *Standebuch* or *Books of Trades*. Here, as Graham Clarke has noted: 'types . . . were imaged as part of a special social organization based on a fixed hierarchy of significance . . . figures are [represented] consistently in relation to their place within an assumed social order: at once traditional, rural and conservative.'[103]

In Jacques LeGoff's terms these embody 'the abstract image of a per-

28 Sergeant Wallace, two Chamars, *c.* 1896.

29 Sergeant Wallace, Mallah, c. 1896.

sonage represented by symbols or signs materializing the place and rank assigned him by God' and in his discussion of Florentine painting come before images that render 'the individual in time, in a concrete spatial and temporal setting'.[104] In an Indian context, the representation of India as a hierarchy of trades is perhaps best exemplified by the work of Sergeant Wallace of the Royal Engineers, who photographed in Mirzapur District in the 1890s. There are large albumen prints of his work in the Royal Anthropological Institute's Photographic Collection and in the Haddon Collection at the University of Cambridge's Museum of Archaeology and Anthropology. His images were used to illustrate William Crooke's multi-volume *The Tribes and Castes of the North-Western Provinces and Oudh* (1896); illus. 28 and 29 depict a Chamar holding a pair of shoes and a Mallah standing by a canoe with a paddle in his hands. Traditionally Mallahs were boatmen and Chamars were tanners and shoemakers. In the context of Crooke's work these images assume a very particular nuance, for Crooke vigorously argued against Risley's claim a few years earlier that caste was the result of the genetic isolation of groups. Crooke revived arguments advanced earlier by Nesfield and Ibbetson that caste was the outcome of 'a community of function or occupation'. Crooke exposed the absurd contradictions in Risley's data and agreed with Nesfield that Brahmans were not 'distinct in race and blood from the scavengers who swept the roads'.[105] Against this backdrop one can identify a tension within the images. In the case of the two Chamars (illus. 28) their erect posture seems to say, 'We have the bodies of Chamars' (Risley's claim), but the quietly held pair of shoes seems to argue against this, saying, 'If we didn't hold these, could you really distinguish us from other castes?'[106]

Risley argued that it was the body itself that demonstrated its caste identity: the external surfaces of Indian bodies were objectified and made to bear the weight of group identity. According to his theory, castes were 'races', separate populations within the population, and their bodies testified to their different genetic constitutions. This approach was most starkly revealed in 1891, in his famous statement in the *Tribes and Castes of Bengal* that:

If we take a series of castes . . . and arrange them in order of the average nasal index, so that the caste with the finest nose shall be at the top and that with the coarsest at the bottom of the list, it will be found that this order substantially corresponds with the accepted order of social procedure.[107]

Risley and some of his followers were later to retract part of this statement, seeking to minimize the wildness of its claims. However, in

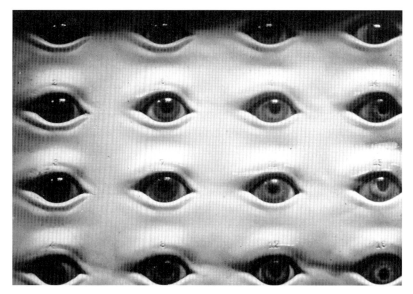

30 Display of glass eyes from the late 19th century. Government Museum, Madras.

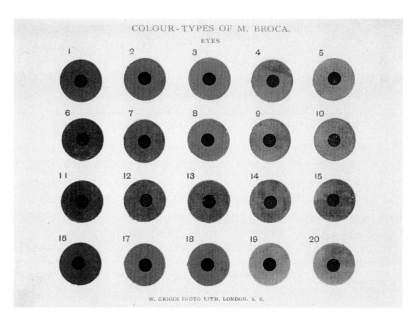

31 Colour photo-lithograph from *Notes and Queries in Anthropology*, 1874.

1891 Risley certainly believed that nearly all north Indian *jatis* (local endogamous groups) bore exterior marks of their social status and that science could rigorously sort and order them into such a hierarchy on the basis of the width of their nose. In his work the body was strongly 'de-Platonized' – its truths came to be rendered increasingly as surface effects and the face became a mere mask of genetically determined widths and angles. If from all the theoretically possible approaches to the face we were to place Rembrandt's epiphanal portraiture[108] at one end of the continuum, then at the other end we would have to place Risley's dolichocephalic and brachycephalic heads, stripped completely of any power to signify except in his tables of 'seriations'.[109]

An elaborate and often bizarre technology of quantification was also brought to bear upon other external surface markers. One barber (a Mr Douglas) in London's Bond Street was prevailed upon to furnish samples of hair to the Anthropological Institute, where it was arranged in accordance with the French anthropologist Paul Broca's system of colour classification.[110] One selection of hair samples – probably used by Edgar Thurston – is still in the anthropology display in the Government Museum, Madras, alongside a selection of glass eyes (illus. 30) which was also inspired by Broca's classification (illus. 31). The process of abstraction evident in Risley is here taken to grotesque extremes: faces are disassembled into constituent parts which are then reassembled in new arcane hierarchies. Thurston, who was Government Anthropologist in the Government Museum, Madras, was later to publish his own 'ethnographic glossary', *Castes and Tribes of Southern India*, whose seven fat volumes appeared in 1909. He describes how, following the establishment of the Ethnographic Survey of India in 1901, he encountered great difficulties in fulfilling his obligation to record the manners, customs and physical characteristics of more than 300 castes and tribes; illus. 32 may well show one of his assistants at work on this project.[111] The suspicions of local populations which gave rise to these difficulties are the object of humour in Thurston's account, but we catch in them another echo of the resentment and terror which Europeans' attempts to capture Indian bodies and faces frequently evoked. On one occasion a Paniyan woman believed that Thurston was going to 'have the finest specimens among them stuffed for the Madras museum'; in Mysore he was mistaken for a recruiting sergeant looking for replacements for those killed in the Boer War; and in one temple town so many had fled that Thurston had 'perforce to move on, and leave the Brahman heads unmeasured'.[112]

32 Quantifying the face: collecting anthropometric measurements, late 19th century.

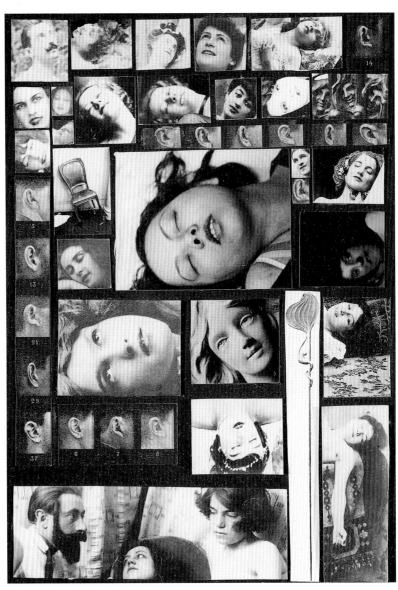

33 Salvador Dalí, *Le Phenomène de l'extase*, 1933.

The excess and desire implicit in these projects were marvellously ridiculed by Dalí in his 1933 *Le Phenomène de l'extase* (illus. 33), which included images of ears from Alphonse Bertillon's system for the anthropometric identification of criminals. Bertillon advocated the close scrutiny of ears as components of the 'word portraits' he used to supplement the complex measurements of the criminal bodies which he believed allowed the establishment of an individual's identity: 'The ear is most clearly superior for identification purposes . . . in cases where the court requires an assurance that a particular old photograph "beyond doubt represents the person here before us".'[113] Bertillon confessed to being an admirer of Sherlock Holmes and there is an uncanny echo of Holmes's declaration to Watson (in *The Cardboard Box*) that 'each ear is as a rule quite distinctive, and differs from all others'. The Bengal Police introduced an 'improved' version of Bertillon's system in 1891, together with experimental dactylography (fingerprinting), to complement the photography of suspects and criminals on their new 'measurement roll card' (illus. 34). Anthropometric data, photography and dactylography are equally triangulated in this appropriation by the state of indexical technologies.

A similar fascination with Indian bodies as semiotic complexes is apparent in another Conan Doyle story, *The Sign of Four*, which leads us back to one of the most ambitious of all official photographic projects in colonial India. *The Sign of Four* follows the activities of Tonga, an Andamanese escapee from Agra Jail. Sherlock Holmes summarizes the evidence:

'. . . consider the data. Diminutive footmarks, toes never fettered by boots, naked feet, stone-headed wooden mace, great agility, small poisoned darts. What do you make of all this?' . . .

'Some of the inhabitats of the Indian Peninsula are small men, but none could have left such marks as that. The Hindu proper has long and thin feet. The sandal-wearing Mohammedan has the great toe well separated from the others, because the thong is commonly passed between.' . . .

He stretched his hand up, and took down a bulky volume from the shelf.

'This is the first volume of a gazeteer which is now being published. It may be looked upon as the very latest authority. What have we here? "Andaman Islands, situated 340 miles to the north of Sumatra, in the Bay of Bengal." . . . The aborigines of the Andaman Islands may perhaps claim the distinction of being the smallest race upon this earth . . . Their feet and hands . . . are remarkably small.'[114]

Having made his identification, Holmes then took up his violin and 'began to play some low, dreamy, melodious air'. We should recall that Sherlock Holmes was a member of the Anthropological Institute;

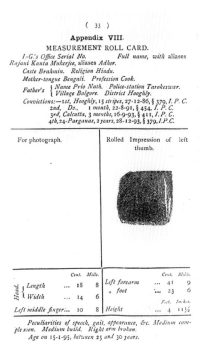

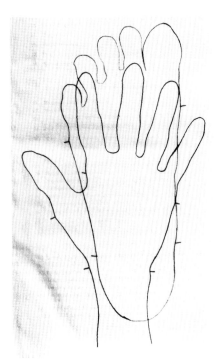

34 From Colonel H. M. Ramsay, *Anthropometry in Bengal, Or, Identification of Criminals by Anthropometric Measurement and Thumb Impressions,* 1895.

35 Maurice Vidal Portman and W. Molesworth, tracings of Andamanese hands and feet, 1894.

he had penned two short articles on the subject of the morphology of the ear for its journal[115] and would certainly have been familiar with Maurice Vidal Portman's work. Portman was Officer in Charge of the Andamans and in 1889 had offered to make a series of photographs for the British Museum showing different stages in the manufacture of Andamanese artefacts. These were completed by 1893 and, together with full-face and profile studies of Andamanese photographed against a Lamprey grid, were sent to the British Museum and the Government of India. One year later, with the help of W. Molesworth, he completed a compendious survey of physical characteristics, several volumes of which recorded their 'Observations on External Characters'. These consisted of printed schedules detailing fifty-four items of information to which tracings of the subject's hands and feet were appended (illus. 35).

Portman and Molesworth's work reveals that photography was to become but one of the means of producing evidence which could be

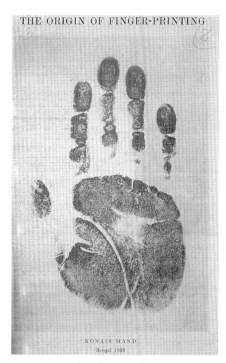

KONAI'S HAND
Bengal 1858

36 'Konai's hand, Bengal 1858'. From
W. J. Herschel, *The Origin of
Fingerprinting*, 1916.

termed, in Peircean terms, indexical. In addition to photographs, life
and death casts[116] and 'paper squeezes'[117] were also made, and the
dactylograph has a significantly Indian origin. It is no coincidence
that fingerprinting was first developed within India and exported by
Herschel from Bengal to England, where it was taken up by Francis
Galton.

Galton argued that the fingerprints were necesssary for the identification of imperial subjects: 'In India as in other British colonies the
natives were illiterate, disputatious, wily, deceitful, and to the eyes of
the European all looked the same.'[118] Galton's source for the 'persis-
tency' of the dactylograph was Sir William J. Herschel, who had first
thought of experimenting with dactylographs in 1858.[119] Prior to this,
his experience as a magistrate in Jungipoor formed in him 'a distrust
of all evidence tendered in Court which did so much to cloud our faith
in the people around us'. He inhabited a universe of 'slippery facts'
which brought him close to despair. However, in July 1858 he accept-

ed a tender to supply 'ghooting', a road-building material, from Rajyadhar Konai of Nista village. Konai was about to sign the contract when, on a whimsy, Herschel insisted that he provide a stamp of his hand (illus. 36). This handprint was used by Galton in his famous lecture at the Royal Society in 1890.[120] In time Herschel isolated the lower surface of the end of the finger as containing the most complex information[121] and as early as 1862 he tried to persuade the government of Bengal (without success) to use fingerprints as a means of enforcing lease agreements. In 1877, Herschel was made Magistrate and Collector at Hooghly, near Calcutta, and proceeded to conduct his own experiments, but it was not until 1891 that fingerprinting (together with photography and anthropometric measurements) was taken up by the whole of the Bengal Police.[122] Herschel lavished praise upon Edward Henry (then the Inspector-General of the Bengal Police and subsequently Commissioner of the Metropolitan Police) for the part he played in 'fashion[ing] a weapon of penetrating certainty for the stronger needs of Justice'.[123]

The earliest uses of photography in India contained the possibility of dialogical encounters between photographer and sitter in which the intimacy of the event created some additional force capable of collapsing colonial distance. A few images are indissolubly linked to the personal names of the sitter and achieve what Nadar termed a 'familiar likeness'. By the end of the century, however, the 'portraiture event', with its creative unpredictability, was completely dead. Official photographers no longer placed individuals in front of their lenses, being interested only in bodies that could testify to abstracted and generalized social identities. Internal qualities were abandoned in favour of external traces of a collectivity. By contrast, photography's sister science, dactylography, sought out external traces that uniquely positioned solitary individuals. Official photography had flickered across 'a field of institutional spaces'[124] and was then partly extinguished. It was replaced to some extent by a new, more powerful indexical technique – the fingerprint – which was able to meet an anxious state's new concern with identifying individual miscreants, rather than potentially troublesome social groupings. In any case, the face had proved an insufficiently stable and quantifiable object for photography ever to succeed. The signs that state-inspired photography had elevated were inherently insecure and unreliable: Waddell's caption 'not so typical as No. 30' can be taken as symptomatic of the fugitive state of all physiognomic generalization. The triumph of the fingerprint within Indian legal discourse also entailed a recognition of this fractured nature of the face:

We may classify human beings and human features but cannot bring about or find a precise agreement between any two; we have white men, red men, and yellow men; we have well ascertained and defined types of humanity; we have in each type classifications of hair, eyes, noses, mouth and so on; but a large residue of difference between any two individuals remains as it were a recurring decimal which cannot be distinguished. The difference between each human face and every other of its species, upon which evidence of identity has always so firmly rested, can be easily observed, but it cannot be specifically and completely isolated. We know that it is there, but we cannot in any case completely define its details.

But in the case of finger impressions, there is no question of dealing with those evanescent expressions which so largely contribute towards recognition of the identity of the human face. The exact differences in such impressions can be pointed out with as much certainty as the differences between the maps of two countries.[125]

2 Indian Eyes

Is there a ruling chief or a petty chief in India that has not got an outfit consisting of several cameras and lenses and all the rest of it? In fact, every tenth person you meet is a photographer, or at least carries a camera in his hand, if not with a strap over his shoulder.[1]

Parallel to the immense and anxious endeavour which I have traced in the preceding chapter, vast numbers of local Indian-run studios were also producing photographs. Several were in business as early as the mid-1850s[2] in Calcutta and Bombay, and two to three decades later there were hundreds all over the country. In 1857, about thirty of the 100 members of the Photographic Society of Bengal were Bengalis. The Bengal Photographers (illus. 37) was started by the Bengali Nilmadhav De in 1862[3] and the *cartes-de-visite* and cabinet cards they produced are images of individuals and families set within conventional photographic-studio settings of the time. The images are strikingly different from anthropometric photographs, but they are not strikingly different from the self-commissioned images that Europeans collected of themselves.

This should not surprise us: early Indian photographic practitioners were part of an élite that mimicked key colonial aesthetic forms. Besides this, the technical expertise necessary to produce photographs during this period came ensconced in a repertoire of pre-existing practices that were easily replicated. In one of the earliest photographic manuals published in India, *A Guide to the Indian Photographer* (1860),[4] the author, F. Fisk Williams, after noting the desirability of locking darkrooms to prevent native servants stealing silver solutions to sell to electro-platers in Calcutta's bazaars, gives extensive advice on 'manipulation for portraits'. He doubtless saw his main audience as European, but we can be sure that comprehensive technical manuals such as his were also consumed by indigenous studios. He stresses the necessity of both the naturalism of pose and the artistry of context:

. . . all awkwardness and stiffness must be avoided, and the person should be made as far as possible to assume an easy natural manner, devesting [*sic*] himself of the idea that he is sitting for a portrait . . .[5]
. . . something more than a carefully prepared plate and correct focusing are required to obtain a good portrait, too much attention cannot be paid to the arrangement of drapery, light and shade &c. The juditious placing

The Bengal Photographers.

19-3, Bow Bazar Street.   CALCUTTA.

37 The Bengal Photographers, cabinet card, late 19th century.

of vases, books and other articles of vertu in the picture will often greatly contribute to its beauty . . . in fact to take a really good portrait the operator must be an *artist* as well a photographer.[6]

Looking at early *cartes-de-visite* and cabinet cards produced by Eng-
lish- and Indian-run studios in Bombay, it is difficult to tell them
apart. All frequently mobilize painted backdrops of classical interiors,
and standing figures often lean against pillars or pediments on which
books or other objects are placed. These images, like European photographs of the same period, bear the dilute trace of the traditional
encumbrances of painted portraiture, especially the style that has
become known as the 'swagger portrait'. Like the painter's studio, the
photographer's premises became a space in which a visual record of an
elevated and intensified identity could be acquired.

The 'swagger portrait' is a term recently given by Andrew Wilton to
a style of imagery that 'puts public display before the more private
values of personality and domesticity'.[7] Associated more with artists
trained in Continental Europe rather than Britain, key practitioners
were Van Dyck, Batoni and Winterhalter. The British tradition
stressed 'the Protestant virtues of civic worth, domestic honour and
administrative probity',[8] whereas the swagger genre exaggerated the
glamour and theatricality of the individuals it depicted. As Sarah Kent
has illuminatingly observed, these images are the obverse of Rembrandt's investigation of his sitters' souls. They are complex fictional
visions, inflected by a theatrical excess in which the sitters inhabit
extravagant and often absurd roles:

We are in the realm of theatre – elaborately coded fictions. The silks,
satins and taffetas worn by these men and women, the ermine, periwigs
and braid that artists painted with such finesse and brio, are not clothes
so much as costumes: signals of rank.[9]

Portrait of a Gentleman by Pompeo Girolamo Batoni (1708–87) (illus.
38) perfectly exemplifies the glamorous transformations effected by
swagger portraits. The subject of the image – probably an English aris-
tocrat visiting Rome on a Grand Tour – may have been a drunken lib-
ertine of modest learning, but in Batoni's image he is transformed into
a dashing intellectual and adventurer, a master of geography and of
the classical heritage. This is the persona available in all of Batoni's
portraits and reflects the space of the painting rather than anything of
the sitter's own character or disposition.

P. Gomes and Co. was a flourishing studio in the late nineteenth
century, based, like numerous others, in Kalbadevi Road, Bombay.[10]
Proclaiming themselves 'Artists and Photographers' on the reverse of

38 Pompeo Girolamo Batoni, *Portrait of a Gentleman*, c. 1760s,
oil on canvas.

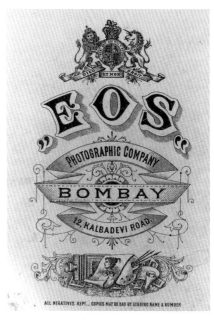

39 EOS Photographic Company,
cabinet card, late 19th century.

40 Obverse of EOS Photographic
Company, late 19th century.

their cabinet cards they boasted of their prowess in photographing children, their 'special arrangements for babies' and their ability to make copies of old and faded photographs whose quality exceeded that of the original. Other claims included 'wedding, picnic, and family groups photographed in an artistic manner' and the promise that 'people who have never come out well in a photograph are especially invited to give us a sitting as no matter where previously taken we can insure [sic] a successful portrait in any case without exception'.[11]

The Parsi photographer S. Hormusjee, also based in Kalbadevi Road, declared on his *cartes-de-visite* 'enlargements made and painted in the most artistic style' and the 'EOS Photographic Company' included a standard motif of the photographer-artist on some of its cabinet cards (illus. 39 and 40). A small engraving, of the sort which can also be found on numerous European products of the time, represents photography as a sort of painting and depicts a camera in front of which are an artist's palette and brushes, amidst various cartouches, photographs and paintings.

The contrast with the indexical idiom, which was repeatedly stressed by the anthropologists and others we encountered in Chapter 1, is striking. In official usage it was precisely its perceived freedom from aesthetic convention that made photography uniquely valuable. Within other spheres, however, its relation to art was the subject of constant debate and negotiation. It was commonly held that its indexical quality inevitably removed it from the realm of the arbitrary and conventional within which art functioned. This is certainly the view of a correspondent in the *Athenaeum*, quoted in *The Photographic Journal* in 1859:

. . . to shape out an ideal purity, nobleness or bravery, that it will do – never. It is at best an angel copier; a god-like machine of which light and sunshine is the animating Promethean fire. Put it higher and you degrade Art to the worshipper of a machine.[12]

This was the dilemma confronted by Henry Peach Robinson, Julia Cameron and Alfred Stieglitz in different ways as they sought to emphasize the pictorial and downplay the documentary function of photography. But there is no need to relate the EOS Photographic Company's motif to such élite global debates. The apparatus of the painter's studio was easily adopted by photographers, and the idiom of art and the persona of the artist – replete as they were with the transcendent and scarce – were much more amenable to commercial manipulation than those of the technician, whose mere proficiency was less marketable. Studios were commercial concerns in competition with others, and 'artistry' was an obvious realm in which individual excellence could be demonstrated. In 1931 an advert for the Vanguard Studios (illus. 41) combined an emphasis on artistry with a declaration of their nationalist credentials: it depicted a nymph with a palette and described its services as 'certified' by nationalists such as Sarojini Naidu, Kamala Nehru, Subhas Chandra Bose and K. M. Munshi.

We should not lose sight of the significant fact that for Indian practitioners the application of paint to the surface of the photographic image did not appear to raise the same paradoxes that it did for many European practitioners. Judith Mara Gutman's path-breaking study of early Indian photography, *Through Indian Eyes*, throws up many troubling questions, but she is surely correct in her estimation of the dramatic role of overpainting in the period she describes. The question here is one of degree: European photographers also used paint, both to retouch negatives and to enhance colour on the final print, and Fisk Williams's book, cited above, lists three imported volumes concerned with the painting of photographs.[13] However, numerous Indian examples dating from the 1860s deploy paint as much more than a supplement to the photographic image; rather, the overlay of

41 Printed advertisement for Vanguard Studios, Bombay. *c.* 1931.

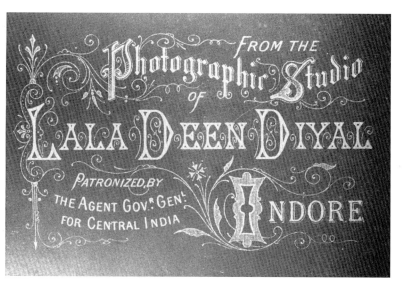

42 Obverse of Lala Deen Dayal cabinet card, *c.* late 1870s–80s.

paint completely replaces the photographic image in such a way that all or most of it is 'obscured'. A *carte-de-visite* taken in Bombay in the late nineteenth century (illus. 43) has been elaboratedly worked over with gouache. Only the faces, hands and feet of the Parsi couple and their daughter have not been overpainted. The studio carpet has been lovingly re-created with minute attention to its floral pattern and the mother's sari and daughter's dress have been worked over with an intricate and delicate tracery.

Some painted photographs also reflect the interpolation of this new technology into long-established painters' workshops. The English portraitist Val Prinsep, who toured India in 1876, recorded the centrality of photography to many Indian artists:

To-day I have received visits from the artists of Delhi: they are three in number, and each appears to have an *atelier* of pupils. The best one is Ismael Khan. Their manual dexterity is most surprising. Of course, what they do is entirely traditional. They work from photographs, and never by any chance from nature. Ismael Khan showed us what his father had done before photographing came into vogue, and really a portrait of Sir C. Napier was wonderfully like, though without an atom of *chic*, or artistic rendering.[14]

The Nathdvara painter Narottam Narayan Sharma (1896–1986) started his life working for the Udaipur court, before finding fame as the originator of many of the twentieth century's most influential chromolithographic images. In illus. 44 we see a photograph of an Udaipur prince painted by Narottam in the 1920s or 1930s: all of the photographic image has been overpainted and only the thinly washed face and hands of the subject reveal its photographic origin.

The oldest remaining studio based in Kalbadevi Road is the Premier Palace, also known as the Indian Art Studio, on the corner of Princess Street. Founded in 1917, its ornate antiquated basement studio with painted backdrop was featured in Mira Nair's 1988 film *Salaam Bombay!* Beautiful heavily painted portraits are still displayed in the windows and in glass panels that line the main space of the ground floor, and the studio still employs two painters. Gutman reproduces many examples of painted photographs, noting their 'explosive and glorious new range of tones',[15] suggesting that the production of painted photographs was central to most Indian studios' business in the second half of the nineteenth century and revealing that some studios employed up to twenty-nine painters to do outlining, background scenery, retouching and oil painting.[16]

She also observes that the peculiar power and fascination of such images to a Westerner stems from their apparent pollution. Within

43 Painted *carte-de-visite*, late 19th century, watercolour on albumen print.

44 Narottam Narayan Sharma, portrait of Mewar prince, *c.* 1930,
watercolour on albumen print.

the dominant Western semiotic order, paint seems to be a lower iconic sign and its application to the semiotically superior indexical photograph inverts this hierarchy: '. . . painting on photographs suggests a kind of impurity – on the one hand an excuse for failing to reach more perfect heights, on the other, a device for watering down what should be a purely photographic statement.'[17]

In the next chapter I will be looking at contemporary photographic practices in the town of Nagda, in Madhya Pradesh, and will return to this question of the relationship between photography and painting. Nagda was nothing but a small village until the early 1950s, when it developed as a significant industrial centre. There were certainly no photographic studios in Nagda in the late nineteenth or early twentieth centuries. However, significant developments were occurring to the east and west of this small community, in the nearby towns of Indore and Ratlam.

The significance of Indore to most Nagda photographers of the late twentieth century is as the location of various colour processors and as the main regional source of imported Japanese cameras. No photographer in Nagda knows the name of Lala Deen Dayal[18], or is aware that he started his phenomenal career in Indore (illus. 42). In 1881, five years after Deen Dayal founded his studio, Indore's population was 75,401.[19] The city was already home to cotton mills, which were to become its staple industry, but also bore many marks of projects implemented by the Maharaja Tukoji Rao II. In addition to his own palace, which could be seen from all over the city, there were the Lalbag gardens, with a small summer palace and a reading-room, and, on the west of the city, 'an antelope preserve where sport with hunting leopards may be enjoyed'.[20]

Some sense of the 'hollowness' of this local crown can be gleaned from the report that the Resident's announcement in an open Durbar of the selection of Tukoji Rao II, after the previous ruler, Khande Rao, died without issue in 1844,[21] met with the disapproval of the Governor-General. This direct announcement amounted almost to a recognition of hereditary entitlement and the opportunity to enforce the formal protocols of subservience had been missed: 'the investiture of the young chief, instead of bearing the appearance of a free act of grace on the part of the British Government, had assumed more the form of succession by legitimate right.'[22] For the next century the ruling of Indore was to be intimately bound up with British aspirations and machinations.

It was in such a setting that Lala Deen Dayal, a young Jain who had been trained in a Civil Engineering College in Roorkee, took up a post as Head Estimator and Draughtsman in the Indore Public Works Secretariat in 1866. In 1874 he began his amateur photographic studies with the encouragement of Sir Henry Daly, the Agent to the Governor-General in central India. Deen Dayal was able to photograph Lord Northbroke during a visit to Indore and the Prince of Wales in 1876. He accompanied Daly on a tour of Bundelkhand, 'photographing views, native chiefs, etc',[23] and in 1882–3 worked with Sir Lepel Griffin, contributing eighty-nine photographs to his *Famous Monuments of Central India* (London, 1886).[24] Deen Dayal also won the appreciation of Tukoji Rao II, who granted him a *jagir* (rent-free land).

It is not clear what public facilities there were in Deen Dayal's establishment in Indore. He opened a commercial studio in Bombay in 1886 and in 1892 he was to open a *zenana*[25] studio in Hyderabad, where he had already become the Nizam's court photographer in 1884.[26] Existing stock and catalogues kept by his descendants in Secunderabad reveal several studio images that may well (although it is impossible to be certain) have been taken in Indore between 1874 and 1884 (illus. 45), in addition to an album, *A Souvenir of Indore*, which included views of the Maharaja and his palaces.[27] What we can easily establish, however, is that throughout his career Deen Dayal's major patrons were local courts and British officials and agencies. The testimonials that his family collected throughout his career clearly demonstrate the élite niche he occupied as a photographic recorder of elaborate state ceremonial and painterly landscapes that captured 'the beautiful, the characteristic, and the picturesque'.[28] When the Equerry to HRH The Duke of Connaught wrote in 1889 to tell him that 'His Royal Highness is of the opinion that you are decidedly the best native photographer he has seen in India' he was affirming Deen Dayal's mastery of a photographic practice that was completely accessible to his imperial patrons. This was a verdict confirmed by a writer in *The Times of India* in 1886,[29] commenting on Deen Dayal's views of central India and Rajputana: 'They are admirable specimens of photographic arts and would do credit to any European firm.'

During the Prince of Wales's visit to India in 1875–6, Deen Dayal took a series of photographs showing the state entry into Indore, Delhi and Jaipur.[30] It would have been during this last visit that he met Maharaja Sawai Ram Singh II, who had been experimenting with photography since the early 1860s under the tutelage of T. Murray, formerly an 'artist-photographer' based in Nainital. In 1870 a Dr de Fabek created a photographic section in the Maharaja's School of Art,

45 Lala Deen Dayal, portrait study.

of which he was Principal, and the presence of Thomas Holbein Handley also added to this nucleus of photographic enthusiasts in Jaipur.[31] Ram Singh's oeuvre[32] includes portraits of visiting dignitaries such as the Duke of Edinburgh, ceremonial arches ('Peace and Prosperity Attend Thee'), the city's new gas streetlights and rephotographed copies of images by Bourne and Shepherd and Ritter & Molkenteller of Bombay and Pune. It also includes images of a sadhu (illus. 46), a group of tribal women and a copy of a German *carte-de-visite* of a fez-wearing Turk (captioned 'Thronfolger der Türkei'), suggesting that Ram Singh also saw one of the objects of photography to be the 'typological' documenting of society. Perhaps most interesting, however, is an image taken by T. Murray,[33] Ram Singh's chief photographic mentor, which shows the king seated in a yogic posture by an open window (illus. 47). The image is clearly a collaborative venture, a joint communiqué about the natue of an idealized ruler. Ram Singh adopts the persona of a devout and simple worshipper of the gods. He wears only a dhoti and various ritually powerful necklaces, and sits on a mat surrounded by the paraphernalia of worship – a small bell, a brass *lota* or pot and a plate used to prepare offerings to the gods. There is a quiet, intimate theatricality in this image of a pure and simple king attending to his otherworldly duties that alerts us to a quality of photography we will soon encounter in much stronger forms. In this image, jointly constructed by Ram Singh and Murray, photography does not seek to impose a category of identity plucked from a pre-existing structure but emerges rather as a creative space in which new aspirant identities and personae can be conjured.

Similar developments can be seen in Indore in the early twentieth century. Lala Deen Dayal left the city in 1884 to take up his post as the Nizam of Hyderabad's court photographer, although his Indore *atelier* functioned until 1904. Reminiscing in 1899, Deen Dayal recalled that his services were 'much appreciated' by the Indore Maharaja. Tukoji Rao II died in 1886, two years after Deen Dayal shifted to Hyderabad, and was succeeded by his eldest son, Shivaji Rao, who was to rule until 1903.

It was Shivaji Rao who initiated the expansion of the buildings in the Lalbag palace into a vast royal complex. The core of the palace was built on the orders of Shivaji Rao Holkar in the 1890s and was further extended by Tukoji Rao III (1902–25).[34] The building is a monument to the creative appropriation of different styles – French, Italian and German – and is characterized by a rich baroque exuberance. Vast iron lions guard gates emblazoned with the Holkar motif, and inside stuffed tigers cavort among the debris of Holkar kings. Kalyan Kumar

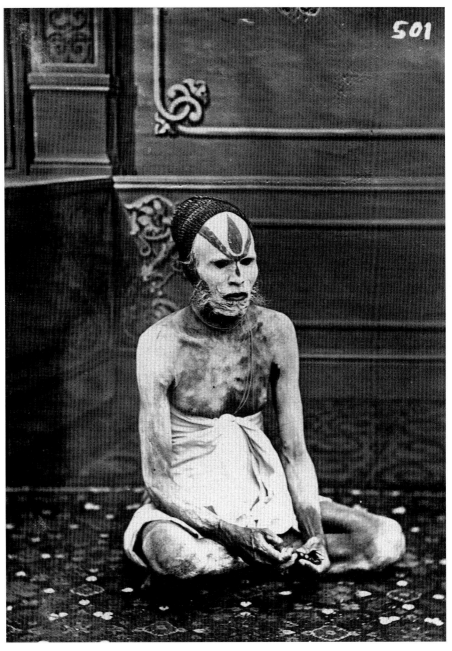

46 Maharaja Sawai Ram Singh II, sadhu, modern print from original negative
c. 1870s.

47 Maharaja Sawai Ram Singh II and T. Murray, portrait of Ram Singh, modern
print from original negative *c.* 1870s.

Chakravarty evocatively conveys something of the richness of juxta-positions: 'The walls, the mirrors and the paintings are hung with meandering floral scrolls, choked full of vine . . . flowers, tendrils and leaves, wheat sheaves . . . pineapple, pomegranate, apricot, grape . . . peacocks and snakes' and perceptively notes of this phenomenal pas-tiche that:

the artifice, variety, esoteric and antique allusions in the palace . . . sug-gest a successful baroque attempt to boost royal and civic pride. The outer façade of Lalbag impresses us overwhelmingly with its massive powerful presence, while inside we are transported into a decorative world of muted extravagance and fantasy. The overbearing impression as we leave Lalbag, is of a gentle colossus with a severe, rather forbidding external presence, concealing a jubilant, ever playful heart within.[35]

Something of the same duality is apparent in images made by another renowned studio which was to find Indore a hospitable place: Ramchandra Rao and Pratap Rao, the Indore State Photographers. These practitioners, probably brothers, undertook a variety of work. They made cabinet-card portraits in a studio with the conventional paraphernalia of a Victorian photographic parlour – cloth-draped tables, floral backgrounds, ornate furniture and that perennial reflex-ive sign of the studio portrait, a photograph album (illus. 48). They also produced some photographic prints of paintings of mythological subjects and were best known for their work with the Holkars. Two photographs of Shivaji Rao Holkar by Ramchandra and Pratap Rao on display in the Lalbag palace mobilize elaborate painted backdrops to depict him flying an early monoplane (illus. 49) and in charge of a row-ing boat travelling down a decidely European-looking river (illus. 50). Aviational backdrops were used in photographic studios in European fairs – for instance, at the L'Exposition de Gand in 1913,[36] but the public use of such images among the paraphernalia of royal rule is intriguing.

The same building also exhibits a life-size painted photograph by Ramchandra and Pratap Rao of the later Maharaja, Yashwantrao I, c.1917, demonstrating that this studio was also equal to producing the standard formal signs of royal power. These photographer-artists were clearly masters of many idioms and their royal Holkar clients were adept at using photography both to project dignified formal rep-resentations of royal grandeur and to exploit its ability to create dreamworlds.

Rather like the architecture of Lalbag, these images spring from a representational strategy that is concerned not with categorization and the closure of identity but with the manipulation of a repertoire

48 Ramchandra Rao and Pratap Rao, woman with photograph album, *c.* 1900.

49 Ramchandra Rao and Pratap Rao, Shivaji Rao flying, *c.* 1890s.

50 Ramchandra Rao and Pratap Rao, Shivaji Rao rowing, *c.* 1890s.

51 Krishna killing Kaliya (still from D. G. Phalke's 1919 film, *Kaliya Mardan*). National Film Archive of India, Pune.

of signs signifying possible states of being. Just as in architecture king-building involves the accumulation of different national styles, and rooms associated with different places and epochs, so these photographic images suggest a person-building in which different performances are acquired. In both domains, the person or thing represented is merely a starting point for a much wider confabulation. In this respect architecture and photography operate as parallel technologies of augmentation, both working to leave substantive traces of what otherwise would be mere dreams.

At the same time that Ramchandra Rao and Pratap Rao were starting their business in Indore, a soon to be famous master of cinematic dreams was resident in Ratlam, a town lying to the west of Nagda. A catalogue of Lala Deen Dayal's work lists several studies of Ratlam. They include views of the approach road to the palace showing the clock tower, the Rambagh summer house and 'a triumphal arch made of brass utensils in honour of a visit by the Agent to the Governor-General'.[17] D. G. Phalke, the film-maker and the master of dreams referred to above, probably saw it in a very different light. He was to emerge in the second decade of the twentieth century as probably the most important figure in the emergence of mass-mediated visual culture in India (illus. 51).

Ashish Rajadhyaksha[38] has noted the significance of Phalke's multi-media apprenticeship at a time when representational forms in India were undergoing profound cultural and technological transformations. In 1875, aged 15, he studied at the J.J. School of Art in Bombay. This institute, which had opened in 1857, was a Parsi contribution to the British project to (in Lord Napier's words) 'Romanize' the 'Indian pencil'.[39] Phalke then moved to an art school in Baroda. It was here that he purchased his first camera and learned how to paint photographs. The principal was so impressed with his photography that he was sent to Ratlam, where he learned three-colour blockmaking, photolitho transfers, colotype and darkroom printing techniques under the guidance of one Babulal Varuvalkar. It was in Ratlam that he decided to become a professional photographer and he soon opened a studio in Godhra, in Gujarat. During this period Phalke was so impressed by the performance of an itinerant German magician that he set about instructing himself in magical arts and gave public performances using the professional name of Professor Kelpha.

The Marathi biographer Isak Mujavar[40] comments on the difficulties Phalke faced in his early career. It was felt by many people that having a photograph taken was as inauspicious as insuring one's own life: both were intimations of and provocations to mortality. Phalke encountered such resistance from a Baroda prince who refused to allow him to take his likeness on the grounds that this would surely shorten his life. The prince was also afflicted by troublesome *bhut pret* (ghosts and spirits) and Phalke arrived at an ingenious solution to his dilemma: he told the prince that he could banish the ghost with his camera. Having thus convinced the prince of the benefits of photography, Phalke prepared a painted negative depicting the sort of monstrous ghost from which the agonized prince was suffering. He then seated the prince under a tree and photographed him, as he had wished to do all along. The negative exposed by Phalke was kept hidden (and was later used to produce saleable images of the prince), while the pre-prepared image of the ghost was shown to the grateful prince, who then rested content that the ghost had been captured and neutralized.

Although the prince went on to convince others in the court of the benefits of photography, Phalke failed to generate a sufficiently large income and was forced to take up a job as a draughtsman/photographer in the local Archaeology Department, recalling Lala Deen Dayal's original employment. Subsequently he worked as a painter of theatrical scenery in Baroda and latterly in Pune. Phalke was then to move to Lonavala – mid-way between Pune and Bombay – the site of the Ravi Varma Press, one of the nation's most important chromo-lithographic printers, by now run by the German technician Schleicher, to whom Ravi Varma had sold his interest in 1901. Here he would run his own printing press and, according to some accounts, work in the Ravi Varma Press. The chronological coincidence of Ravi Varma's departure and Phalke's arrival amounts almost to a succession of leadership in the field of popular visuality.

Ravi Varma was an oil painter who had been tempted into mass picture production in the hope of 'raising' popular taste, a project from which he would retire disillusioned. In one of his early paintings of the artist Chitralekha (illus. 52), he clearly saw a parable of his own abilities. Usha, the daughter of King Banasur, dreamt one night that a handsome prince had kissed her while she slept (this was also the subject of another painting by Ravi Varma). She told this to Chitralekha, a skilled portraitist, who then produced likenesses of all the local princes. Through this gentle identity parade, Usha was able to identify Aniruddha, the grandson of Krishna, whom she would eventually marry.[41] Imagination, in the form of a dream, is clearly at the heart of this story, but it is eventually disciplined by mimesis, and it is this mimetic precision that appealed to Ravi Varma, searching for an allegory of his own talents. Phalke's experience in Baroda is instructively different: the space of the photographer's cloak allows a new creative intervention that transcends mimesis, opening up a new space of magical conjunctions of the sort which Phalke was to explore in his films from 1913 onwards.

Phalke's period in Ratlam was a small fragment of an extraordinary and lustrous career. But in looking at images taken in Ratlam photographic studios at the turn of the century (illus. 53)[42] it is fascinating not only to speculate on whether Phalke might have been involved in some aspect of their production but to peer into a representational world in which many different media – photography, theatre, chromolithography and film – were all starting to work together, creating a distinctive aesthetic which, like Phalke's training in magic and his sleight of hand under the photographer's cloak, opened up a new space within photography where powerful and extravagant visions could be conjured.

This historical conjunction of different media, at a particular moment, provides a more satisfactory framework in which to understand the emergence of new forms of visuality than the culturally essentialist argument advanced by Judith Mara Gutman. Gutman has made extravagant claims for the 'Indian-ness' of locally produced photographs. Drawing on a significant body of images, she valuably

USHA AND CHITRALEKHA (THE ARTIST).

52 Ravi Varma, *Usha and Chitralekha, c.* 1890.

attempts to '[throw] open the history of photography'[43] by revealing how 'Indian photographers used the camera to reflect and extend an Indian conception of reality'.[44] Gutman's observations contain insights but are too broadly stated and need to be relocated in a more sensitive reading of both colonial and local practice.

Paralleling a thesis advanced by Peter Galassi, that photography in the West echoed the proto-photographic syntax of earlier European painting,[45] Gutman agues that 'Indian photographers followed in painters' footsteps' in such a way that 'everything in the picture field happens at once . . . in an idealized space over a timeless identity'.[46] Whereas 'Western' images (Gutman discusses a landscape by Samuel Bourne) involve a gentle narrative that leads the eye through the picture and the choreographing of light to produce images that were consonant with expectations created by a pre-existing tradition of visual and literary representation, 'Indian' images participate in a completely different aesthetic.[47] Gutman describes her frustations with a photograph showing a large number of women at a fair:[48]

. . . with no 'invitation' into the picture, my eyes did not know how or where to enter. So they leaped in and were surrounded by one group of women. Even then, inside the picture my eyes could not move around. They were locked into one part alone. There were no leads as you find in Western imagery . . .

Gutman's verdict is too determined by a hyperbolic essentialization of an Indian alterity, but there are valuable observations to be extracted from the exaggeration and excess. It is plausible that the retraining of court painters as photographers and the relatively closed aesthetics of many courts led to direct overlaps between painterly and photographic practices and imagery. However, such observations need to be carefully situated historically. We shall see in Nagda and Bhatisuda practices many apparently similar overlaps between painting and photography but within the idiom of commercial popular culture. Dramatic changes in patronage structures and the public sphere undercut any possibility of generalizing about the 'Indian-ness' of this relationship.

The attempt to sort images and practitioners into the categories of 'Indian' and 'Western' (as Gutman does) is also fraught with difficulties since many Indian studios had largely European clienteles, and many studios had mixed ownership or became Indian-owned without visible changes in the product. In some respects it makes more sense to contrast official and personal photography. Thus what differentiates the images we have seen in the earlier chapter from the cabinet

53 Portrait of four unknown males by unknown Ratlam studio, *c.* 1900.

cards and *cartes-de-visite* being produced by the sundry Indian studios is, first and foremost, the field of power around the camera rather than cultural practice. It is the continuities between most private nineteenth-century photographic portraits of Europeans in India and Indians which is striking, and Indian photographers were just as capable as Europeans of participating in the project of ethnological surveillance.

The new visual culture that emerges around the turn of the century does, of course, make a direct appeal to 'traditional' motifs and concerns, but I would wish to stress how these are mediated through a particular historical context. They are not the eruption of some unchanged Indian psyche, as in Gutman's version, but highly complex, 'modern' attempts to formulate visual identities under specific historical and political conditions. Thus both Ravi Varma, the painter who played a significant role in defining a new aesthetic in oil painting and mass-reproduced chromolithographs, and D. G. Phalke, who was to make a similar impact in film, both consciously articulated their work as responses to specific predicaments of their time.

Phalke, for instance, was propelled into film production by his viewing of the film *The Life of Christ*. This was to effect a personal transformation which was also imbued with a huge political potentiality: '. . . while the life of Christ was rolling fast before my eyes I was mentally visualizing the Gods, Shri Krishna, Shri Ramachandra, their Gokul and Ayodhya . . . Could we, the sons of India, ever be able to see Indian images on the screen?'[49] Phalke's own political intentionality is never far from the surface in his writings and he saw his own film-making practice as a contribution to a fluid contemporary political reality.

In addition to the anthropological projects mapped in Chapter 1 which were concerned with categorical difference and the body as an external sign, there were other projects concerned with particular notions of 'portraiture'. A key difference here was the class of person depicted: the anthropological works dealt with anonymous 'typical' representatives of particular categories, whereas 'portraits' were concerned with individual members of an élite within which markers of ethnicity were downplayed.

An example of this is Sorabji Jehangir's *Representative Men of India: A Collection of Memoirs, with Portraits, of Indian Princes, Nobles, Statesmen, Philanthropists, Officials, and Eminent Citizens* (1889). Edited by the Parsi Chief Magistrate of Baroda and dedicated to Victoria Queen-Empress of India, this sumptuous volume was

the first of a proposed series of drawing-room table volumes of photographic portraits of contemporary Hindus, Mahomedans, Parsis and Englishmen, who, however they may be otherwise discriminated, are all connected together by the honour they share in common of having, in their various spheres of Imperial and Civic duty, won the confidence and affection of the people of India.

The introduction by George Birdwood positions the volume between an audience eager for a new vision of a de-ethnicized élite at ease with itself and an atavistic desire to position members of this élite within an ethnological hierarchy: 'These portraits of Native Indians are deserving of observation also in more than their individual aspects. They present a wide ethnographical range, and are illustrative of many races.' But this is a troubled hierarchy, one in which the ties of friendship have attenuated and disrupted the anonymous certainties of science:

There, among the rest, is the portrait of my revered and saintlike friend, Mr Dadabhai Naoroji [illus. 54], formerly a Member of the Legislative Council of Bombay, and now a candidate for a seat in the Imperial Parliament. The most cursory examination of it will suffice to show how altogether inaccurately, through the casual use of a colloquialism, Lord Salisbury applied to the owner of so Caucasian a head the descriptive phrase of 'black man'![50]

Dadabhai Naoroji, Esq.

54 'Dadabhai Naoroji, Esq.', 1889, from Sorabji Jehangir, *Representative Men of India*.

The value of the work, Birdwood wrote, was that it would enable English newspaper readers to see 'depicted after the true, substantial mould of frame and face, in which they breathe and move'[51] those individuals who would otherwise be mere names in newspaper accounts. Implicit in this desire is a complex notion of portraiture in which the face becomes a valuable supplement to mere action and thought. In our televisual world the possibility of such a severance never arises since the person never appears in advance of his/her face. The Jehangir volume marks out a historical moment during which photographic technology was able to retrospectively supply the 'frame and face' of those who had made history, but up till then invisibly and in a disembodied way. *Representative Men of India* is thus a catching-up exercise, a retrospective supplement dispatched from the colony to the metropole to fill in a missing part of personages who were already familiar.

The attempt to link 'frame and face' with a de-ethnicized identity reaches its apogee several decades later in Indore, the very city we encountered earlier. The crucial agent in this development was the idiosyncratic theosophist G. S. Arundale.

Arundale had previously been Principal of the Central Hindu College in Benares, where he resided for many years with Annie Besant, the founder of the college. His long-standing interest in theosophy can be traced to his aunt, Francesca Arundale, who raised him as her own son, and he was tutored as a boy by the Reverend Charles W. Leadbeater, an Anglican who became a Buddhist and theosophist and was later to be closely associated with Annie Besant.[52] Arundale had been Organizing Secretary of the All India Home Rule League and was interned with Besant and B. P. Wadia under the Defence of India Act in 1917 (illus. 55).[53] He became head of the Education Department in Holkar State in 1920, the same year that he married Rukmini, the daughter of Pandit Nilkantha Sastri of Madras, an action which, according to Nethercot, sent the Brahman community into 'an angry dither'.[54]

Theosophy, a complex mystical movement which flourished greatly in India, was started by Madame Helena Petrovna Blavatsky and Captain Henry Steele Olcott. They travelled to Bombay in 1879 and, after a brief alliance with the reformist Hindu Arya Samaj, gained the patronage of Damodar K. Mavalankar, who purchased the property on the Adyar River in Madras which remains the headquarters of the movement. Key elements in Blavatsky and Olcott's belief system were Tibetan *mahatmas*, able to project their astral forms and to communicate telepathically and through long-distance writing and draw-

55 L. P. Wadia, Annie Besant, and G. S. Arundale during internment in 1917.

56 Portraits in the Nara Ratna Mandir.

ing,[55] and among the Theosophical Society's aims were the formation of a Universal Brotherhood of Humanity 'to study Aryan culture and to explore the hidden mysteries of nature and the latent powers of man'.[56] Theosophists were disciples or *chelas* of these *mahatmas* and they were the objects of much contemporary ridicule in Britain, as is clear from the September 1891 *Punch*:

I AM KOOT HOOMIBOOG.[57] There are more things in my philosophy than were ever dreamed of in heaven and earth. You are POONSH. You are a Thrupni but you are not a Mahatma. Be a Mahatma and save your postage expenses.[58]

But theosophy, for all its Blavatskian lunacy, took aspects of Indian and Tibetan philosophy and religious practice seriously. It placed a colonized culture in the role of spiritual teacher and for many adherents, including Arundale, this had important political consequences. Besant and Arundale were at their most political in 1916–17 when with Wadia they organized the Home Rule League agitation. This involved convening discussion groups, lectures and the dissemination of vast numbers of pamphlets, and Besant's League was to find its main support among Madras Tamil Brahmans and Gujarati professionals in Bombay, who were attracted by theosophy's 'theories of ancient Hindu wisdom and glory, and mystic claims that all the achievements of the modern West had been anticipated by the *rishis* [sages]'.[59] Besant, Arundale and Wadia's internment in June 1917 provoked talk of passive resistance among many of these followers.[60]

It is this theosophical and political context that makes sense of Arundale's involvement in 1923 in the creation of a remarkable picture gallery in Indore. Known as the 'Nara Ratna Mandir' (literally 'Temple of the Jewels of Mankind' but Arundale reads it as 'Temple of Human Greatness'), this stressed the putative unity of all Indians. Whereas the anthropological investigations discussed earlier dwelt on difference and separation, the faces and bodies deployed in the Nara Ratna Mandir were conceptualized as elements of a wider human unity. This attractive building still exists and now serves as the sculpture section and exhibition hall for the Indore Government Institute of Fine Arts.

The Nara Ratna Mandir was inaugurated by His Highness the Maharaja Tukoji Rao II in the presence of representatives of 'all the great religions of the world' and a commemorative brochure issued by Indore State documented the philosophy that lay behind the creation of this 'very interesting institution':

It is nothing less than a special building wherein will be housed portraits of all the greatest men and women in the world irrespective of religion, race or colour as well as a library containing biographies and autobiographies of great people, so that the public may see the pictures of the world's greatest, and read of great deeds, great words, great thoughts.

Portraits of great people were intended to introduce the population of Indore to their ideas and written works, which would be available in the adjoining library. Before its inauguration Arundale delivered 249 framed portraits of great men and women, although only sixty of these were displayed when the building first opened (illus. 56). These included major religious figures such as 'Shri Rama in exile', Guru Nanak, Mohammed, Moses and (unsurprisingly) Madame Blavatsky and Colonel Olcott; Indian historical figures such as Asoka, Jehangir and Akbar; Western classical figures such Cicero, Pythagoras and Petrarch; a cluster of nineteenth-century literary figures (Blake, Shelley, Keats, Thomas Carlyle); a number of Italian nationalists (Garibaldi, Mazzini); and a scattering of European scientists (Huxley, Kepler, Leibniz, Newton) and philosophers (Descartes, Pascal).

The images were of necessity a mixture of paintings and photographs and Tukoji Rao was to praise the artistry of his own State Photographers in his reply to Arundale's speech:

Presiding over the Picture Gallery room in the Home of Greatness is the portrait of Devi Sri Ahilyabai, the great ornament not only of the Holkar House, but equally of the whole of India, a fine picture generously presented by the State Photographers, Messrs. Ramchandrarao and Prataprao, who are not merely photographers but artists too, as a visit to their beautiful picture gallery would show.

A 'substantial annual grant' had been promised to expand the collection and in 1925 further additions were made which included Tulsidas, the twenty-four Jain Tirthankas, the Rani of Jhansi and various members of the Holkar dynasty. In addition, portraits of Charles Darwin, the German anthropologist Virchow, William Herschel and Sir William Ramsay (the Scottish discoverer of argon) appeared. By 1946 the gallery displayed a total of 377 portraits. The library's collection of biographical and autobiographical works also grew (in 1932 there were 483 English, 149 Hindi and 81 Marathi books), and regular lectures were arranged (in 1925 there were thirteen public lectures, in 1927 there were five, in 1929 there were ten).

Arundale's motivating idea was that 'the lives of great men all remind us, we can make *our* lives sublime'. In a speech made at the opening his egalitarian instincts are clear, for he observed that the Nara Ratna Mandir was the first 'Home of Greatness' in the whole world 'where true greatness, irrespective of all distinctions of race, of faith, of sphere and line of activity, is to find an honoured and a worthy home'. He continued:

True greatness is universal, belongs to all nations, is the property of the world, be its race and its faith what they may. And if we are to hope for the advent some day of the universal brotherhood of mankind, we must begin to take stock of what we share in common, so that little by little we may perceive that the essential unity is above all differences, may some day dominate them, however opposed the differences may just now seem.

But this implicit political programme was tempered by paternalistic advice:

If there is unity among the British to-day, it is, I venture to think, because they have – if I may use the expression – pooled their heroes, their saints, their martyrs; and that they share them in common, even though these very heroes, saints and martyrs may in the past have been in fiercest opposition. Robert the Bruce, William Wallace, for example, are as much honoured by the English youth as by his Scotch comrade, for, at least with regard to the heroes of the two islands, greatness has transcended the borders between Englishmen, Welshman, Scotchman and Irishman.

For Arundale, then, the myriad faces in this gallery would serve as moral exemplars of a grand human project in which Indians were centrally situated. The public's first point of contact would be these great persons' physiognomy, and he hoped that through encounters with these wise faces the public would be encouraged to discover more in the library.

There is here a clear continuity with the founding idea behind London's National Portrait Gallery, where these words by Lord Palmerston are to be found inscribed at the entrance:

There cannot, I feel convinced, be a greater incentive to mental exertion, to noble actions, to good conduct on the part of the living, than for them to see before them the features of those who have done things which are worthy of our admiration, and whose example we are more induced to imitate when they are brought before us in the visible and tangible shape of portraits.

Arundale's theosophical engagements may well have made him more susceptible to the powers of 'the visible and tangible shape of portraits', for in the Adyar Theosophical Society headquarters, images purporting to be of the *mahatmas* acted almost as letterboxes, literally conveying their messages from distant Tibet. These were memorably, and sceptically, recollected by Moncure Conway after a visit to Madame Blavatsky in the 1880s. At the heart of the Adyar bungalow lay the 'sacred room' in which was a shrine constructed inside a cabinet. On either side of a small Buddha were 7-inch-high pictures of

Blavatsky's two main *mahatmas*, Koot Hoomi and Morya. Conway was convinced that one was based on a painting of Rammohun Roy and the other was perhaps a chromolithographic image of the god Rama which had been 'manipulated'. Blavatsky, on the other hand, contended that they were 'done by some process said to be occult'.[61] This shrine was a posting point: 'Letters were deposited and swift answers received from the wonderful Mahatmas.'[62]

The image of Rama is not all that Blavatsky appropriated from popular Hinduism, for images – whether stone or paper – are commonly endowed with a great power. One contemporaneous example must suffice to illustrate this: Ramakrishna, the great Calcuttan sage, frequently entered *samadhi*, a state of suspended animation, after seeing pictures of deities, and when shown a photograph of himself in *samadhi* taken at the Dakshineshwar Temple in 1883–4, he predicted that 'this photo will be worshipped in every home'.[63] Many images of Ramakrishna reproduce this famous photograph. Ramakrishna, Swami Vivekenanda and the Mother are shown seated in front of the temple's statue of Kali (illus. 57). To the right is the framed photograph about which Ramakrishna commented, garlanded with marigolds. The question of the power of images within the Hindu tradition is elaborated in Chapter 3.

As the name indicates, the Nara Ratna Mandir was a 'temple' and both the language used to describe it and the rules regulating public access emphasized this very explictly. Rule number 2 of the 'Conditions of Admission and Temporary Rules' laid down by D. B. Ranade, the Director of School Education for Holkar State, stipulated the following: 'Persons entering the Picture Gallery of Greatness will remove their shoes and while in the gallery will observe Silence.' Devotees would remove polluting footwear before entering any religious temple and the symbolism would not be lost on the visiting public. The temple metaphor receives its most grandiose articulation in Arundale's inaugural speech: '. . . I would ask that reverent silence be maintained within the Picture Gallery itself – the *sanctum sanctorum* of the Shrine itself, so that in quiet peace the seed of greatness, surely within each pilgrim, may be stirred to growth by contact with flowers of greatness without.' The Maharaja's reply to Arundale pursued the divine analogy with reference to Tennyson and Ruskin:

Many years ago Tennyson, with the true vision of the poet, exclaimed:

> Let knowledge grow from more to more
> *But more of reverence in us dwell*
> That we may make one music as before
> But vaster.

57 Photolithograph showing Ramakrishna, Vivekananda and The Mother with the Dakshineshwar temple Kali image.

'More of reverence' is the crying need of to-day, for we are building a world on the ruins of the old and, if we would build to the glory of God we must build in a spirit of humble reverence, not only to God, but to all whom we recognize as great. Ruskin rightly said: 'To yield reverence to another . . . is not slavery; often it is the noblest state in which a man can live in this world.'

Reports on the administration of Holkar State indicate the annual numbers of visitors to the Home of Greatness as 2,000 in 1925, 1,000 in 1927, and 1,150 in 1929.[64] These are paltry numbers, especially when set against the annual figures of one million visitors each in 1936 to the Indian Museum, Calcutta, and the Victoria and Albert Museum, Bombay.[65] Apart from the visitor figures to the Nara Ratna Mandir, we have no information concerning the reactions of the local population in Indore. However, it is clear that the gallery was a failure. Part of the reason for this may have been the conflict between the two idioms appropriated by Arundale.

There was something hybrid and confused about Arundale's intentions, for he sought to collapse local practices of image use with Palmerston's high Victorian notion of moral portraiture. The phrase 'contact with the flowers of greatness' contains and conceals this complex hybridity. Local practices of *darshan*, of seeing and being seen by the divine, involved a process of divine contiguity between seer and seen in which the benefits of the viewing event would be the outcome of the physical visual 'contact' with the image. Arundale invoked some of these local expectations, but he tried to fuse these with a quite antithetical notion that desirable qualities such as intellect, moral example and sensibility could be read in the lines of the face. This Victorian notion of portraiture presumed that the viewer would find in facial 'features', and physiognomic aspects of a likeness, a model of morality and action worthy of emulation. The differences between these two idioms can be stated in another way: *darshan* invokes a generic type of image whose potency and efficacy are contingent on the images' conformity to certain typological constraints. 'Moral physiognomy' is dependent on a very particular transparency of moral worth, on the visibility of a specific character and action in a specific and unique face. We will soon see how different this is from the expectations that contemporary Nagdarites have of portrait photography.

Before returning to Madhya Pradesh in the 1990s, however, we shall make a brief detour to 1880s London, where, as a student at the Bar, Mohandas K. Gandhi approached Dadabhai Naoroji (whom we encountered above in *Representative Men of India*, see illus. 54) for advice as to what an aspirant lawyer should read to succeed in his job. Naoroji responded that 'a vakil should know human nature. He should be able to read a man's character from his face.' To this end he suggested that Gandhi read Lavater's and Shemmelpennick's books on physiognomy. Gandhi records:

I was extremely grateful to my venerable friend. In his presence I found all my fear gone, but as soon as I left him I began to worry again. 'To know a man from his face' was the question that haunted me, as I thought of the two books on my way home. . . I read Lavater's book and found it more difficult than Snell's *Equity* and scarcely interesting. I studied Shakespeare's physiognomy, but did not acquire the knack of finding out the Shakespeares walking up and down the streets of London. Lavater's book did not add to my knowledge. . .[66]

Gandhi's reaction suggests a rather different perspective on the readability of the body, one which was perhaps always at variance with the readings which were brought to bear in nineteenth-century anthropological projects, and in the Nara Ratna Mandir.

3 Chambers of Dreams

. . . photography is an imprint or transfer off the real; it is a photochemi-
cally processed trace causally connected to that thing in the world to
which it refers in a manner parallel to that of fingerprints or footprints or
the rings of water that cold glasses leave on tables. The photograph is thus
genetically distinct from painting or sculpture or drawing. On the family
tree of images it is closer to palm prints, death masks, the Shroud of
Turin, or the tracks of gulls on beaches.[1]

Babulal asked me to accompany the Mahavir Jaynti procession around
Nagda. The day before this he described the form it would take. Young
girls would assemble with *kalashs* [brass pots filled with water and
topped with mango leaves and a coconut] outside the Rajendra Suresh
Temple in Rani Lakshmibai Marg together with the Nav Prabhat Band
and a huge 'photo' of Mahavir (the founder of Jainism), drawn on a tractor.
It would of course be remarkable for a photograph of Mahavir to be
produced, rather I expected a photograph of a *murti* [statue] of Mahavir.
In the event it turned out to be what I would have called a large painting
garlanded with marigolds. Later Babulal told me that whereas 'artists'
[painters] used to be known as *chitrakars* this sounded very quaint and
old-fashioned – nowadays they were called *photobananevale* [photo-
makers].[2]

In the previous two chapters we have encountered two moments in
the photographic representation of body and face. In the first we
traced an official anxiety about the identity of colonial subjects and
an attempt to fix these photographically. In the second we encountered a quite different desire to use physiognomic imagery to communicate ethical ideals. This final chapter presents another twist in
the tale of photographic practice in India. Here we will look at contemporary portraiture in Nagda, the industrial town in central India
which was introduced in the prologue.

In the first chapter, photography's 'indexical' status was repeatedly
appealed to by colonial photographers. The chemical trace that constituted the photographic image was deemed to be of a higher semiotic order than the vagaries of the pen or the brush or the dishonesty
of local testimony. These practitioners also considered photography
to be a radically new technology. To many it was a sign of Western
technological prowess and a symptom of a modernity that they
opposed to the culture of the subjects they coaxed and dragged in front
of their equipment. In Nagda, very few people are willing to privilege
this technology, on the grounds either of its inherent semiotic quali-

ties or its history of cultural diffusion. In Chapter 1 I traced the institutional fields across which official photography flickered; in a similar way we need to map a set of cultural fields across which a wider class of images flicker if we are to understand the role of photography in contemporary Nagda.

The chief reason for this is that the enormous stress on visuality endows a great range of images with extraordinary power. A key concept here is the notion of *darshan*, of seeing and being seen by a deity, which also connotes a whole range of ideas relating to 'insight', 'knowledge' and 'philosophy'.[3] Recent anthropological and philosophical critique[4] has attacked the visualist bias in the Western tradition, but such a bias is equally evident in an Indian context.

In the cases of some temple statues there is a process of what might be termed 'indexical' replication – that is, the image is considered to be some self-willed simulacrum of a divine original. Many of these are *svayambhu* or 'self-born' images, such as an image of Hanuman that rose from the ground in the middle of Nagda in late 1982.[5] Fortuitously it erupted on a plot of land by the Civil Hospital which was under dispute with a Muslim landlord and the vast numbers of eager Hindus who hastily erected a makeshift temple around the *svayambhu* image the next day rendered the pending legal cases concerning ownership of the land irrelevant. Perhaps the most celebrated self-made image is the Shrinathji *svarup* whose left hand emerged from Mount Govardhan near Mathura in 1410.[6] Shrinathji's face did not appear until 1479 when Vallabhacharya, the founder of the Pushtimarg sect that venerates the image, was born: 'At first only one arm was visible but on the day of Vallabha's birth the face also appeared and from this time it was fed miraculously each day by a cow which poured milk into its mouth.'[7]

There are also images – and this would describe the majority of main temple images – which are elevated by a process of what we might term indexical contiguity or transference. Here, everyone knows that the image of the deity has been constructed by men (artisans of specific castes, some of whom are Muslims), but there is a process of induction and transformation that converts the previously lifeless image into a powerful receptacle of divinity. This is usually known as *pranpratishtha* – literally, 'establishing the breath'[8] – a consecrational ritual conducted by an *acharya* of suitable power who is able to transmit recondite divine power, and who inducts the *pran*, the breath of the deity, into the image with the aid of *mantras* – that is, sacred formulae. The ritual involves the replication and relocation of a pre-existing power and authority into a new location and the eyes of the deity play a crucial and revealing role in this. Frequently in these rites the eyes are opened last of all: sometimes they are smeared in honey and this is wiped away; or, if an image is painted, they are 'opened' with a final flick of the paintbrush; or, as in the case of most village images, artisanally produced enamelled pairs of eyes are stuck to the image. It is at this point that the image frequently acquires a liminal and ambivalently dangerous excess. Mirrors can be placed in front of the deity's own eyes, or they are shielded to protect onlookers from the unpredictable surges of energy that occur during this period. The tactile and visual relationships that devotees seek with their gods also have a negative undertow, for deities' glances can also be destructive. Some humans too are capable of deploying potentially fatal *nazar* or 'evil eye'.[9]

A third form of empowerment is grounded in a much more personalized and diffuse relocation of divine potency as the outcome of a relationship between the devotee and the deity. Historically this goes under the name of *bhakti*, or 'devotion', denoting a variety of medieval movements that increasingly stressed individual devotion and a set of interiorized emotional states in the devotee. These various movements and sects privileged these intimate gestures and engagements against the external play of ritual signs controlled by a hierarchal social and religious order. In Bhatisuda village, which lies 4 miles south of Nagda, *bhakti* has ceased to have any subversive implication and is the dominant idiom of ritual engagement that also centrally articulates a dualism between interior truthfulness (attached to intentionality and the heart) and publicly displayed exterior signs. We will later encounter this dualism as an important (and in some senses surprising) element in local discourses about photographic portraiture.

In the everyday lives of Bhatisuda villagers, encounters with the divine most frequently occur through the medium of chromolithographs (confusingly, for the reader, these are usually called *photos*), although photography can also be the medium for such encounters, through either photographic reproductions of statues of gods, photographs of saints and gurus, or photographs in which devotees pose in front of painted images of deities. These vividly coloured images of deities have a long, complex and fascinating history,[10] and are purchased as loose paper ('framing') prints in Nagda. Although I have never heard a villager express any interest in the details of the artists or the publishers that produce these images (most of these details being clearly identifiable on the print), they understand with admirable clarity that these are commodities churned out by some industry somewhere in the hope that people like them will purchase them. As they carry an image home in their bags (usually rolled up and tied with a piece of old string) from the main Sunday *hat* (market), jostling against a small paper packet of rice, perhaps some sugar, some incense sticks and a few fresh vegetables, it is just one of a number of purchases, and when they arrive home other family members may unravel it and finger it, demanding to know how much it was, rather as they might ask how much okra cost today.

Until this point the images are mere pieces of paper, recalling John Tagg's description of photographs as 'paltry paper sign[s]'[11] whose apodeisis is achieved socially rather than technologically. What gives the images power is the relationship that the devotee comes to have with the deity mediated through the image; and this is power that comes to inhere in the actual image itself in such a way that it requires to be formally 'cooled'[12] in a tank, well or river, as and when it is disposed of. Although some households replace all their chromolithograph images every year at Divali, most have a number of old images which continue to accrue potency as they become accreted with the marks of repeated devotion – vermilion *tilaks* placed on the foreheads of the deities, the ash from incense sticks, smoke stains from burning camphor. In this respect chromolithographs are similar to most Bheruisthans (clan deity shrines) for these are merely stones which are endowed by faith with potency. Although the particular siting of a Bheruisthan is usually authorized by a particular myth (for example, it is on the site of the home of the earliest clan member, or it was there that a snake bit an itinerant ancestor who then settled in the village where he recuperated), the stones from which they are constructed don't have any particular ontological quality – they just happen to be the stones which were to hand, any other stones would have done as well and it is repeated worship and attention that endow them with cumulative power. Like chromolithographs, the stones in a Bheruisthan have not been indexically authorized with potency by an *acharya* through *pranpratishtha* but have acquired their energy through 'faith' (*shraddha se*).

The 'inter-ocular' field[13] that photography enters is one already suffused with potent technologies of representation. In Chapter 1 we encountered critiques of the reliability of pre-photographic imagery and examined the ways in which photography (for certain purposes, at least) came to be regarded as possessing a 'penetrating certainty' denied to other media. In contemporary Nagda and Bhatisuda, photography is not semiotically marked out in such strong terms and, accordingly, its analysis needs to locate it at the centre of various overlapping visual practices, rather than at the apex of other media that it claims to have vanquished.

It is not clear to me how, without falling into the kind of pitfalls that Bourdieu[14] warns against (in which the anthropologist gets the answer s/he anticipates through questions that are asked in a theoretically overdetermined manner), one could ethnographically focus on the intriguing question of whether photographs, through being looked at over the years accrue a potency that in some way parallels that acquired by these other old images whose power is enhanced by the mutual visual contact and the images' intuitive awareness of the love in the devotee's heart. However, it seems at least worthwhile to frame this as a possibility. In Nagda and Bhatisuda, as also surely elsewhere, photographs are, like the Baruya of Papua New Guinea's soot-stained salt bars, 'good for thinking'.[15]

Partly because of this semiotic and lexical slippage, the 'photo' is not clearly marked as 'modern' because its functions are duplicated by so many other forms of palpably ancient representation. It is certainly true that the object that Nagdarites and Bhatisuda villagers most frequently ask me to bring on my next visit is a camera from Japan. This is testimony to product awareness, but not to any profound xeno-identity attached to photography. In Bhatisuda people know, as indeed do I, that Japan produces the best cameras. Although at one level there is an acute awareness and evocation of a (generally negative) 'West', as for instance in popular film,[16] in other respects that awareness remains exceptionally hazy. Photography does not come bearing any particularly visible xeno-trace, since it is so firmly inserted into everyday practice, not only in the functioning of the state but also in local temples (the Badrivishal Mandir in Nagda has supplies of photographs of the central temple statue for those devotees who require one), and into the emergent visual biographies of many people in both Nagda and Bhatisuda. In this sense there is no work of conversion to be done between different value systems.[17]

To be unaware of the intricacies of a particular technology does not imply that Nagda clients and photographers are not keenly aware of photography as a rapidly developing medium, subject to fashion and desire (and, as we will later see not without some nostalgic reinventions):

4.4.91: Shukla Studio, Rani Lakshmibai Marg: collected watercoloured photographs – very 'realistic' colouring of the Victorian variety, no heavy overlay as in Venus Studios. The proprietor's brother (a permanent worker at the local factory GRASIM who was away filming a wedding video) and his assistant were adamant that nowadays people didn't request studio watercolour photos because now they could get colour-processed ones. *Before* colour, people had black and white ones painted ('If you can get colour process why get a watercolour one?'). He understood that I had requested my painted photographs for 'research', to recapture a practice that no longer existed. Nowadays people only request colouring of pre-existing black and white photographs of the deceased.

A similar point was made by Suresh Panjabi of Suhag Studio:

Nowadays you can get everything, colour photos, good cameras, auto-focus. Before you had to be a great artist and have a special interest; nowadays anyone can be a photographer. All the functions in a camera are auto: auto-forward, auto-rewind, everything is auto. When we were making those black and white photos the cameras weren't that good.

I have already suggested that we will discover substantial differences between the motives for portrait-making in Nagda and those which motivated Arundale. One further difference with earlier practices should be stressed: whereas much British colonial photographic imagery sustains a Foucauldian stress on the links between visibility and power, comparatively little of Nagda's photographic portraiture is implicated in the processes of state surveillance. This is not to deny that the requirements of the state do motivate some image-making, for full-face photographic images are required for use on driving licences, railway season tickets, college admission forms, bank loan forms and ration cards, in addition to various identity cards required by government agencies, insurance corporations, schools and colleges (illus. 58). In 1996, for the first time, those wishing to vote in the national elections had to show a new ID card bearing a digitized photographic image. The Indian state, like all states, places great faith in photography's ability to capture vital aspects of its citizens' physiognomy. This faith in the simple truths of photography, however, stands in contrast to prevailing popular photographic ideologies and practices in Nagda.

Suhag Studio, whose proprietor we met at the start of this book, is the oldest studio in Nagda. However, the oldest photographs to be found in the town were brought by the migrant industrial workers and merchants whose arrival in Nagda from places such as Marwar in Rajasthan and diverse parts of Gujarat and Uttar Pradesh have transformed what was once the village of Nagda (with a population of a few thousand in the early 1950s) into a bustling township in excess of 90,000 in the late 1990s. In Nagda's main bazaar one can see, displayed on shop walls and at the rear of tea shops and other establishments, the traces of images that predate the practice of photography in Nagda. These are memorial images of ancestors and are often

58 The late Manohar Singh's driving licence, 1986.

recent handpainted photographic enlargements of old prints made many decades ago in remote parts of Rajasthan and elsewhere.

Over the last decade, about half a dozen major photographic studios have been in operation at any one time, although there were a notional seventeen studios registered as members of the Nagda Photographers' Samiti (Committee) in 1996. Some of these are long-established (like Suhag), while others have much more ephemeral existences. Several (such as the Venus Studio – illus. 59) have closed and reopened over a period of several years as proprietors pursued other business opportunities. There is also one studio, Sagar, established only a few years ago, which because of the technical expertise and inventiveness of its proprietor has acquired a loyal clientele and a reputation for quality that rivals that of Suhag, the studio which most Nagdarites would acknowledge to be the leader in its field. In addition to these studios, out of the 150 photographers registered with the Photographers' Samiti, there are about a dozen independent photographers whose main income is derived from work in the gardens of the local Birla Temple. This is a curious hybrid temple, rather like a cross between Khajuraho and a multi-storey car park, which was completed in 1974 and lies near the factory complex. The industrialist G. D. Birla funded many such temples during his career and although the Nagda

59 Manoj Jha, proprietor of Venus Studio, Nagda.

temple has a full complement of well-paid and learned Brahmans, it is viewed by the vast majority of Nagdarites as a place of *tamasha* (fun) rather than worship. The temple is set in beautiful gardens and attracts many families during the clement weather who picnic and relax in this (by Nagda standards) atypically sylvan setting. Like all tourist sites, it attracts photographers, and Nagda tourists at the Birla Temple commission sufficient images to sustain a large number of photographic careers. The images taken at the temple reveal a photographic itinerary, a route that takes in a large pond in the middle of which is an extravagant image of Vishnu reclining beneath the cosmic snake, and various shrubs providing floral backdrops in front of which families and children can pose. Beyond these Birla Temple image-makers, there is an even more precarious rank of photographic worker – the itinerant lensman who spends his days travelling around local villages. We will shortly encounter several examples of their work. Like other categories of photographers, their numbers are in a state of constant flux, but over the last decade there have been something in the range of ten to twelve active intinerants. Our typology is not yet exhausted, however, for there is another type of itinerant, but one with a much rarer skill on offer: the memorial portraitist. Nanda Kishor Joshi, whose work adorns the largest number of Nagda shops and homes, will also feature in due course in this account.

A popular chromolithograph shows the gods Shiv and Parvati and their two sons, Ganesh and Kumar (also known as Kartikey), having their photograph taken (illus. 60). Shiv, clad in a leopard skin and with a writhing cobra around his neck, sits comfortably with Ganesh, his beloved elephant-headed prodigy, seated on his right knee. Parvati clasps Kumar, who has insisted on bringing along an arrow, and we can almost hear the cosmic photographer politely urging her to squeeze closer to her husband to fit into the picture. Shiv and Parvati clearly visited this studio some time after their marriage, but it is marriage, and the fruits that flow from it, which is celebrated here. Parvati's pride and pleasure are those of being a married woman. This theme of patriarchal encompassment is continued in another popular image which was widely distributed throughout India in the 1980s in the form of a calendar (illus. 61).[18] Here Shiv and Parvati are depicted within the confines of a *shivling*, the phallic representation of Shiv's enormous power which is immediately recognizable to all Hindus. Within the *ling* Shiv literally encompasses Parvati and hierarchy is denoted spatially. In this image we see the notion that within each consecrated image or *murti* there lives the *pran* of the gods: the external form of the image contains the form of the god who contains the

60 Painter unknown, Shiv, Parvati, Ganesh and Kumar, *c.* 1980, chromolithograph.

61 Calendar depicting Shiv and
Parvati within the form of a *shivling*,
1983.

goddess. It is precisely this image which is cleverly reworked in a
sophisticated montage produced by Suhag Studio (illus. 62). Part of a
wedding album – the production of which still forms the staple activity of Nagda photographers – the image is the result of the complex
printing techniques at which Suhag Studio excels. Using carefully cut
card templates to mask the photographic paper during printing, a full-
face portrait of the bride wearing her *mangalsutra* (a necklace worn by
a married woman) is interpolated into a profile of the groom and both
these images are encompassed by a large shadow profile of the groom.
The montage clearly replicates the calendar image of the *shivling*, and
like that it plays upon the nature of representation, for the encompass-
ing shadow also refers to the literary Hindi term for photograph –
chhayachitra (shadow picture).

This image might serve as a motif for Suhag Studio, not only
because of its characteristic brilliance but more pointedly because of
its dramatization of the auspicious state of being *suhag*, of wifehood
or of having a husband. Becoming *suhag*, through all the activities and
performances that lead up to marriage, is what sustains Suhag Studio
and most other photographers in Nagda, and it is the centrally important representation of marriage that I will now consider.

The actual marriage ceremony is but the climax of a complex

118

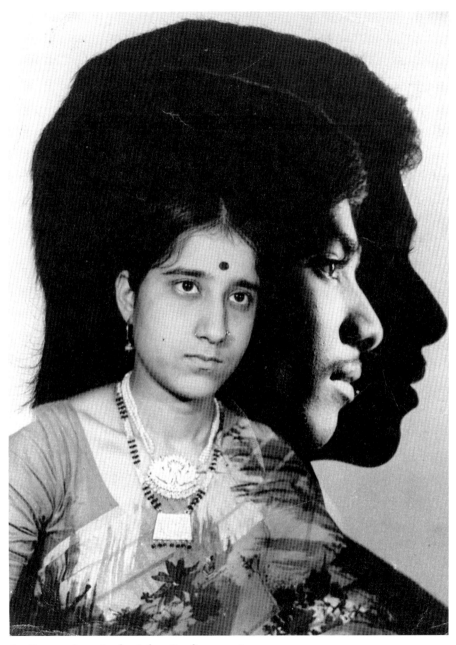

62 Composite print by Suhag Studio, *c.* 1980.

process of search and negotiation by the parents of prospective brides and grooms. Almost without exception mariages are the responsibility of parents, although ultimately the choice that prospective partners have is often considerable. The method of search varies according to family, caste and socio-economic group. Most caste groups prefer spouses from outside Nagda and often searches are made over a great distance. In Nagda, as elsewhere in India, marriages are seasonal. The four months of the monsoon and certain other months, fortnights and specific days are considered inauspicious and very few weddings take place at these times. The busiest time is after Divali (October/November) when the cool weather arrives, and at the height of the season up to half a dozen wedding parties might be simultaneously processing around Nagda's streets on any one night.

All but the poorest groups will commission a photographic studio to record different aspects of the wedding. Geographic exogamy, combined with patrilocal residence, is almost universally practised. This means that the bride and groom are rarely both from Nagda (and, in the case of village weddings, almost never from the same village), and that following the marriage the bride will leave her natal home for that of her husband. The costs of wedding photography can be borne by either side, but the norm seems to be for the bride's family to pay for the services of a studio from the bride's home town, where the wedding will be performed. This, however, is highly variable. In the mid-1980s, the record of the wedding would have taken the form of albums of black and white photographs. Poor urban families might have commissioned only a few dozen images, and many impoverished villagers would be content with one group studio photograph after the marriage (illus. 63). The majority of middle-income Nagda residents, however, commissioned albums comprising upwards of 200 images. After the mid-1980s the availability of video eradicated most of this market and the majority of clients sought moving colour images.

These videos record the sequence of events as they occurred in real time and post-production editing is limited to the addition of title sequences. They dwell chiefly on the arrival of the *barat*, the groom's wedding party, in the bride's home town. In some videos this will include their departure by bus or train; others merely show them arriving. Then there are long and often intimate sequences in which the bride, seated in a special pose, is virtually scanned by the camera, almost as one would input text into a computer. Starting at her feet (which will be covered with delicate henna patterns), the camera moves up her body to her face, before supplying close-ups of nose

63 Colour print of village wedding party in the Venus Studio, *c.* 1988.

rings, other pieces of jewellery, and her eyes. The camera moves down her shoulders and towards her hands, also covered with henna patterns prepared by female members of the bride's family.

In these sequences, the spectacle of the bride almost halts the narrative motion of the film. This interruption is often visually marked by camera angles that invert the bride so that she cuts into the screen horizontally or upside-down, and the lingering looks of the camera suggest Laura Mulvey's description of a parallel phenomenon in Hollywood melodrama:

The beauty of the woman as object and the screen space coalesce; she is no longer the bearer of guilt but a perfect product whose body, stylized and fragmented by close-ups, is the content of the film and direct recipient of the spectator's looks.[19]

The videos may include long sequences of feasting in which all the relatives and friends of the groom are shown enjoying the hospitality of the bride's family. The timings of marriages are closely circumscribed by astrologers' evaluations of the most auspicious moments for the commencement of the various elements. Thus sometimes a *barat* arrives in town very shortly before the actual wedding, at other times they may arrive in the dead of night and wait twenty-four hours for the most auspicious time for the central wedding rite. The timing of all these elements is highly variable and contingent on the star charts of the bride and groom. The problems that this poses for the videographer are sometimes compounded by the fact that he may be contracted to film two or three other weddings at more or less the same time. As a result videos frequently have a discontinuous feel: there may be very long sequences where nothing in particular happens and what appear to be the most crucial sequences may be hastily filmed. Similarly, if the videographer feels that he has not captured sufficient action during the main events of the wedding, he may pad out the tape with seemingly endless group shots of relatives posing in front of the bride and groom's thrones on the specially erected dais.

Next comes the actual procession of the groom's party around Nagda. The groom mounts a mare and to the accompaniment of a raucous brass band and surrounded by a dozen or so tribal children bearing neon tube lights powered by a mobile generator (for these processions are nearly always in the evening) a lengthy circumambulation takes the party through the town. The *barat* reaches the bride's home and the groom announces his presence by striking the ceremonial *toran* (wooden frame) with a wooden staff or sword. Various prestations are offered by representatives of the two families and the groom then proceeds to the place (usually within the bride's house) where the actual wedding rite, involving seven circumambulations of a fire in the presence of a Brahman, will take place. Following this the couple move to a pair of thrones on a stage which is usually to be found directly outside the house, often partly obstructing busy roads. Here further prestations are exchanged, some (or all) of the dowry may be visible, and finally numerous complexly differentiated groups of relatives pose on the stage.[20]

The earlier black and white images, many of which were complex montages, were immediately rendered archaic and quaint by video and it appeared that an irrevocable shift in the register of realism had occurred. However, this technological transformation contained its own internal contradiction. Very few people in Nagda have their own video players and video cassettes thus quickly became prisons, much less willing than old-fashioned albums to relinquish their information. Immediately after weddings, families would frequently rent a video player and repeatedly watch the footage of the wedding. But after a day or so these machines had to be returned and families were thus left with the video, but no easy means of bringing their images to life. The several occasions on which I have watched these tapes give an indication of the constraints involved. Many, perhaps most, households in Nagda have televisions and many of these subscribe to a local cable/satellite operator. In return for a monthly payment (in 1996 it was forty rupees per month), subscribers receive (via a cable) a mixture of programmes scheduled by their local operator. He will have a satellite dish through which he can get channels such as DD Metro, Zee and Vee,[21] and he blends these into a single offering. Sometimes it is posssible for this line to be disconnected and used to show individual video films from a separate VCR. In such cases arranging to see a wedding video is no more complicated that visiting one's local operator, bearing the video in question, and asking him to temporarily rewire your link. Just as often, however, because of complex intermediate junctions, a client's line cannot be so easily isolated and in such cases a new temporary line has to be run between the operator's shop and the client's house. This can be immensely complex, since there may be busy roads in the middle and electric and telephone wires causing obstructions.

Following the initial euphoria over this new technology and the vastly greater number of images it provides for roughly the same cost as an album of 200 still photographs, the experience of its practical inaccessibility (by those who did not possess VCRs), combined with an awareness of the improved quality of colour photography, led to different decisions being made about future weddings. From the early 1990s those same families who had opted to video the wedding of a elder son or daughter often chose colour still photography to document the alliances of younger sons and daughters. In all cases, accessibility and the ability to instantly produce such records to show to visitors were cited as the reasons.

The different temporal frame in which video and still photography are read was also commented on. Most wedding videos lasted one to two hours and even with the assistance of the fast-forward button were hard to edit for the benefit of the casual visitor – for example, a distant relative not present at the wedding who was changing buses in Nagda and had forty-five minutes to spare. Albums, by contrast, would repay even two minutes' attention and the central images – for example, the most complex montage – could be quickly located and dwelt on.

The film theorist Christian Metz has contrasted the different spatio-temporal sizes of the lexis – the totality of units of reading – of film and photography. According to Metz, the lexis of these respective media is radically different, both formally and socially. Formally, the photograph is a 'silent rectangle of paper',[22] whereas film, even if only a few minutes in duration, assumes a much larger lexis constituted by the size of the screen and the presence of sounds and movements. Metz stresses that the social context within which films and photographs are consumed also differs markedly, with film being by and large a collective and photography an individual pursuit. This also pertains to an extent when contrasting Nagda photographic albums and wedding videos. With the former I was almost always left alone to browse or had the assistance of one family member to elucidate various images, whereas the showing of a video invariably encouraged the whole family to materialize. But perhaps more significantly, Metz notes that the temporal lexis of film is *relatively fixed* while that of the photographs is *completely free*, even when confined to the syntagmatic narrative structure of the album. The video spectator is trapped within a temporal regime in which (except with a fast-forward button) s/he is completely unable to intervene. By contrast, the viewer of the still photograph has total temporal control over the image and decides for her/himself how long to gaze at it. As Metz concludes, 'Where the film lets us believe in more things, photography lets us believe more in one thing.'[23]

The nature of the moving film immerses the image in 'a stream of temporality where nothing can be kept, nothing stopped'.[24] By contrast, photography's suddenness and fixity parallel, for Metz, the childhood glance which fixes for ever the fetish: 'Photography is a cut inside the referent, it cuts a piece off a piece of it, a fragment, a part object, for a long immobile travel of no return.'[25] This dismemberment from the flow of reality produces images that have a greater fixatory power for most people in Nadga, so that it is always easier to point to a single image that summarizes a wedding than to a single sequence in a video.

The wedding album recording the 1983 marriage of Pukhraj Bohra and his wife Pritibala is one of the more spectacular examples of the work of Nagda's Suhag Studio. The bulk of the 200 images are ordinary photographs, showing no trace of 'cutting' or combination printing, but the dozen or so montage images are placed prominently at the beginning and end of the album. The images (illus. 64) are arranged two to a page and inserted in clear plastic pockets. The top image on the first page acts as a title and depicts a vignetted Pukhraj riding his mare *en route* to the bride's house, and around this image is a large black *svastik* (an auspicious Hindu symbol) and in Devanagari lettering (the script used in Sanskrit and Hindi) *shubh vivah* ('auspicious [or happy] wedding'). Below this is a stunning double image of Pritibala, the bride, achieved through masking part of the photographic paper and then reversing the negative to complete the rest of

64 Composite print of Pritibala from her wedding album, by Suhag Studio, 1983.

the print. In other montages the couple appear on television (illus. 65), and travel the length and breadth of India, appearing by the India Gateway in Delhi, the Tower of Victory in Chittaurgarh and the Birla Temple in Nagda.

Suhag Studio had been in business for five years when they printed the images in this album. The proprietor recalls that he would often stay up until four in the morning printing black and white images on the premises. In part this was because of the sheer numbers of images to be processed during the busy wedding season, but also because of the extraordinary complexity of some images. When colour processing first became available there was a radical change in his work pattern, for all the processing was now done by colour labs, initially in Bombay and subsequently in Indore and Ujjain. As colour became increasingly popular (and cheaper), the photographer's work was progressively confined to exposing the film, dispatching it to the processing labs and returning the results to the customers. Currently all Nagda studios use the services of a courier who travels by train to Indore each day to deliver and collect film and photographs. In the late 1980s, Suhag Studios (and later several other studios) acquired a video camera and added the slogan 'Video Shooting' to their shop hoarding and business cards. With the advent of video, clients' requests for photographic records of the wedding declined dramatically. In the words of Suresh Panjabi, the people of Nagda 'forgot' photography: 'They said don't take photos, only do video shooting.' By 1995, however, it was video that was on the wane and the demand for systematic photography at weddings returned. The numbers of photographs requested varies: 'It depends how much money the party has, 150, 200, 250, 300. If the party has lots of money then they want lots of photos.'

Suhag Studios were also responsible for another album dating from the late 1970s which records the marriage of Dinesh and Pushpa Khandelwal. Khandelwals are a middle-ranking merchant caste and Dinesh runs an electrical repair shop with a reputation among local villagers (who frequently bring him irrigation pump motors for attention) for absolute probity. Perhaps the most inventive work in this album depicts multiple images of Dinesh positioned in a strip of film (illus. 66). The same negative has been used to print images of different sizes within a silhouette of a film strip and canister created with a cardboard template. We have already, in the case of the wedding montage which echoes the *shivling* calendar, seen something of the subtle allegories of the nature of representation that Suhag excels in; here it is photography itself that forms the subject of the photographic image.

65 Composite print of Pritibala and Pukhraj from their wedding album, by Suhag Studio, 1983.

66 Composite print from wedding album, by Suhag Studio, *c*. late 1970s.

Suhag Studio is the longest-established in Nagda and perhaps the most renowned for the quality of its work. Sagar Studio is a relative newcomer in the world of dream production, but its talented proprietor, Vijay Vyas, is gaining a reputation for innovation and accomplishment to rival that of Suhag. Until six years ago Vijay worked for a haulage firm based in the local administrative headquarters of Khachraud. In 1990 he set up his studios in Nagda and quickly carved a customer base for his technically innovative colour double-exposure work, as well as a marketable competence in black and white portraiture and handpainted memorial enlargements. In addition to this, he also supplements his work with press photography commissioned by his younger brother, who edits a local paper, *Chhota Sansar*. In 1994 his big scoop was dramatic images of an exploding oil train, captured during an accident in one of Nagda's many railway sidings, and in 1996 his most significant images depicted the film stars Reena Roy and Jackie Shroff during their recent stay in Nagda. They were on location, filming in the gardens of the Birla Temple, and lodged for several days at a new luxury hotel constructed by a Nagda family who control all the local liquor franchises.

As a new studio, Sagar initially derived most of its income from studio portraits of near residents. Many of these were taken on particular festival days on which it is almost customary to have portraits made. As Vijay Vyas consolidated his local reputation, he was increasingly asked to photograph weddings and it is this activity which now accounts for about three-quarters of his income. The proprietor of Suhag Studio stressed the importance of wealth as a determinant of the number of images of wedding ceremonies which clients request; Vijay Vyas, by contrast, stressed the importance of religious affiliation. Hindus frequently request as many as 300 or 400 photographs, but Muslim clients request many fewer. The chief reason, Vijay suggested, was that in Muslim ceremonies there is less to photograph since they have less *riti rivaj* (customary ritual):

All communities (*samajs*) want photos to be taken at weddings. Muslims also want photos of weddings but their *samaj*'s *riti rivaj* is less, there isn't a big 'programme'. They have a simple 'programme': the girl comes, the boy comes, the agreement letter is produced, there is a *maulvi*, a judge (*qazi*). But with Hindus you have Brahmans and all the rest. Muslims have the *qazi* and the boy and girl sign the agreement . . . just like you have church weddings. There isn't a lot of ritual (*zyada riti rivaj nahi hota hai*). With Hindus, Panjabis, Sindhis, you have a lot of *riti rivaj* and you need to take lots of photos – a minimum of 300.

67 Colour double exposure by Sagar Studio, c. 1993.

Until recently, colour photography did not permit composite printing, although Vijay Vyas has always experimented with double exposures (illus. 67). This involved simply exposing the same negative
twice to produce superimposed images, and from the processing lab's
point of view there was, of course, no difference between such images
and single exposures. Composite printing, however, is a much more
complex operation and labs in Indore have offered this service only in
the last year or so. The restricted range of composite images offered
by labs contrasts with the limitless range of black and white possibilities, where the imagination and energy of the photographer/printer
were the only constraints. Vijay has also always continued to use
multi-image lenses, which are placed in front of the lens and are used
to create between three and nine images of the sitter (illus. 68). These
are also frequently used in wedding videos and occasionally in mainstream Hindi film.[26]

We have seen some examples of Suhag Studio's use of card templates of lettering, televisions and other xeno-objects to construct
extremely complex black and white images (illus. 69). These montages structured around linguistic signs and the signs of other orders
of representation are not Dadaesque subversions of photographic
authority through what Rosalind Krauss terms the 'language effect';[27]

68 Colour print made with a 'multiple image' lens by Sagar Studio, *c.* 1995.

69 Suresh Panjabi holding a 'Ring Ceremony' card template of the sort used in 1970s and 1980s black and white composite prints.

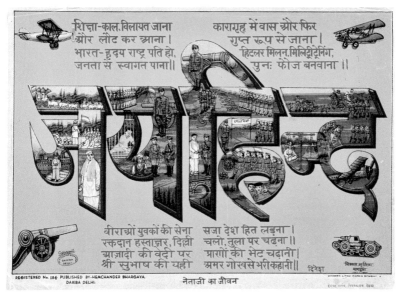

70 Khubiram, *Netaji ka Jivan* (the Life of Netaji [Subhash Chandra Bose]), *c.* 1946, chromolithograph. Bose's biography is pictured within the frame of the Hindi slogan, *Jay Hind* (Victory to India).

they are almost the opposite of this. Linguistic signs are viewed in broadly pre-Saussurean terms and in popular art Devanagari is frequently used (as in illus. 70, an image of Subhash Chandra Bose) to inscribe history as an immutable, indexical script. As we have seen, photography, by contrast, is not lexically or semiotically marked in local discourse as indexical, and in most cases is not differentiated from other techniques of iconic representation.

One possible reading of the Suhag montages might emphasize the homology between the complexity of the montage suspended in what

71 Composite print from Pritibala's
and Pukhraj's wedding album by
Suhag Studio, 1983.

is viewed locally as 'the non-symbolic' webs of language and the
astrological destiny of the couple (illus. 71). Marriage marks the alignment of human bodies whose compatibility is dependent on the time
and place of their birth; it is the final point of astrological knowledge.
The union is in this sense non-arbitrary, 'non-symbolic' and there is a
need to find an image that transcends the symbolic. In black and
white images this was performed through linguistic signs; colour
images achieve this through naturalization, through the interpolation
of the bride and groom into a realm that stands opposed to the arbi-
trariness of culture. Among the photographic templates used in contemporary composite colour printing are courting peacocks, the
wings of butterflies (illus. 72) and pairs of flowers (illus. 73) within
which the faces of the bride and groom appear. Colour processing
offers a new repertoire of signs, a different ratio of realism.

Vijay Vyas is still able to manipulate colour images through collage,
however, and he has recently started to use this to produce startling
covers to his wedding albums (illus. 74). The example reproduced here
is typical: at the centre the groom is shown garlanding his bride and
on either side they are represented in portrait close-up. Below this two
separate photographs showing different groupings of relatives with
the couple have been carefully cut and pasted. Working around this
basic structure, Vijay has infilled with a line pattern in yellow, green
and red, contributing to the sense of repleteness and density of the
overall image. His inspiration here is clearly the genre of posters and
hoardings used to advertise Hindi film. These also characteristically
superimpose large images of the main actors' faces with subsidiary
images of the support cast. Vijay was explicit about this link:

the [collage] is in *filmi* style. There are film posters which depict all the

72 Colour composite print produced by an Indore colour lab for Sagar Studio. 1996.

73 Colour composite print produced by an Indore colour lab for Sagar Studio. 1996.

74 Vijay Vyas, colour collage, 1996, photographs, watercolour and ink.

major episodes and show who the hero and heroine are. Their photos are cut and then pasted and a new background is painted. This is the method used to make film posters. So I have made the groom and bride the hero and heroine of this image. And it looks very good; no other studio does work like this. People really like this sort of work.

These remarkable collages exemplify in two dimensions all that photography represents in the Nagda context. The first dimension is the compacted and constructed dream world, set free from any arbitrary frame, that this local photographic technology makes possible. Released from its habitual chronotopic imprisonment, these photographic images conflate time and space, so that at least several temporally discrete moments come to coexist within the same fabulous space. The second dimension is the fractured picture plane, ruptured by the exuberant materiality of the collage composed of photographic fragments and areas of painted patterning with overlaid pen work which coils around the main portrait images.

The continuing (and increasing) demand for double-exposure and composite printed colour images suggests that, in this context, new forms of technology do not precipitate any trend towards a more realist chronotope privileging what Gombrich termed the 'eyewitness

134

75 Hand painted photograph by Suhag Studio, 1991.

principle'.[28] Indeed, as Vijay Vyas noted, the new generation (*nai pirhi*), by which he meant those aged under 35, had a liking for trick techniques. This was part of a wider trend in which earlier practices were now once again in fashion: 'College girls want to wear village blouses, and trick photo, double-exposing, and "design mixing" are again in demand.'

The proprietors of both Sagar and Suhag Studios are clear, however, that there has been an irreversible change in styles of portraiture, which they associate with poorer peasants' increasing access to photography. Many studios still display (and will happily take, if asked) portraits in which qualities of the face are accentuated through heavy shadow (*chhaya*). English terms are used to describe these – 'art photo' and 'shade light photo' – and photographers evaluate them positively when contrasted with the 'simple' or 'plain' photos (full-body poses with no shadow) which peasants always request. For Vijay, this is a frustrating constraint on his own creativity: 'Nowadays village people don't understand photography. They say that we are like this and we want to look like this in the photographs – for this reason they don't like "shade-light" photos.' Suresh Panjabi is perhaps the most accomplished in producing this style (illus. 75) which was elegaically described as being like an image from an 'old movie'. For Suresh, this is a disappearing art which is hardly ever requested by the masses seeking clarity and completeness. His sense of loss evokes the nostalgia one occasionally hears for the early films of Raj Kapoor and Guru Dutt from those alienated by the brashness of contemporary Hindi film.

It is clear that Nagda photographic studios are caught up in a complex nexus of changing tastes and aspirations on the part of their clients. But within these changes and recurrences, the daily life of photographers is structured by the timing of wedding seasons, the increased demand for portraiture on certain key festival days and the lack of business that attends various adjustments in the Hindu lunisolar calendar.

In Nagda, Hindus visit photo studios in large numbers during Rakshabandhan (a festival in which real and fictive siblings reaffirm their bonds) and on the day after Divali (known locally as *parhava* but also the day on which villagers celebrate Govardhan puja). Divali marks the start of the financial year and during this time hierarchy and order are especially stressed. Urban families come together for an elaborate *puja* to the goddess Lakshmi after which junior members of the family give *pranam* (a reverential bow) to senior members: sons touch the feet of fathers and mothers and younger brothers touch the feet of elder brothers. There is an important gender dimension to this in that wives touch the feet of husbands. This is also a day when many gifts of cloth are made by senior family members and by employers to employees. The day after this, male members reinforce their wider ties in the community as they wander around, usually in their best clothes, meeting friends and work mates. Many people choose to record these meetings photographically and extended families, husband and wives and, most commonly, male friends will visit their local studio for a permanent memento of the occasion.[29] Wearing one's best clothes improves the likelihood of the desired sort of photograph emerging, but there is also a sense that Divali marks the perfection of the social order and the idealized kin relationships and friendships that underpin this. As we shall see, almost no one in Nagda is interested in acquiring photographs created within a naturalist idiom: it is formalized and theatrically staged images that are most desired. Accordingly, Divali – the most orderly and highly structured period of the year – is an ideal time to visit the photographer.

Muslims, by contrast, arrive at the studio to have their photographs taken at Id, the end of Ramazan, and on the day of Moharram. On Moharram, Shiites mark the martyrdom of Inam Hussain and participate in a large procession, and after this many groups of Muslim

76 Bina and Pushpa, c. 1980.

friends meet (*milte-julte*) and visit Nagda studios. On both the day after Divali and the two Muslim festivals as many as 200 people may turn up in one day, according to Vijay. On the day after Divali, Hindu and Jain women also visit photo studios, although in smaller numbers than men (illus. 76). In Nagda, Muslim women very rarely arrive unaccompanied by male family members. This, together with obvious differences in dress and ornaments, marks the only differences between Hindu and Muslim portraiture practice. The preference of urban couples of both communities on such occasions would be for half-pose, full-face portraits, with the wife seated to the left of the husband. Much more will shortly be said concerning strategies of 'posing', but here we can note that in Nagda Muslim women occasionally don the 'Hindu' costume and ornaments kept by Vijay for the use of female clients.

Festival times can be very busy, and they often coincide with periods of intense wedding activity. Muslim festivals, calculated by a lunar calendar, can fall on any day of the year, and Divali, which always falls between October and November, comes after *dev uthni*, the eleventh day of the bright fortnight of the month of Karttik. This is the day that the gods awake after their slumber during the monsoon, after which the number of weddings increases dramatically. Within the Hindu calendar, however, lunar days, fortnights and months are occasionally added or deleted. Added, or intercalary, days, fortnights and months (*malmas*) are considered inauspicious and during these periods there can be little auspicious work (*shubh kam*). Vijay Vyas describes the consequences: 'There are no marriages, no openings [*muhurt*[30]] of shops or any openings of factories.'[31]

Vijay occupies a particular niche in the market for memorial images (*yadgar*), for his clients are mostly villagers who lack sufficiently large or defined images of the deceased individual whose images are offered for treatment. The cheapest service Vijay Vyas offers involves simply overpainting existing images, and an example of this sort of work can be seen in the examination of photographs in Bhatisuda. For 200 rupees and upwards he will copy the existing image and overpaint an enlargement. This is very time-consuming work and requires great concentration, but can be undertaken during slack periods. Many of the images he works with depict groups from which individuals have to be extracted:

Mostly village people want these because in the villages there aren't that many photos – they may have photos from an engagement or a wedding or some function like that. A group photo may have been taken at these functions. If someone dies, then if there is a single photo of them fine, but otherwise I will [have to get the portrait] from a group photo. I'll extract [*nikalna*] the person's photo and do an enlargment. But this is mostly in villages: in towns most people have photos of themselves.

In overpainting images he uses poster paint, oils and Fuji 'transparent watercolour folios'. These are booklets of coloured papers in twelve hues, specifically intended for 'professional photographers and artists to change ordinary black and white prints into beautiful natural colour photographs'.[32] A small square of the paper is cut and the colour dissolved in water. The photograph is then dampened and the colour applied.

From the point of view of Peircean semiotics, the occlusion of the photograph with a non-indexical veil of paint is surprising, for one might anticipate that in the attempt to recover the individual as a permanent visual trace one would relinquish indexical traces last of all. Seen as the technological apotheosis of perspectival picturing, photography is – within Peircean theory and Western folk ontology – privileged over its earlier painterly antecedents grounded only in mere resemblance. The historical narratives which mark this invention record the supersession of the handwrought icon by the machine-made index. Indian practice inverts this archaeology, for whereas in

77 Post-mortem photograph, *c.* 1975.

Western practice paint lies under (before) the photographic image as 'painterly referent', or a negated 'lack', in Nagda paint can be found over (after) the photographic image as part of a semiotic democracy.

Vijay is sometimes asked to take, or work from, post-mortem photographs, usually (though not always) because the subject was not photographed during his or her lifetime. His own father, of whom numerous photographs exist, died in October 1996 and he took a photograph similar to illus. 77, with family members surrounding the deceased father. Vijay saw this as an expression of a combination of the love that (Indian) children have for their parents, and the need for grief-stricken relatives to cling to memories of the deceased, just as it was common practice to keep clothes or shoes which had belonged to the deceased. Also significant, perhaps, is the fact that since an individual's *pret* (spirit) is not released from the body until cremation, Hindu death is comparatively slow and inert bodies are able to retain vital qualities.[11]

Vijay Vyas incorporates changes requested by relatives into the final enlarged and overpainted image, albeit not systematically: 'People give instructions that "I want that colour", "I want that *pagri* [turban]", "give me a garland"; they ask and I do.' In some cases images are simply enlarged and coloured as in illus. 78, a reworking of

78 Painted memorial image by Sagar Studio, 1996, and original photographic referent, *c.* 1975.

a wedding image. In others the interventions are more obvious, as in illus. 79, in which a moustache has been trimmed and an open collar replaced with a closed Jodhpuri coat.

Looking at my own painted memorial image (illus. 80) revealed how these images conform to a very particular set of rules. As a comparative stranger to the genre, one is initially struck by what one might term a hyper-reality, a solidification of certain features and an intensification of the gaze through the sharp reworking of the eyes. Here is proof that, in the words of Nelson Goodman, 'realism is a matter of habit' and the 'correctness' of a picture within any system 'depends upon how accurate is the information about the object that is obtained by reading the picture according to that system'.[34]

I have returned to Bhatisuda, the village south of Nagda, many times over the last decade, usually bearing copies of photographs I have taken at the request of villagers. On two such occasions I was approached by Manaklal, my old Jain neighbour and a rich and powerful person in the life of the village. Both times he quizzed me about a photograph of him that I had taken during my previous visit. Ashamedly, I had to confess that I had not brought the large colour print he had been expecting and Manaklal responded indignantly with the cry, 'So what will happen when I'm dead?'

79 Painted memorial image by Sagar Studio, 1996, and original photographic referent, *c.* 1985.

This riposte alerts us to the fact that photographic portraiture is as important (perhaps more so) in the village as it is in Nagda for its role after the death of the subject. Manaklal here alluded to photographs' frequent role as a sign of the ancestor in various ritual procedures. The use of photographs in this way is very widespread but it is appropriate that the most visible sign of this practice in the village is in the form of large images of Manaklal's brother, Bhairav, who died in 1977. It was indeed a gift of his portrait at the conclusion of my first period in Bhatisuda that led me, on further visits, to investigate more closely the role of photography in constructing the present and the past. This portrait had been given during a *bidai samaroh*, a departure ceremony organized by Bhatisuda Jains, and the giving of Bhairav Bharatiya's portrait was itself photographed by an employee of Suhag Studio, the resulting photographic album becoming – after a short delay – the last in a long list of presentations (illus. 81).

Bhairav, Manaklal and Hukmichand were all sons of the the village zamindar, Khubchand (illus. 82), an itinerant Jain merchant who had bought the revenue rights to the village at an auction in 1934 organized by Gwalior State, the princely state of which the village was a part prior to Independence. Khubchand and his family then threw themselves fully into rural affairs, playing the part of traditional vil-

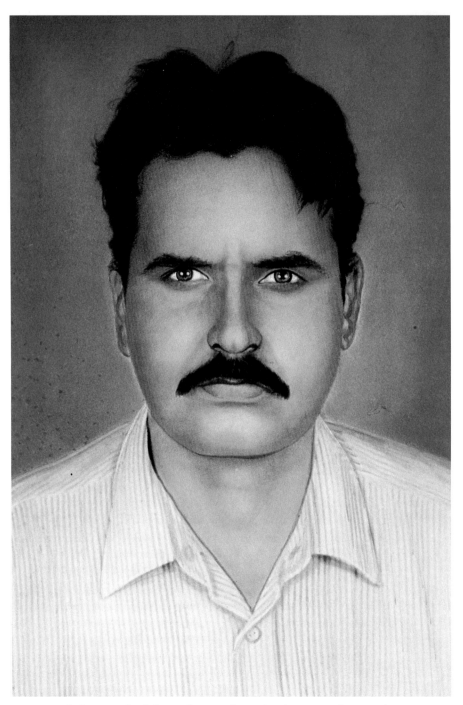

80 Painted photograph of the author, in the style of memorial image, by Sagar
Studio, 1993, watercolour on photographic print.

81 Presentation of a photographic portrait of Bhairav Bharatiya to the author in
1983.

lagers. Bhairav, the middle son, was always rebellious and sided with
poorer peasants in the region against oppressive local zamindars (one
of whom, of course, was his own father). Bhairav, who was an important figure in the freedom struggle in this region, was imprisoned several times before Independence, and in due course became the local
Communist (CITU) member of the State Legislative Assembly in
Bhopal. After the 1950s, his politics were increasingly configured by
struggles against the management of the industrial complex which
was to so radically change the Nagda area. Forming a *kisan-mazdur*
(farmer and industrial worker) alliance, he led several high-profile
campaigns against G. D. Birla, the proprietor of GRASIM, and against
local management on a variety of issues, ranging from pay and recruit-
ment policies to pollution. Over the course of two decades' agitations
involving court cases, *gheraos* and strikes, local managers came to
identify him as the major oppositional figure and one who consider-
ably hampered their activities. It came as little surprise that during

82 Studio portrait of Khubchand, former zamindar of Bhatisuda village, *c.* 1940.

the Emergency from 1975 to 1977, he was arrested. Shortly after came the tragic news that he had died in jail, the result, so his family and many local supporters believe, of a high-level decision to eliminate him.

Bhairav's political legacy has been immense, and although I never had the pleasure of meeting this clearly remarkable man (he died in 1977 and I did not visit Bhatisuda until 1982), he has been a very tangible presence during all my time in his village. Many villagers directly benefited from his activities and have land and loan facilities which perpetuate his memory, but this work is also done in part by the large image which his son, Manoharlal, keeps prominently displayed in the front room of his house in the village's central square (illus. 83). This framed black and white photograph is worshipped with burning incense sticks each morning and evening, and is the subject of more elaborate procedures on the lunar day that marks his death. The Hindu lunisolar calendar divides each of the twelve months into two fortnights (*paksh*) each of which comprises fifteen lunar days (*tithi*). The same *tithis* are repeated in each light and dark fortnight. Various moments of remembrance can be observed: the annual *tithi* on which a person died (and in the case of Bhairav the calendar date), the *tithi* in *pitr paksh* or *shraddh*, the first fortnight of the month of Kvar (also known as Ashvin), the *tithi* in the relevant light or dark fortnight within each month which serves as a more regular (though less significant) marker of that annual event and the day of the week on which the person died. In Bhairav's case a coconut is broken and the photograph is offered a marigold garland on each *panchami* in the bright fortnight of every month, and his son Manoharlal fasts every Thursday. On Kvar *krishna panchami* (the fifth day in the dark fortnight of the lunar month of Kvar), that is during *shraddh*, a more elaborate *puja* is offered, all family members fast and special foods are prepared and given to village Brahmans, and also to cows, dogs and crows, which are able to pass these on to the deceased. Specific ancestors can be propitiated on their appropriate *tithis*, but frequently in Bhatisuda all ancestors are worshipped on a day associated with the oldest-known forebear, or on the fifteenth *tithi*, the day of the new moon (*amavasya*).

Sadly, Bhairav's death was not the only tragedy in Manaklal's life, for as a child his youngest son died of a snakebite. Manaklal's house is opposite a shrine to the god Tejaji, who provides protection from snakebites. Tejaji, a truthful warrior, had been granted a boon by a cobra and on several occasions I have witnessed distraught bitten villagers rush into the precincts of the shrine and, on prostrating them-

83 Manoharlal Bharatiya worshipping a photograph of his father, 1991.

selves before the images of Tejaji on horseback and an angry cobra, receive its benefits. Their panic gradually subsides and after a hour or so they are able to rise and return to their homes to recuperate. Manaklal's son, however, did not make it to the shrine in time and he died.[35]

After his son's death, Manaklal took a photograph of him to the Bombay Photo Studio in Ujjain, where a beautiful montage was made (illus. 84) that interpolated the boy's image into the centre of a rose, a visual reference to the local frequently invoked link between scent and memory. The pain of such a tragic death is compounded in Bhatisuda by the knowledge that the soul of those who meet violent and untimely deaths will frequently encounter great difficulty in finding repose in the abode of the ancestors (*pitr lok*). In the case of timely deaths, the soul will find this repose only after eleven or more days' wandering, during which time relatives remain in a state of pollution. In Bhatisuda, when a person has met a good death, people will say that *sho din puri*, 'all the days have been been completed', and that the deceased has gone readily (*khushi*) to his or her *dusri shadi*, a 'second marriage' with god. In such cases, if the necessary complex mortuary procedures are followed, the deceased person's soul will almost certainly be peacefully relocated to its new abode. In the cases of *achanak*, 'sudden', or *ekdam*, 'immediate' or 'all in one breath', death,[36] however, the prognosis is much less certain and expectations will be high that the deceaseds' souls will be trapped to roam the world unhappily for ever as *bhut pret*, ghosts and spirits.

In Bhatisuda the victims of sudden death are classed either as *jhujhar* or as part of a residual category known variously as *sagas*, *sagat* or *pattarbabji*. *Jhujhar* are warriors who have died in battle, decapitated with a single blow, and there are many shrines to such figures in and around Bhatisuda. Like other *bhut pret* they make themselves manifest in the bodies of the living. Perhaps the most spectacular local example of this is an English soldier who regularly speaks in English through the mouth of an illiterate woman in a village near Nimach, some distance north from Bhatisuda. Several people in Bhatisuda are regularly host to known and identifiable *sagat* who appear throughout the year, but the majority of *sagat* make themselves manifest during two periods of nine nights associated with goddesses. These occur during the months of Chet and Kvar and it is generally agreed that during the former more powerful *bhut pret* are to be found.

Manaklal's son's *pattarbabji* did not appear until twenty years after his death and he was to do so while Manaklal's family were worship-

84 Composite print by Bombay Photo Studio, Ujjain, of Manaklal's son, *c.* 1965.

ping their lineage goddess in April 1994. The *pattarbabji* chose to use his elder brother Prakash as his *ghorla* (vessel). From my fieldnotes:

All the three families were crowded into the *puja* room; there was an extraordinarily tense and expectant atmosphere, almost as though everyone had waited all these years for this to happen. Prakash was in front of the main *havan* [a sacrificial fire], pounding the floor with his hand, passing his hand over the fire so as to burn it, and occasionally putting his face above the fire, all the while shouting lucidly. *Pattarbabji* spoke about the necessity of the family all coming together for *mataji puja* [worship of the lineage goddess]. Motilal (a cousin) interjected and defended the absence of various children.

Pattarbabji was at times excessively angry, berating the gathering. Pukhraj's mother [i.e. Prakash's aunt] hugged him and tried to calm his agony; Prakash's mother also did this but with more restraint. She seemed shocked and overwhelmed by the events. This shock was shared by everyone, but there was also a powerful sense that they were witnessing something very important: Pukhraj sat nearby with his son Tapish perched on his knee, ready to thrust him forward at any moment for *pattarbabji*'s blessing.

Many of those present found *pattarbabji*'s comments about disputes within the family painful to listen to, and his discourse had an apocalyptic air to it, peppered as it was with predictions of *tufan* [storms] and *dukh* [sorrow and suffering]. At points, *pattarbabji*'s energy contorted Prakash's body towards the display of chromolithographs and photographs surrounding the *mataji* shrine. His outstretched hand seemed to draw the energy down from the images.

Afterwards there was frantic, scurrying activity to communicate the productive energy that *pattarbabji* had left and to solemnize this eruption in the interests of family harmony. *Tilaks* were given to all present by Pukhraj. Prakash's mother distributed *prasad* [offerings consecrated by the gods] and all present touched the feet of those senior to them in a collective gesture that affirms family hierarchy and the authority of elders. Afterwards there was almost no discussion of the episode. I ate lunch [*puri* and *lapsi*] with Pukhraj's family and all talk was of crop prices.

The trace that ancestors are able to leave in their photographic portraits is one reason why Bhatisuda villagers' engagement with photography is so different from the French peasants analysed by Bourdieu. In the French village of Lesquire, the density of their local knowledge makes photography almost wholly redundant: '". . . it's not worth it!" "We've seen each other too many times already! Always the same faces all day. We knew each other down to the last detail."'[37] In Bhatisuda, conversely, photography never seems to merely duplicate the everyday world, but is, rather, prized for its capacity to make traces of persons endure, and to construct the world in a more perfect form than is possible to achieve in the hectic flow of the everyday.

Photography has potentially enormous implications for biographical perceptions and the development of new intimate forms of historicity. This hugely significant effect of photography has received surprisingly little attention from commentators. Indeed, some of the most penetrating suggestions are to be found in Alan Trachtenberg's analysis of American Civil War photograph albums, a context which may seem infinitely remote from Bhatisuda. Trachtenberg writes of what he calls 'historicism-by-photography', the notion that 'historical knowledge declares its true value by its photographability',[38] and stresses the narrative-making possibilities of albums which by their 'very blankness . . . prompt us . . . to ask whether it is possible to imagine photographs without narratives, without configurative structures to focus isolated images into a meaningful sequence or diegesis'.[39]

More will be said later about the narratives that surround individual images, but I want first to briefly consider the effects, what Umberto Eco once described as the 'syntagmatic concatenations imbued with argumentative effect',[40] of displaying images in albums and frames. We have seen that wedding images are customarily arranged in albums in which chronological sequence predominates. Montage images sometimes interrupt this, but the dominant narrative replicates the sequence of events as they happened. This is also true of the only two (non-wedding) photographic albums in Bhatisuda, both of which are owned by Pukhraj Bohra, a highly educated Tolstoyian figure who lives in the central square, near the Tejaji shrine.

The older of the two albums (illus. 85) is a cloth-bound landscape-format book with black pages. The images in it are arranged in chronological sequence and trace Pukhraj's student days and various special occasions in Nagda and Bhatisuda. On the first page are three small portraits in the 'poet' style, tipped in at a slight angle in a manner that replicates the idiom once used to display film stills. The images bear the very marked imprint of a particular historical moment. Later images are larger, clearer and show Pukhraj at a local *mela* (fair), posing in front of a painted backdrop with a rifle. There are photos taken during the festival of Holi, a spring saturnalia, in which Pukhraj and friends are shown elaborately disguised as ascetics, and pictures taken in the central square at Krishna Janmaasthami (Krishna's birthday) showing a tower of figures reaching for an earthenware pot full of *ghi* (clarified butter) in a re-enactment that resonates deeply with every Hindu in Bhatisuda. The exploits of Krishna the 'butter thief' are also familiar to villagers through chromolithographic representations. There are photographs taken on Rakshabandhan, a day when links between siblings are affirmed; in this case Pukhraj's

85 Pukhraj Bohra displays his earliest photograph album.

86 Pukhraj, Manoharlal and Rajendra on Juhu Beach, Bombay, *c.* 1975.

87 Kachru's son's only photograph of his father. Bherulal Kachrulal Ravidas.

cousin drapes his arm around Pukhraj's shoulder. Other village scenes include several of an all-night dramatic recitation (*katha*) in honour of Tejaji and an elderly Brahman reading from a vast religious text. And then there are images taken outside the village that record various perambulations: a visit to Bombay poignantly inscribed in peeling scenes of Pukhraj and two cousins at the water's edge in Juhu (illus. 86), a 1970s bus outing to Mandu, a decaying Muslim citadel south of Indore, where the group was fortunate enough to find two Westerners (*hippis*) and persuade them to join their group pose.

For Pukhraj, this album has historical veridity, for compressed into its pages are the conjunction of village festivals repeated from year to year and singular events and journeys that permit the attribution of dates to what so easily slips into amnesia. The historicity that springs from this intersection of the cyclical and the unique is compounded by the materiality of the images, the small early sepia images, the disintegrating records of early travels and the much more stable trace of the recent past.

Photographic technology's insertion into historical awareness is further demonstrated in the second album, a small plastic folder which allows the insertion of one image per page. This contains images taken in the late 1980s and 1990s and many are already beginning to fade, assuming a characteristic rusty aura. Whereas the earlier album depicted Pukhraj as a student – an aspirant poet and explorer of his Indian heritage – the second album records him as the father and family man. All the images were taken in Bhatisuda and show Pukhraj with his wife, with his sisters, feeding his cattle and working alongside his labourers in the cattleshed. One striking image shows him and his wife and sister closely grouped together under a guava tree in a small grove in one of his fields: the harmony of family life and the harmony of nature are depicted in a perfect alliance.

However, it is not only albums that create a space for 'syntagmatic concatenation'. Several individuals in Bhatisuda do not have albums, but they do have large numbers of images that form temporally stratified archives of personal and family experience that heighten and concretize historical experience in importantly new ways. But, equally, there are many individuals for whom single photographs record singular stark traces of loved relatives. Where many images are possessed, there is always an implicit narrative to be elucidated: 'This is x in such and such a year, when he went to y, and had this photo taken.' Where there is just one photo, as was the case with Kachru Ravidas (illus. 87), then that image comes to serve *in toto* for the individual and, forced to serve this more ambitious function, is stripped of its spatial and temporal specificity. Kachru, who died in 1985, was a landless Chamar labourer who was bonded for most of his life to one of the Jain families. He often worked sixteen hours a day and then slept in his employer's house so as to be on hand to deal with any emergencies in the night. The tiny image of Kachru, photographed in front of a painted cloth backdrop in some travelling photo studio, was the only visual trace that Bherulal, his son, possessed of him when I copied this image in 1991. His son continued to live in Kachru's tiny shack in the Chamar *mohalla* (neighbourhood) on the east side of the village and also worked as a field labourer until his premature death in 1996.

Small colour prints cost between eight and ten rupees, a substantial amount when set against the average daily agricultural wage in 1997 of twenty-five to thirty rupees. There are, accordingly, obvious financial reasons that make it difficult for the marginalized rural poor to build up complex photographic narratives of their lives (and equally to explore the fantasy trope that photography offers many people in the Nagda area), but this absence also mirrors a wider disengagement from and inability to challenge the narratives that control their lives. Bheru was one of the most widely respected men in the scheduled caste Chamar or Ravidas community, but though a person of very great wisdom he was never able to respond to my attempts to explore what I hoped would be oppositional theories of history held by Bhatisuda's poor. A conversation recorded in 1992, when I tried to create an opening in which he could articulate his own sense of how dominant theories of history did or did not relate to his own experience, captures this unwillingness to occupy oppositional ground:

We don't have the information. Those people who have written all the histories know. In the Ramayana [it tells] how many years of the *yugs* [different epochs] there are, how many births we people will take in the *yugs*. It's a very complex matter and you should go and meet those people to discuss this. We don't know things that are complicated – the pandits (*pandit log*) can show the meaning of all this. Those *yugs* which exist – they [the pandits] can tell you about them. Whatever there is – such as like Vishnu, Krishna, Ramchandraji, their births, who was in which *yug*, what happened in each *yug* – those people can tell you. Because we haven't studied that much. Those people can read and write and they know the history [*itihas*], so however much you need to know, how many births there were, who took birth, who is this god, they can tell you the whole history. What do we people know?

In Bhatisuda, photographs are often displayed alongside commercially mass-produced chromolithographs of deities, but whereas it is possible to discern elements of an oppositional strategy in the creation of visual pantheons through the display of images of deities, this is not at all apparent in photographic portraiture. I have found no evidence of different photographic practice among poorer villagers and among Untouchables. While several Chamars and other Untouchables possess only one or two photographic images, some have extensive collections.

Since the establishment of the viscose rayon plant in the early 1950s, large numbers of the landless poor in the village – who are nearly all members of Chamar and Bagri *jatis* – local endogamous communities or castes – have been employed in industrial work in a variety of capacities. A very small number have had access to highly paid work as 'Permanent' labourers, but most have had occasional and unpredictable access as 'Badli' or substitute workers, or more commonly 'Temporary' or contracted workers subject to recurring short-term contracts which prevented them acquiring a record of service which would entitle them to a more exalted status under Indian industrial labour law.

Kanvarlal Ravidas (Chamar) worked in the chemical division of the factory in Nagda continuously for fourteen years and then, after a break, for a further six years before losing his job because of an injured arm. He is the only person in Bhatisuda to maintain an exceptional display of chromolithographs and photographs on the external wall of his house. All are framed and jostling among the dozen or so chromolithographs are two frames of photos. One of these shows him giving *pranam* to his guru in Bhilwara, Rajasthan, whom he visits every two years (illus. 88). The other frame coalesces nine fragments from a complex life (illus. 89). In the top left of the frame is a photograph taken by me in 1992 which shows Kanvarlal with his younger brother (since deceased) holding one of the framed chromolithographs which are also displayed. Next to this is a small image of Ramdev, a popular deity among Chamars, and a colour print of a female relative. Beneath this is a photograph taken in the factory of a crusher machine on which Kanvarlal worked for some time, small passport-size photos of his brother, his *bhatija* (brother's son) and Kanvarlal himself. In this latter, taken in Birlagram to submit with a compensation form, he holds out his injured left arm. At the bottom of the frame are images recording a pilgrimage to Haridwar, where he visited the Mansadevi Temple, and family members touching his elderly mother's feet.

The industrial complex in Nagda also features in Pannalal Nai's collection of seventeen images which are all kept loose, unframed.

88 Framed colour photograph of Kanvaralal Ravidas touching the feet of his Guru, *c.* 1990.

89 Large frame containing black and white and colour photographs belonging to Kanvarlal Ravidas, *c.* 1985–92.

90 Photograph of Pannalal Nai's work group in the Engineering Section, GRASIM, *c.* 1970. Pannalal is standing on the far right.

91 Photograph of Pannalal Nai's son seated in front of painted backdrop of the Taj Mahal, *c.* 1980.

The largest of these was a group portrait of Pannalal's co-workers in the engineering section of the factory (illus. 90). Pannalal was one of the very few industrial workers in Bhatisuda to have 'Permanent' status, entitling him to comparatively high wage rates, and this had enabled him to acquire reasonable agricultural holdings and even to employ a bonded labourer to work his fields in the village while he created and dismantled vast boilers in the factory. Another photograph (illus. 91), which was taken some fifteen years ago in a small travelling studio at a *mela* in Ujjain, captured his son and another much younger relative seated in front of a painting of the Taj Mahal. Responding to my query as to whether this was the real Taj Mahal,

Pannalal said amusedly, 'No! It's a cloth painting. The original[41] is in Agra, near Delhi. It was made by Shah Jahan.'

Two small black and white quarter-length portraits of Pannalal's sons had been prepared to include with job applications submitted to GRASIM personnel office, and another black and white studio image recorded one of the sons as a 5-year-old boy with fully grown hair prior to its removal in a life-cycle rite which marks the transition of the male boy into childhood. In Bhatisuda this rite, which is performed at the appropriate Bheruisthan (clan-shrine), is of great significance for many people and large numbers of printed invitations are commonly sent to kin, and Nagda-based photographers are hired to visit Bhatisuda to document the event. The final black and white image in Pannalal's collection depicted a deceased relative and was partly handcoloured. All the other images were more recent colour prints taken by itinerant photographers. These individuals, of whom there are about a dozen in Nagda, roam neighbouring villages on a speculative basis in search of commissions and are also available by prior arrangment for life-cycle rites and other events (for instance, the inauguration of a new well).

Four of these images were taken by Diamond Studio from Nagda and are formal yet intimate portraits of Pannalal's wider family posed in various groupings in front of a bedspread which has been neatly tacked to one of the walls of his substantial *kaccha* (mud-built) house. It is perhaps significant that Pannalal's very elderly mother is photographed full-pose, whereas the three groups of younger family members are photographed three-quarter-length. We have already encountered the strong preference among many subjects for full-pose images: these images suggest perhaps that the preference is less strongly marked in younger individuals. The same photographer was responsible for another image taken on another occasion which shows one of Pannalal's sons with his two finest bulls on the occasion of *Govardhan puja* (illus. 92). This rite occurs on the morning of Karttik sudi 1, the first day of the bright half of the month of Karttik, the day after Divali. Cattle are decorated with henna, their horns are painted, and other decorations purchased in the Nagda bazaar are applied before they are taken to the River Chambal to bathe. *En route*, the cattle trample through cow-dung representations of the gods Radha and Krishna and a small hill. This later denotes Mount Govardhan, a hill in Braj which Krishna had raised on the tip of his little finger in order to protect the local cattle from torrential rain. The rite is essentially a celebration of rural wealth and marks the continuing centrality of draught animals to Bhatisuda's economy; it is also the

92 Colour photograph of Pannalal Nai's son holding two bulls on the day of *Govardhan puja*, *c.* 1990.

day on which contracts between landowners and yearly paid field-labourers are renewed. The final six images were made by a photographer from Pavan Studio (also from Nagda) during the wedding of Pannalal's son, Radheshyam. Three of the images show the bride and groom together just prior to the *phera* ceremony, the critical part of the rite in which the couple circumambulate a fire seven times; one shows other family members seated in front of the fire; another shows members of the *barat* (the groom's marriage party from Bhatisuda village); the final one shows the groom kneeling in front of a statue of Hanuman in the village Ram temple upon his return with the bride from her natal village.

The contrast with the elaborate and expensive Nagda wedding imagery discussed earlier is striking. The Nagda albums comprised a great many more images and also bore the traces of numerous, often exceedingly complex, interventions in the studio darkroom. The photographic traces of Bhatisuda weddings, by contrast, are inflected by an intriguingly different aesthetic. The itinerancy of the photographer, the relative poverty of most village image commissioners and the difficulty of intervening in colour processing conspire to ensure that, paradoxically, village images lie closer to what a Western tradition would recognize as a 'realist' aesthetic. Whereas Nagda images tend to have a greater formal symmetry and preparedness, combined with a greater frequency of montage effects, images circulating in villages capture more of the randomness of everyday life: they are less constructed, less filtered. The more casual framing and composition reflect both the relative inexperience of itinerant photographers (as opposed to wealthy studio practitioners who trade on their reputations) and also the villagers' greater lack of familiarity with the spatial and behavioural circumspection that highly staged and artificed images require. This difference is compounded by the infinitely greater theatricality of urban weddings, which are much more likely to be hosted in replicas of proscenium-arch stages and other carpentered spaces that lend themselves to a formal aesthetic. Consequently village wedding images more easily conjure a sense of mobility, fluidity and the jagged reality of daily village life.

Despite their status in Madhya Pradesh as a Scheduled Tribe, Banjaras have a rather anomalous status in the Bhatisuda *jati* hierarchy. As a result of this Banjaras – although they live right next to the Bhangi – are permitted to use the *uttam* (high-caste) panchayat well. Lakshman Motilal, a Banjara, has worked in GRASIM on and off since 1974. Initially he found contracted work loading and unloading trucks and rail bogies in the goods yard. He also occasionally worked in the godown (warehouse) and helped load pulping machines with raw bamboo and eucalyptus filament. In 1986 he was lucky enough to get a permanent post. This involved guaranteed work at vastly greater rates with what, by village standards, are extraordinarily good holiday and other entitlements. Now he works in the canteen, preparing vegetables and cooking *samosas*, *kachauris* and *sev*. While he does this comparatively undemanding work, he (like Pannalal Nai) employs a village labourer at a tenth of his own factory wages to tend his fields.

A single large frame included twelve images that captured some of Lakshman's complex biography (illus. 93). The earliest images are identical passport-size black and white images of Lakshman adorned with his purple thumb imprint which were used on application forms. Almost as old is a similarly sized image of his *jiyaji* (sister's husband) which was originally taken for use on a bank pass. The five large colour prints were taken by an itinerant Nagda-based photographer and date from the mid-1980s. All of them make use of backdrops: in two of them the natural architectural qualities of the small *khajur* palms to be found around Bhatisuda, while the other three use coloured lungis and rugs to create an ordered and formal environment. Lakshman appears in three of these. In one he is shown seated with his brother Bhavarlal's new-born son on his lap. Another image

93 Lakshman Motilal's son holding a frame containing photographs collected by his father.

94 Colour printed photographic mount of the sort sometimes used in Nagda and Bhatisuda.

of this child celebrates and confirms his physical wholeness and vividly demonstrates the idiom of repleteness that many in Bhatisuda seek from photography. While a reposeful visage would certainly be deemed preferable to the frozen grimace on the baby's face, the clear delineation of four sound limbs and the proof of the most desired gender identity constitued this as a successful portraiture outcome. Also included in the frame is a small colour print of a guru with a considerable following throughout India, Sathya Sai Baba, and three similar images of deities: Shiv in his androgynous form as Harihara, Hanuman tearing apart his chest to reveal his master Ram, and Shiv and Parvati shown above a *shivling*.

Bourdieu has suggested[42] that many French wedding images are 'sociograms' – that is, figural representations of social relationships – and we might make the same claim for Lakshman's framed archive. Commonly, villagers take photographs to Nagda to be framed at one of the three picture-framing (and, more recently, lamination) shops. When a request is made for a number of images to be included in a single frame, the picture-framer will usually take the lead in suggesting how the individual photographs might be arranged. These are then pasted on the plain mounting paper or, in the case of individual images, stuck to ornate and brightly coloured mounts that Nagda framers buy in from presses in Bombay, Delhi and elsewhere (illus. 94). The client can, of course, make interventions and suggest a particular ordering, and the resulting products might be viewed as collaborations that reflect the desires of individual clients mediated by the framer's sense of conventional practice. A cursory formal reading of Lakshman's frame reveals the centrality of the mother, the vitality of the extended family and the ubiquitous insertion of the divine into the everyday.

Lakshman shares 20 *bighas*[43] of land with three other brothers, one of whom is Biharilal. Biharilal, who has worked as a milkman for one of the Jain households, cycling to and from Nagda, and as a contracted worker in the chemical division, is currently the village *chaukidar*, responsible for notifying the Nagda police of any births and deaths. He has a more general responsibility to ensure good order in the village, and this genial man is often to be seen casting a friendly eye over processions and wedding parties in the village.

Biharilal's house is very large, with space for goats at one end of the single room. On the left, as one enters the door, there is a large display of devotional images centred around a huge mirrored image of Ramdev, hung above a small alcove. Included in the display were a large framed and garlanded image of the goddess Kali, a framed Sharma Picture Publication of Satyanarayan (a form of Vishnu), sheets of miniature film posters and two pieces of incense-stick firework packaging depicting Shiv. There were also two small framed photographs of Pannalal, a mendicant who previously lived in the village and was celebrated for his ability to separate his hands and his feet from his body (illus. 95), and the famous talking bull of Aslod, District Mandsaur, which had spoken sternly to his owner when he had tried to take him to the market to sell him (illus. 96). The handcoloured photo is captioned *shri nandi ke ghar prasann (aslod)* – 'the gracious one from the house of Nandi (Aslod)':

That bull is from Mandsaur. The bull said you mustn't sell me [he spoke from his mouth], but the baniya tied him to the bullock cart to take him for sale, and the bull said [again] you mustn't sell me or you will face ruin [*nuqsan*]. Then the baniya went round from place to place selling these photos, for worship, as a memento [*yadgiri ke liye*]. That's the sort of bull it is.

As well as Biharilal's two photographs – of his guru and the Aslod bull – there are several more ritually powerful photographs in the village

95 Colour photo of Pannalal, an ascetic formerly resident in Bhatisuda.

श्री नंदी के घर प्रसन्न (असलोद)

धानी फोटो फ्रेमिंग एण्ड आर्टिस्ट
चिम्बोद (मन्दसौर म.प्र.)

96 The talking bull of Aslod.

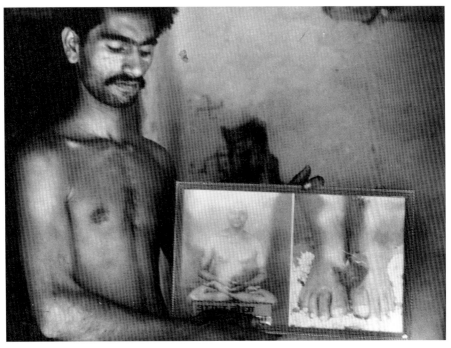

97 Ramesh Suttar holding a framed colour image of Shri Paramhansji.

in addition to approximately 1,000 chromolithographs displayed in homes and temples in the village, all of which possess varying degrees of potency. Among these we should certainly include three framed images of a guru named Shri Paramhansji (illus. 97). He embodies an extreme form of *bhautik* (material) yearning and his transactions with his devotees lie at the opposite extreme to Fuller's memorable vision of *puja* as 'the worshipper's reception and entertainment of a distinguished and adored guest'.[44] All the mass-produced pictures are the same, being double photographs depicting on the left the guru seated in a yogic posture and on the right the guru's feet garlanded with flowers, and they all originated from the same source: C. B. Tiwari, a Nagda resident and employee of the factory fire service. Since he learned about Paramhansji from a doctor in Surat he has become an energetic local proselytizer.

The great appeal of the technique – and this is what Tiwari contin-ually stresses to the sceptic – is that faith or belief is not necessary; desires will be fulfilled without belief (*bina vishvas*). The analogies that tumble forth from Tiwari's lips are all grounded in a technologi-cal world in which all that matters is effect: 'Suppose that you want to use some electric power – you make a connection, fit your tube light, lay the wiring, provide a switch, connect this to the overhead wires. If the power is available, the tube is fine, the wiring is fine, the switch is fine, the tube light will come on – (chalega!) – with belief and without belief' – he flicked his thumb to and fro as though switching the current on and off. To produce surges of energy in one's own life all that was required was the utterance of six sentences. When Tiwari himself first uttered these he had no faith in them; now he claims to have spoken to 25,000 people and 200,000 schoolchildren about the method. He spends all his free time touring local villages and towns, and this was how he came to leave traces of Paramhansji in Bhatisuda.

The six sentences invoke Paramhansji, provide a space for the supplicant to describe the problem, the monetary reward which it is proposed will be sent to Paramhansji by money order and the number of people whom the devotee will tell in the event of a successful outcome. Tiwari describes the intial part of the exercise in which Paramhansji is summoned as being 'just like a code' (on a 'telephone' or a 'computer'). Once connected, Paramhansji will send messages direct to your mind if he feels that the money or the number of people to be informed is not sufficient and the devotee must raise his offer if he wishes his work to be done. Tiwari had several impressive tales of Paramhansji's intervention, among other things in a catastrophic railway fire in which he was badly burned and in bringing a runaway motorcycle to a halt, and Pukhraj Bohra in Bhatisuda had experienced similar benefits in the treatment of a diseased horse. This meritocratic technicity contrasts starkly with other deities for whom 'faith' and 'devotion' are the prerequisites of any divine return.

Earlier we saw Bherulal's tiny image of his late father, Kachru (illus. 88). Bherulal's neighbour is Kesarbai, the widow of Ganpat, who lives with her two surviving sons. One of these is Ramlal, another landless Chamar who works intermittently as a contracted labourer in the chemicals division of Nagda's industrial complex. Like Kachru, Ramlal's late brother Hira worked for many years as an annually paid labourer for one of the village's Jain households. Inside the small house (illus. 98) is a display of laminated prints of two scenes from the Ramayana (Ram with Hanuman and *Sita haran* – the abduction of Sita) and of Krishna as a child. Directly above and below this are a small glass image of Samvaliyaji, a local deity associated with Krishna, and an unframed paper image of Lakshmi of the sort that is the focus of Lakshmi *puja* held during Divali. A very long marigold garland is hung across these and also beneath two large framed photographs which have been mounted almost at the very top of the

98 Interior of Kesarbai's house, showing chromolithographs and framed images of her husband Ganpat and son Hira.

kaccha (mud) wall. One of these is a black and white portrait of Ganpat, Ramlal and Hira's father, and the other is a colour print taken by me in 1989 (illus. 99) shortly before Hira was killed by a train as he hauled his bicycle over the tracks near Nagda station. In the colour image, taken at Hira's request, he cradles the photograph of his father, leaving an enduring visual trace of his respect and devotion. This was taken a stage further when, following Hira's death, Ramlal asked me to take a further photograph in which he held the image of Hira with his father's photograph (illus. 100). There is a powerful notion here of the translatability of an affective to a spatial proximity through re-photography, through a sort of recursive binding in of space, a representational involution, as though this photographic recuperation was capable of arresting time itself. Hira's mother also sought out the services of Sagar Studio. She took some wedding photographs in which Hira's face could be seen in the crowd. The face was then isolated and emphasized by the application of concentric rings of blue, red and yellow paint. These rings were painted on the image and Vijay Vyas then rephotographed the image with an enlarging lens (illus. 101).

There are also parallels here with what we might term the 'montage effect'. We have seen how the technical procedure of 'cutting' and composite printing permits spectacular juxtapositions in wedding

99 Hira holding a framed photograph of his late father, Ganpat.

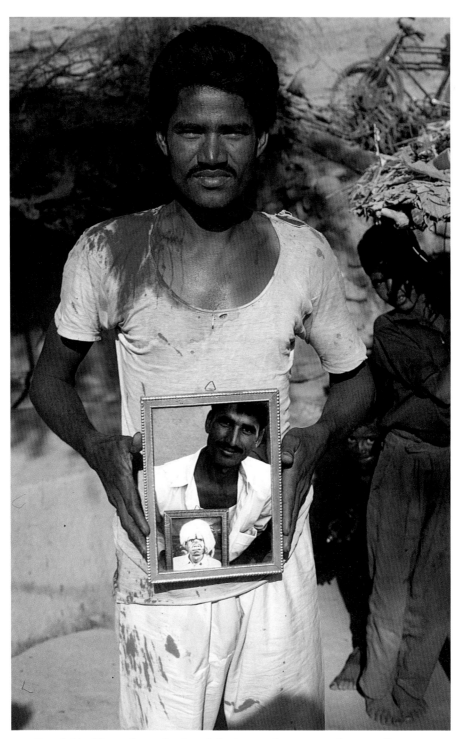

100 Ramlal holding a framed print of the image that appears here as illus. 99.

101 Colour print of Hira, *c.* 1991, overpainted and re-photographed by Sagar Studio.

albums. Similarly, images in Bhatisuda often mobilize an idiom of proximal empowerment through which persons, objects and images can come closer to divine power. Frequently images of household members will be pushed underneath the glass of framed prints of deities. That the principle here is simply value as a function of physical proximity is suggested by the common practice of placing auspicious banknotes against the glass of framed chromolithographs of deities. Sitabai, for instance, the wife of a contracted Banjara worker in GRASIM, once came across a two-rupee note in the mud road to the next village. 'Found' notes are considered auspicious and should not be re-entered into the cycle of exchange from which they have recently departed. Sitabai chose to stick her note on an S. S. Brijbasi chromolithograph of the Ram Darbar. This practice is not confined to Hindus, for there are two prints owned by a Muslim family against which are pasted two-rupee notes which bear a serial number containing sequences (the numbers 786) which Muslims hold to be auspicious. It is also relevant to mention in this context that village families are commonly photographed by itinerant Nagda photographers in front of their domestic shrines and that villagers frequently choose backdrops depicting deities in travelling photographic studios.

'Proximal empowerment' is perhaps nowhere more apparent than

102 Framed black and white photograph of members of Nagu Ravidas' family taken in travelling studio in Nagda *c.* 1980.

103 Framed black and white photograph of Sitabai's son posing in front of painted studio backdrop.

in photographic images that incorporate deities. Most often these are created through the use of painted backdrops, although montage is also sometimes used, as we shall see in the case of images produced in Delhi's Chandni Chowk. In Bhatisuda the most common divine backdrops depict generic versions of deities (such as illus 102, which shows female members of Nagu Ravidas's family in front of a heavily coiffured Shiv in a travelling studio in Nagda), but some also invoke specific places where such photography would not be possible. Sitabai's son doing *puja* in front of the *shivling* in the Mahakaleshvar Temple in Ujjain is captured in illus. 103. This important Shiv temple was the scene of a tragic stampede in 1996 in which more than fifty people were killed and the actual *shivling* is in a cramped underground passageway where such a photograph would be very difficult to stage.

Similar practical considerations may also determine the popularity of studio backdrops such as the Taj Mahal, of which we have already seen an example. In illus. 104, Kalu Singh is photographed in front of the same building in a travelling studio at a fair at Ujjain. As we saw in the earlier case of Pannalal Nai, villagers seldom have doubts about the status of such backdrops. Most of those who chose to be pho-

104 Black and white photograph of Kalu Singh posing in front of painted studio backdrop of the Taj Mahal.

105 A Jain couple posing in front of the Taj Mahal.

tographed in such a way certainly did not have the resources to visit Agra; indeed, no one in Bhatisuda had ever been to Agra. In Nagda, where numerous people could, and have, been to Agra, people still chose to use such backdrops. People who could very well afford to be photographed in Agra were still likely to be photographed in front of painted versions in Nagda. Once when copying an image (illus. 105) of some distant relatives of a Nagda Jain friend, it transpired that no one present could say whether the building in the background was the Taj in Agra or one of its countless copies, for no one could remember if this couple had ever been to Agra.

This suggests that backgrounds are used not simply as a substitute in the absence of their referents, but as a space of exploration. This exploration is often geographic: within Nagda studios one can travel from Goa, to Mandu, to Agra and Kashmir merely by standing in front of different walls. But Nagda studios also function as chambers of dreams where personal explorations of an infinite range of *alter egos* are possible. The younger brother of Kanvarlal Ravidas, Govardhan-lal, has several frames full of photographs. In the centre of one of these (illus. 106) is a quarter-length portrait of him twirling his moustache

106 Framed photographs belonging to Govardhanlal Mangilal, *c.* 1965–80.

107 Studio photograph of Orissan tribal woman wearing wristwatches, *c.* 1990.

108 Early photographic copy of a chromolithograph of Chandra Shekhar Azad, possibly by Rup Kishor Kapur, c. 1931.

109 Studio photograph of Chandra Shekhar Azad on which illus. 108 was based, late 1920s.

with his left hand. What may seem a casual pose is to everyone in Bhatisuda and Nagda a mimetic invocation of a great freedom fighter and a statement by Govardhanlal of his own resilience and independence. The freedom fighter is Chandra Shekhar Azad, who died in a shoot-out in Allahabad in 1931. Azad is nearly always depicted in this posture: he rolls his moustache with his fingers and wears a Brahman's sacred thread across his chest and a wristwatch on his left arm (illus. 108). This early chromolithograph is based on a studio photograph that Chandra Shekhar had taken shortly before his death (illus. 109). The quality of extant copies is poor but one can make out an elaborate painted backdrop of a lake of the sort which is still popular in Nagda. Bhatisuda residents know little or nothing about Chandra Shekhar, beyond his name. However, his attention to his moustache lives on as part of a repertoire of signs offered up to the camera. Chandra Shekhar Azad may also be responsible for another sign that circulates in some regional studios: the wristwatch. In illus. 107, an Orissan tribal girl wears dark glasses and two wristwatches. These are signs of wealth and power, but the majority of chromolithographic images of

Chandra Shekhar may perhaps have sustained the wristwatch as a sign of power. Whatever the precise archaeology of these signs, this is a further example of the way in which the photographic studio is frequently used as a space in which to stage idealized versions of oneself.

The contrast with 1960s popular French photography described by Pierre Bourdieu is striking. For Bourdieu, photography is above all socially regulated and nothing may be photographed which has not already been solemnized. Correspondingly, what is photographed 'is not . . . individuals in their capacity as individuals, but social roles, the husband, first communicant, soldier, or social relationship, the American uncle of the aunt from Sauvignon'.[45]

Now this is certainly true of some Nagda photographic practice – most individuals in wedding photographs, for instance, are depicted in their roles as particular categories of consanguines and affines, and many villagers seek to be photographed in the role of a disciple of their guru. However, the inventive posing that characterizes much of the imagery produced within studios is concerned with the transcendence and parody of social roles. The photographic studio becomes a place not for solemnization of the social but for the individual exploration of that which does not yet exist in the social world. This is not for a moment to deny that Nagda photographic practice is every bit as sociologically revealing as Bourdieu's French material, merely that its characteristics are very different.

Whereas Nagda popular photography does not seem to share much with the solemnizing function of French photography, there are insights to be gained from some West African practices. Kobena Mercer, describes the approach of the Mali photographer Seydou Keita, who was active in Bamako from the mid-1940s onwards:

With various props, accessories and backdrops, the photographer stylizes the pictorial space, and through lighting, depth of field and framing, the camera work heightens the *mise-en-scène* of the subject, whose poses, gestures and expression thus reveal a 'self' not as he or she actually is, but 'just a little more than what we really are'.[46]

The comment at the end is by Seydou Keita himself and uncannily mirrors the obervation by Vijay Vyas, the manager of the Sagar Studio, that Nagdarites rarely desire 'realistic' (*vastavik*) photographs:

They always say I want to look good . . . everyone says I am like this but I want to come out better than this in my photo [*is se bhi zyada acchha mera photo ana chahie*]. So we try.

Vijay's comment also echoes David MacDougall's astute observation that Indian studio photography 'offers us the chance to add something

110 A female sitter dons Sagar Studio's all-purpose Rajasthani costume, 1996.

to ourselves and review our varied appearances'. MacDougall suggests that this style of photography 'increases us' and 'attests to the possibilities within us' and is in this respect the opposite of the 'draining and predatory' photography of the sort that we examined in Chapter 1.[47]

'Coming out better' in a photograph is achieved in two ways: through the adoption of gestures and through the deployment of costume and props. Frequently the one implies the other. Vijay Vyas refers to any photo involving a gesture with the English phrase 'action shooting': 'Action shooting or an action photo means you've got your hand in a certain way – holding it up to show your watch, one leg is higher than another, these are action photos.' This refers to a set of techniques, agreed between the sitter and the photographer, that allow a particular pose to emerge and may jointly involve a gesture or look by the subject and the adoption of an appropriate camera angle by the photographer. Thus there are 'poet' and '*filmi*' (film star) poses which both require low camera angles, and the creation of these involves a sort of theatrical direction by the photographer.

Vijay, like several other Nagda studio owners, also has a collection of costumes available for the use of his clients, although, as we will see, they are the cause of considerable tribulations. The costumes include an all-in-one dress that can be arranged to give different regional, caste and class flavours. Thus, according to Vijay, it can serve as a marker of Malwi or Rajasthani regional identity, or as Rajput or Banjara caste identity (illus. 110). Some of the differences involve minor inflections, such as the number and variety of ornaments in the Rajput and Rajasthani ensemble. Vijay can also supply a T-shirt for use in the 'college girl' persona (a recurrent trope in Hindi movies) and there is a repertoire of 'modelling style' gestures (involving the placing of one foot on a box) which are part of the 'college girl' pose.

The question of exegesis and the pitfalls it provides for the unwary anthropologist has recently been the subject of useful discussion.[48] O'Hanlon has shown how, in a Highland New Guinea context, everyday verbalizations can be empathetically screened for evaluations about the 'meaning' of aesthetic acts. A similar tactic is necessary here and the significances of these small acts in these studios need to be teased out with small questions. In this spirit I asked Vijay why his clients are so keen to wear different clothes when they are in front of the camera:

For *shauq* [pleasure, to satisfy a desire]. Everyone wants to look their best, and they hope that they will look their best in photos. They don't want to wear their everyday clothes. Just like you – if you want your photo taken, you'll brush your hair, wear your best shirt . . . They don't want *vastavik* [realistic] photos. They always say I want to look good, gents and ladies, everyone says I am like this but I want to come out better than this in my photo. So we try. They brush and braid their hair, put on [talcum] powder, put on cream, put on lipstick, they change their dress, they wear good clothes, put on a tie, wear a coat, they make sure their trousers are OK, then they say 'Take an action photo', 'Take my photo with this type of dress, Rajasthani dress, with a *matka* and so on. Women wear lots of ornaments, and then when I've got a good angle I can photograph.

[Female clients] cause me difficulty. My studio is very small, there isn't a lot of space, and when [female clients] change their clothes I have to wait outside. They change their clothes, then they do their make-up and sometimes when I'm waiting outside other customers come and then I have to ask them to come later. Sometimes it takes them half an hour to get ready, a whole hour to get ready, so much time it takes them and at the end I only take one or maybe two photos and all this time I'm turning clients away. This is also a problem with children dressing up as Krishna – customers have to be turned away – it takes too much time. So now women and other people wanting to wear costumes are only allowed in the afternoon between 12 and 6 p.m. The morning and evening are busy with other customers.

I have suggested that the costumes available in the Sagar Studio are associated with various regional, caste and class identities, but they are also deeply bound into particular models of history and India's

111 Two photographs juxtaposed in a Nagda album, *c.* 1985.

place within that. The heavy mirrored embroidery of the female costumes is a transparent sign of the 'traditional' (*paramparik*) every bit
as much for people in Nagda as it is for Western tourists. Conversely,
the accoutrements of the 'college girl', or in other studios the television set and the telephone (also frequently used props) are explicit
markers of what it is to be 'modern' (*adhunik*).

Within the broader spectrum of linkages between gender and historicity, Vijay Vyas's 'college girl' costume is atypical, for, as has
already been suggested, overwhelmingly it is women's bodies that
become sites for signs of the traditional to play over, whereas men are
more usually the surfaces upon which the modern can be written.
This opposition, which appears so often in the history of colonial and
post-colonial India, is perhaps the core motif of Hindi film and is
vividly exemplified by illus. 111, a juxtaposition of two separate
images on facing pages in one Nagda photograph album. The female
on the right, in a pose that would probably have been distributed to
prospective grooms, is shown replete with all the stereotypical village
emblems, whereas the policeman on the left wears the uniform of the
state and sits astride a Royal Enfield Bullet, a mobile temple to the
elegance of twentieth-century engineering.

The binaries of 'tradition' and 'modernity' and their gender linkages

112 Guman Singh astride a travelling studio's Royal Enfield Bullet, c. 1983.

are not obscure motifs to be conjured up through formal analysis by the anthropologist but are rather an absolutely fundamental feature of popular culture. The reinforcement of these oppositions, their inversion and their parody, are saturated into the very fabric of the popular imaginary. A scene in the film *Agneepath* provides one particularly memorable example. Mithun Chakravarty plays a lungi-wearing Keralite ('Krishnan Iyer, M.A.') who courts Amitabh Bachchan's sister, played by Neelam. Mithun's rusticity is initially contrasted with Neelam's urban ways and she is described at one point with the English phrase 'trouser-suit disco girl'. Eventually and inevitably she abandons her Western clothes for a sari whereupon Mithun says, 'I've turned the clock back; I've turned this Indian back from being a foreigner.' A musical sequence follows in which, to the accompaniment of the song 'Mera Hero' (My Hero), these dress roles are inverted to comic effect. Neelam appears in a traditional dancer's outfit and Mithun in a zoot suit with pork-pie hat and ghetto-blaster.

The policeman's Enfield is rather unusual as a photographic subject since it is 'real': it is evidently the machine he uses for work. Within photographic representations, motorbikes are much more likely to be hollow shells, ancient defunct specimens whose utility lies simply in their outward appearance. The travelling studios that frequently used to come to Nagda always had an Enfield or a Yezdi, almost always positioned in front of a dramatic urban scene of bridges, high-rise buildings and a sky filled with planes inscribing dramatic vapour trails. It is against such a backdrop that Guman Singh of Bhatisuda sits astride his bike (illus. 112) in front of a hybridized cityscape more suggestive (to me) of New York or Chicago than anywhere else, but which Bhatisuda villagers and Nagdarites will unequivocally identify as Bombay, the city which for them symbolizes all that is most dramatically good and bad in the modern.

There is a visual tension, an apparent posing of possible worlds, in this image of Guman Singh. He is not fully of this urban landscape, but rather passing by it, a villager getting a frisson of excitement from this passing proximity to a way of life that simultaneously excites and repels. There is an experiment here, through juxtaposition and in-between-ness that is highly evocative of the strategies apparent in the early films of Raj Kapoor.

This paradoxical juxtaposition that simultaneously holds two opposites within the same picture frame is nowhere more apparent than in another image to be found in Nagda, belonging to Sunil Chhajed. This was prepared from paper negatives in Delhi's Chandni Chowk, and shows Sunil on a motorbike outside a large temple (illus. 113). Again it is popular film which provides an interpretive frame for such images. Just as Bakhtin suggests that the time-space of the 'castle' serves as the chronotopic location for the Gothic novel and the space of parlours and salons is the central chronotope in the work of of Stendhal and Balzac,[49] in popular Hindi film the temple frequently features as a sort of courtroom, a space of judgement and resolution to be found in a side-passage off the central chronotopic space where the village meets the city. Time after time it is the temple, and particularly the space outside the temple (where the drama of the decision whether to enter or not is played out), that becomes the space for the articulation of those moral dilemmas implicating 'tradition' and 'modernity'.[50] The power of this image lies in its deliberately unresolved narrative: will Sunil zoom away from the temple, abandoning his duty, or was the motorbike a means of arriving at the temple more speedily?

Commenting on a similar use of props in Mali, Kobena Mercer

113 Sunil Chhajed astride a motorcycle outside a temple. Photographic montage made by cutting two paper negatives, *c.* 1985.

notes the 'banal, everyday objects valued not for their intrinsic worth or meaning, but for the aspirations they come to embody as tokens of exchange in the syncretic imagination'.[51] It is certainly in the world of the imagination, rather than the immediate domain of consumerist aspiration, that these signs take on their most potent function, and it is against a much vaster backdrop of India's history and its post-colonial dilemma that they need to be understood. But perhaps it is popular film which is the primary point of reference here, for it is in both film and photography that we can see most clearly the complex process of what has been termed 'impersonation'. Writing about post-Independence Indian film, Sumita Chakravarty extrapolates the notion of 'imperso-nation' from Salman Rushdie's *Satanic Verses* and provides a description which is profoundly true of popular photography:

Concentrated within this metaphor are the notions of changeability and metamorphosis, tension and contradiction, recognition and alienation, surface and depth: dualities that have long plagued the Indian psyche and constitute the self-questionings of Indian nationhood . . . Impersonation subsumes a process of externalization, the play of/on surfaces, the disavowal of fixed notions of identity. But it also encompasses the contrary movement of accretion, the piling up of identities, the transgression of social codes and boundaries.[52]

Another insight into the significance of posing in popular Indian photographic practice is provided by David and Judith MacDougall's film *Photowallahs* (1992). This presents a detailed account of practices of disguise and posing in the north Indian hill station Mussoorie, although some of the exegesis suggests differences from Nagda interpretations. In Mussoorie, middle-class Indian tourists arrive on Gun Hill by cable car and gaze at the Himalayas, dressed as tribals, sheikhs or parodies of Western guitar-strumming hippies. Bodies can be dressed in a limitless range of identities – as Pathan frontiersmen, Kashmiri women, gun-wielding dacoits and village women posed with decorated earthenware pots in the style of the Midas publicity image (illus. 1). One photographer, H. S. Chadha,[53] offers a client most of the national styles of turban ('Rajasthani, Panjabi, Gujarati'). This cosmopolitan sartorial excess recalls Appadurai's observation that through its inclusion of regional items, much middle-class Indian food simulates a national cohesion[54] and we may suppose that the clients of Mussoorie photographers aspire to a similar ideal. Edibility and wearability stand as parallel idioms of national integration. It is as if contemporary Indians, rejecting aspects of colonial ethnicization through physique, costume and other external signifiers, have arrived at a strategy of mutual mimicry, a reciprocal consumability in which – in front of the camera at least – identities are suspended and inverted. The concern with 'changeability . . . metamorphosis, tension and contradiction'[55] contributes to a strikingly non-essentialist view of the nation.

The predilection for posing can also be usefully contextualized within a century-old practice of photographically representing *bhav* (emotion, or sentiment). *Bhav* has a long classical pedigree but acquired a new expressive form and systematicity in the later nineteenth century with the publication in several Bengali theatre magazines of series of photographs depicting the actor Girish Chandra Ghosh in a series of eight emotive *bhav* poses. This remarkable actor and impresario appears in a variety of poses in illus. 114: disgust, diabolic purpose, high glee and fright.[56] As Rimli Bhattacharya notes, some of these are new, hybrid *bhav* and they formed part of a new genre, the bioscope or visual narrative, which was also to encompass publications such as Dhirendranath Gangopadhyay's *Expressions of a Graduate or a Passed B.A.* (subtitled 'Laughing Scenes of Delightful Humour').[57] Residents of Nagda and Bhatisuda are not familiar with this complex history but are very familiar with the medium in which these formulaic expressions of inner states persist: popular film.

Juxtaposition and impersonation are also achieved through techniques of montage and multiple printing – through 'cutting' and 'trick' photography. We have already seen many examples of the images that result, which combine within a single picture frame more than one image, sometimes the inverted image of a bride or groom, the same person occupying two different personae within the same frame, or a person juxtaposed with a place that is different from the place of the making of the photograph.

To revert, briefly, to Christian Metz, we might say that the lexical spaces of these images are extended, so that more information is presented, but the idiom in which this occurs is very different from attempts to extend the lexical space of images during photography's colonial career. Recall Johnston and Hoffman's full-face and profile images of the 'Khambu or Jimdar of Eastern Nepal – not so typical as No. 30' pasted on facing pages of the album commissioned by Waddell in Darjeeling (illus. 25), or the full-face and profile studies in front of graph paper reproduced in Marshall's 1873 study of the Todas (illus. 23). At one level the desire to see more of the same person parallels the motivation of the Nagda photographer, but the separation of the frame is crucial. The realist chronotope that inflects these early images demands adherence to Gombrich's 'eyewitness principle'.

আহ্লাদে আটখানা !   ভয়ে স্তম্ভিভূত !

ঘৃণা ও বিরক্তি !!   মস্তিস্কে চক্রান্ত !

114 Girish Chandra Ghosh giving form to various *bhav*, or emotions.

Under colonialism, India's people were also doubled through the use of stereoscopy, which was justified through its displacement of monocular with a 'truer' binocular vision. The motivation here is the substantiation of experience through a doubling of evidence. Thus the text printed on the reverse of an Underwood and Underwood's 1903 stereoscope of 'a Hindu devotee doing penance on a bed of spikes' in Calcutta matches the observations of the photographer with the visual experience of the stereoscope viewer:

The photographer who watched him dispose his gaunt frame on this extraordinary bed, says he took a good deal of pains to lie down cautiously and to distribute his weight so that there would be minimum risk to his skin. In fact long exposure has rendered his skin so tough that it would not easily be punctured by those rather blunt spikes. Notice how his knees and soles are calloused by long familiarity with stone streets and floors.[58]

The doubling that stereoscopy provided received its most eloquent support from Oliver Wendell Holmes. In a series of celebrated early essays, Holmes suggested that whereas the humble *carte-de-visite* was a mere 'sun-picture', stereoscopes were 'sun-sculptures' which gave the viewer 'solidity' rather than mere surface. In the stereoscope, he wrote, 'the mind feels its way into the very depths of the picture' and whereas the ordinary photograph was easily falsifiable, the stereoscope was incapable of 'perjuring itself':

'At the mouth of *two witnesses*, or of three, shall he that is worthy of death be put to death; but at the mouth of one he shall not be put to death.' No woman may be declared youthful on the strength of a single photograph; but if the stereoscopic twins say she is young, let her be so acknowledged . . .[59]

So the spacing in the stereoscope exists only in its pre-processed state, before its insertion in the viewer when the two images coalesce to provide a higher legalistic truth.

Clearly, Nagda images do not strive for this: their spacing is of a different order. Do Surrealist images provide a useful point of departure, for these too are marked by spacings, what Rosalind Krauss calls the 'two step that banishes simultaneity'?[60] Krauss's analyses suggest a number of illuminating parallels which I will briefly review before considering the fundamental difference in these two photographic practices' logics of refusal.

First, we need to follow Krauss's differentiation of Heartfield's montages (and collages), intended as decodings and interpretations of reality, from Surrealists' use of photography to present 'that very reality as configured, coded, or written'.[61] Heartfield's work evokes parallels with the wave of hermeneutical doubt that has swept anthropology since the publication of Marcus and Clifford's *Writing Culture*.[62] The desire has been to disassemble the fictitious seamless reality in both monological ethnographies and the frameless photo that pretended to be a slice of reality. Both Heartfield and Brecht (and latterly Clifford and Marcus) were motivated by a desire to reveal that the image, or the play, or the ethnographic monograph, is not to be mistaken for 'reality' but should rather be recognized as 'the world infested by interpretation or signification, which is to say, reality distended by the gaps or blanks which are the formal preconditions of the sign'.[63]

Crucially, Krauss notes that whereas Heartfield used photocollage, Surrealists eagerly sought the 'seamless unity of the print'. For reasons that we have already examined, this is not a significant principle of differentiation in Nagda practice, where seamless prints, photomontage and overpainted photographs all compete in the same space. Surrealists' concern was to infiltrate their prints with the spacings that were part of reality in such a way that their indexical power was not compromised. As Krauss notes, 'The spacings and doublings are intended to register the spacings and doublings of that very reality of which *this* photograph is merely the faithful trace.'[64]

Nagda studio photographers producing wedding montages are clearly not Brechtian critics of the nature of representation. There is a consonance and a harmony between the images they produce and plausible versions of the world, and it is here that we encounter a difference in what Jurij Lotman termed the 'poetics of refusal'[65] that starts to separate Nagda photography from the work of Surrealists. Surrealist photography is grounded in a negation, a deliberate refusal of the dominant representational codes of early-twentieth-century Europe. Nagda photography is not: it reflects the dominant codes to be found in other media and narratives.

Before we can elucidate this further, we need to explore some aspects of the aesthetic inculcation that contribute to the production of dominant versions of visual reality in different societies. A great insight in this area has been provided by Gerald Mast in a consideration of the choices with which early European film-makers and their audiences were faced. Mast sets out to explore the thesis expounded by the German film theoretician Siegfried Kacauer that the triumph of the Lumière brothers' 'realist tendency' over Méliès's cinematic fabulism was inevitable. The Lumière brothers seemed to be concerned with the world as it was, whereas Méliès strove to create a fantastic world of journeys to the moon. It was inevitable, Kracauer asserted, because film ineluctably redeemed the physical world; there was a contradiction between fabulism and the filmic experience of the world. Subsequent events, Mast notes, would appear to confirm Kracauer's position: 'faster film stocks, faster lenses, the wide screen, the conversion to colour, and higher fidelity sound have steadily permitted each to admit . . . and thereby redeem more physical reality than its less seeing and hearing ancestors.'[66]

Through a comparison of two early films that exemplify aspects of these two traditions, Mast then proceeds to question Kracauer's stress on the visual texture of reality, suggesting that it is narrative structure, and the familiarity of those narrative structures, rather than visual acuity, or photographic surfaces, which is a far more potent creator of a sense of the real. I find Mast's argument wholly convincing and the key point to extract here is that it is cultural familiarity that establishes the horizons of reality and plausibility. These horizons are established within different media such as theatre and literature:

Perhaps film must be seen as the logical extension and culmination of the richly textured realist and naturalist novel of the late nineteenth century, extending the novel's inevitable progress in weaving complexly patterned fictions out of the apparent flow of life itself.[67]

Within what horizons of expectation, then, does Nagda photography operate? We have already encountered numerous shadows of the 'inter-ocular' field within which photography does its work – we have seen chromolithographs of gods having their photograph taken, we have seen Nagdarites inhabiting personae immortalized through Hindi film, we have seen the emergence of a new form of wedding album montage inspired by Hindi film posters.

I am not able here to thoroughly map the dense 'inter-ocularity' that characterizes the last century of popular visual culture in India. Some fragments from a broader genealogy must suffice. The first of these occurred in 1918, when D. G. Phalke, the founding father of Indian cinema, released *Shree Krishna Janma*, of which a portion survives in the National Film Archive in Pune. The resources of the Hindustan Film Company enabled Phalke to present a greatly more sophisticated product than in his earlier attempts[68] and, as Suresh Chabria notes, the film 'contains sequences of amazing virtuosity' which suggest comparison with Méliès.[69] From the very start, Chabria continues, Phalke 'dazzles his audience with magical transformations appropriate to the subject of Vishnu's *avatars*'.[70] In his 1919 film *Kaliya Mardan*, Phalke's daughter Mandakini played the part of Krishna and at the very beginning she appears as herself sitting on a stool reading a notebook; in the next shot she is gradually trans-

115 D.G. Phalke's daughter transmogrified into Krishna in *Kaliya Mardan*, 1919.

formed into Krishna playing the flute and wearing a peacock head-dress (illus. 115).[71] Phalke's film is not concerned here with producing a seamless 'reality effect' but rather with an exploration of film's own transformative powers. He is not interested in reflecting what Nelson Goodman terms 'a ready-made world', but rather with creating a new world through film.

Popular Hindi film has undergone enormous changes since Phalke's pioneering work, but it has mostly been inclined more to what Mast terms the 'Méliès's tendency than the Lumières'. For instance, in one of the most popular films of the 1970s, *Jai Santoshi Ma* (1975), which helped popularize the goddess Santoshi Ma, there are several sequences which Méliès would have enjoyed greatly: dishes of food fly magically through the air and a goddess falls from the sky.[72] But almost every Hindi film contains sequences of the sort described earlier in the account of *Agneepath*: moments when melodramatic excess is released in a chronotopic delirium which takes the audience across 2,000 miles in three minutes and in which the heroine changes her clothes half a dozen times.[73]

Much photography, like the popular film to which it so often refers, is concerned with the creation of worlds, rather than their duplication. Nelson Goodman argues that we should not talk of true or false versions of the world, but rather of right or wrong ones. What matters is the rightness of fit within specific frames of reference, for 'worlds are as much made as found': 'Truth,' he argues, 'must be otherwise conceived than as corresponding with a ready-made world.'[74] These concepts are articulated in the theoretical language of twentieth-century philosphy but there are fascinating echoes in enduring Hindu narratives. In both classical and vernacular texts one encounters the idea that there are multiple worlds and that one is no more 'real' than another. Many Indologists have noted the absence of a Hegelian synthesizing desire, and a contentment with what the Sanskritist Wendy O'Flaherty calls the opposites of 'fire and water'.[75] W. Norman Brown, another Sanskritist, has noted that:

Heresy has hardly been known in the native Indian tradition and a persecution for novel or startling ideas has been a rarity. Mutually contradictory doctrines have been allowed and are still allowed to stand side by side in argumentative and unreconciled, but not violently hostile, coexistence. [There is] a generally accepted theory that no one knows the ultimate truth.[76]

Photography also acknowledges this, as when it shows Sunil Chhajed and friends inside the mouth of a frightening beast, or *rakshas* (illus. 116). The image was made in Chandni Chowk by 'cutting' two paper negatives and Sunil chose this style from the numerous examples displayed by the photographer. Sunil would provide no interpretation beyond the descriptive but we might see it as a visual exemplification of theories of parallel worlds and magical doubling to be found in both classical and popular vernacular texts. These often take the form of the metaphor of the mouth of god. Thus Yashoda looks into the mouth of the child Krishna and 'saw in his mouth the whole universe, with the far corners of the sky, and the wind, and lightning and the orb of earth with its mountains and oceans, and the moon and stars, and space itself'.[77]

Similarly the sage Markandeya lives inside the mouth of Vishnu, believing his belly to be the real world:

he roamed inside his belly for many thousands of years, visiting the sacred places on earth. One day he slipped out of the God's mouth and saw the world and the ocean shrouded in darkness . . .'Am I crazy, or dreaming? I must be imagining that the world has disappeared, for such a calamity could never really happen.' Then he was swallowed again, and, as soon as he was back in the belly of the God, he thought his vision had been a dream.[78]

116. Black and white montage made by cutting two paper negatives
showing Sunil Chhajed and friends inside the mouth of a mythical
beast, c. 1985.

A variant of 'doubling' is to be found in the genre of popular Hindi movies whose narrative is structured around the contrasting deeds of a 'good and bad brother' in which two caricatures of *dharma* and *adharma* (duty and the negation of duty) struggle against each other. The clichéd form is a contest between the upright chief policeman of Bombay and a gang boss flooding the city with guns, gold and drugs who finally discover as they lie dying in the arms of their widowed mother that they are in fact brothers separated at birth. As Sudhir Kakar notes:

In many movies, the 'split' in the self is highlighted by the brothers getting separated during childhood, the development fate of each remaining unknown to the other, till the final climactic scene in which the confrontation between the brothers takes place and the two selves are finally integrated.[79]

A variation on this can be seen in the film *Ghazab*, released in 1982 and recently reissued. This stars Dharmendra in the classic double role, playing a doomed weak brother in the first half of the film and in the second half an avenging strong brother who rights the wrongs done earlier to his sibling. My notes after seeing this film:

. . . playing Vijay, his muscular Bombay brother, he returns in the second half to settle the score although he is ultimately only able to do this with the help of the deceased brother (now a ghost, referred to as *atma bhai sahab* – 'respected soul brother').
. . . near the finale Vijay takes his brother's energy (*shakti*) into his own body. Through trick photography we see a literal merging of the two bodies. Vijay's biceps bulge, his shirt rips apart and all the villains are then vanquished. . .

But in addition to the role of the wider inter-ocular field in determining the horizons of expectations within which versions of the world are judged, we need also to consider a more conventionally anthropological topic: the construction of the person. Double and triple portraits (illus. 117) place a person beyond the space and identity which certain forms of Western portraiture enforce. These and trick techniques of montage which are so common in Nagda portraiture testify to the lack of any desire to 'capture' sitters within bounded spatial and temporal frames. The replication of bodies and faces brought about by doubling and tripling not only fractures the spatial and temporal correlates that are implied by the perspectival window created by photography but also suggests a different conceptualization of the subjects who are made to appear within this window. It is as if there is a homology between the spatial and temporal infractions of this

117. Triple portrait by Suhag Studio, composite print, *c.* 1980.

representational window and the fracture of these local subjects that prevents what LeGoff describes as the 'rendering of an individual captured in time'.[80] Or, as McKim Marriott might argue, we are confronted with the visual trace of 'dividuals' (rather than 'individuals') – persons who are 'permeable, composite, partly divisible and partly transmissible'.[81]

This is not by any means to suggest that the photographic portraits people seek of themselves are not expressive of agency and individual desire. Clearly they embody highly personal, non-collective yearnings and fantasies. In this sense I would emphatically affirm Mines's[82] and Inden's[83] claims that in privileging esoteric ideology over seemingly 'banal' popular practice and private voices, the extraordinary creativity of many Indian self-representations gets lost. The question here is not so much the presence or absence of 'the individual', but rather the nature of the chronotope in which the body is made to appear. Louis Dumont's claim that in India what he terms the basic 'sociological unit' – the Western individual – is entirely lacking since it is subordinated to the interests of the whole is too simplistic to account for Nagda portraiture strategies.[84]

The preference for 'poses' and the geographic dislocation provided by backdrops reflects, I think, the difficulty of capturing internal qualities through photography. In Nagda, photographic portraiture rarely involves the exploration of the relationship between 'character' and externality within a concrete spatial (and temporal) setting, but rather is more likely to represent bodies and faces as infinitely multiple and contingent and as relatively unanchored in the qualities of the persons that they cloak. Nagda inhabitants are reluctant to concede that one can 'know a man by his face', but this reflects more than failed casual experiments of the sort undertaken by Gandhi in the 1880s; it is a reflection of a pervasive dualism in which a contingent and mutable external surface is contrasted with a moral character which can be made visible only through action. The customers of Nagda's photographic studios are hugely concerned that their faces should appear free of blemish and shadow, but this is to facilitate a simple recognition of a likeness of the living body of the person depicted. They are much less interested in any more ambitious revelation of internal character (illus. 118).

On the face of it, this is extremely surprising, for many anthropological accounts testify to the interpenetration of physical and mental qualities. Thus two recent studies of different aspects of the holy city of Banaras have stressed how the external qualities of the body function as a sign of internal moral qualities. Joseph Alter, who has made an imaginative study of Banaras wrestlers, writes of their 'somaticity', the signifying qualities of their skin. There is a near consensus among anthropologists, Alter notes, that Hindu persons cannot be understood in terms of a Cartesian mind–body duality: 'Rather, the whole person is regarded as a complex, multilayered indivisible synthesis of psychic, somatic, emotional, sensory, cognitive, and chemical forces.'[85] Similarly, Jonathan Parry, in his brilliant study of mortuary practice in Banaras, suggests that 'the state of the body . . . provides an index of the state of the soul', noting, 'a whole and perfect body is both a sign of one's moral state, and a prerequisite for making sacrificial offerings to the gods and ancestors'.[86]

It was similar beliefs that I expected to encounter in studying studio portrait in Nagda. I imagined that photographs would be endowed with a peculiarly intense power precisely because they recorded external signs. Sontag has suggested that in the West photography has had a 'de-Platonizing' effect and it seemed probable that such a technology would be used in a potently forensic manner in a society in which, so it appeared, external signs signified internal states in a very precise manner. I already knew that in Nagda, as elsewhere, some

118. Over-painted black and white photograph by Venus Studio, 1991, watercolour on photographic print.

bodily phenomena (such as leprosy, or the unwillingness of some corpses to burn) *were* explained in terms of the interior qualities of these bodies (they were full of sin). Similarly, I was also to encounter many people who were able to 'read' external surfaces. In 1992 I had the pleasure of attending all of the *Simhastha (Kumbh) mela* in Ujjain, an enormous gathering of ascetics, saints and other religious adepts. On most days I travelled from Bhatisuda to Ujjain with villagers and I hoped in this way to acquire some sense of the impact that this colossal accumulation of the greatest Hindu thinkers and practitioners had on this relatively small village. I imagined that I would sit with villagers as they listened to discourses by learned *acharyas* and that Bhatisuda would be abuzz with new theological ideas acquired through such intellectual engagements. In fact, nothing could have been further from the truth.

11/5/92: Bhatisuda: so far not a single villager has been able to name a sadhu or swami they have seen or heard. They recount their sightings in terms of physique or *tapasya* [ascetic austerity] (five hundred kilos; dwarf; has stood for the last eleven years). But perhaps I am missing the point. True Mahatmajis can read your mind, see your thoughts and know why you have come to see them. This is why it is usually unnecessary to speak with them for all is laid bare by mere physical proximity. Maybe it is hopeless to attempt elucidation through discourse and analysis when what is needed is a phenomenological study of the gestures and subtle inflections involved in these encounters.

When discussing photography in Nagda, I also encountered one voice which argued for the semiotic transparency of the photographic face and body, in the hands of experts at least. Vijay Vyas of Sagar Studio agreed that there was frequently a discrepancy between the exterior and the interior: 'in every place there are people who look good but whose *adat* [habits] are bad' and it also happens that 'inside there is one thing and outside there is something else'. But against this, Vijay argued, there are certain people with a special knowledge (*gyan rakhnevale*) who can look at a photograph and see what lies beneath external surfaces: 'Just like we have astrologers who can tell the future, they can look at the head [*mastak*], at the face [*chehra*], and tell the future. So they can also tell by looking at a photo.'[87] What is proposed here is that certain skilled individuals possess this power of reading, but that most people do not.

Most people in Nagda, while conceding that certain esoteric ritual specialists may indeed be able to read surfaces, espouse a striking dualism which stresses the occlusion of character and the mystery of external surfaces. The majority of people in Nagda are clear that these portraits are capable of depicting only the external characteristics of the sitter, his or her *vyaktitva*. What *vyaktitva* refers to is best denoted by the term 'the signs of being a person'. In Hindi *vyakti* denotes a person, and *vyaktitva* signifies 'person-ness', although it is usually translated as 'personality', 'individuality'[88] or 'self'.

In central Indian photographic portraiture the body (*sharir*) is a ground for the physical and visual aspects of *vyaktitva* (complexion, sharpness of features, dress sense – usually ranked in this order of importance) and, of course, these can be captured through photography.[89] What photographs are nearly always completely unable to capture, however, is the internal moral character and biography of a sitter, his *charitra*. *Charitra* reveals itself only through actions (*karma*), through past history and future eventualities. Whereas for the eighteenth-century physiognomist Johann Caspar Lavater, Socrates' immense ugliness posed a problem for the science of physiognomics (he concluded, after numerous pages of discussion, that he was the exception that proved the rule), the inhabitants of Nagda would not be surprised by this disjunction between the external surface and the moral interior. For them it would simply be evidence that one cannot read *charitra* from *vyaktitva*. This is a view expressed in several proverbs, such as *bahar se kuchh aur andar se kuchh aur* (one thing outside and something else inside), and *shakal se sidha, lekin kam mem terha* (direct in appearance, but crooked in deeds).

A Jain shop owner stressed this difference: *vyaktitva* had to do with the exterior surfaces of a person, and was concerned with the body (*sharir*) and the soul (*atma*) working together. Thus one could at a glance discern the *vyaktitva* of a living person or his/her photo and conclude, for instance, that such-and-such a person did indeed have the *vyaktitva* of, say, a Collector or some other important official. In this context *vyaktitva* denotes 'deportment', 'demeanour' or social 'appearance'. Quite distinct from *vyaktitva*, there was also the question of *charitra*, which was an essentially internal moral quality or character which was apparent only in deeds – that is, in those activities and existential moral decisions which photography, by and large, could not lay bare. So, photographs will reveal only *vyaktitva*, not *charitra*, or it will only reveal the *charitra* of 1 or 2 per cent of photographic subjects. The other 99 per cent will look like the film actors who make themselves look like *mahatmas* and saints, although in fact they are all really dacoits. The quality of dacoitness is a manifestation of *charitra* and can be known only as a result of circumstance – by talking and living together.

One might also draw attention here to the observation that in Hindi films disguises are nearly always successful. Usually accomplished by remarkably convincing latex masks worn by the villain, there are no clues of mannerism or voice which serve to reveal the deception. An outstanding example would be the Manmohan Desai film *Mard* (1985), starring Amitabh Bachchan. At one point in the film both Amitabh – the hero of the title – and his father are convinced by each other's doubles staged by their imperialist enemies and are thus goaded to engage in a gladiatorial father–son duel. When Amitabh goes to rescue his father, who is chained to a grindstone in a British concentration camp, it is only his perspicacious horse – endowed with supernatural insight – who senses the deception.

The significance of the distinctions made between *vyaktitva* and *charitra* must also be understood in the context of the widespread acceptance within India of the transience of the body and its status as a contingent receptacle for the soul. R. S. Khare has described the expression of this view by Chamar intellectuals in Lucknow, for whom it articulates a political yearning: 'A person's body and caste are his exterior (*ūparī*) and temporary (*naśvāna*) sheaths (*cāddar*), while the soul is the imperishable one, which neither dies nor can be higher or lower, but is always equally present in every living being.'[90] Khare suggests that this Untouchable view overlaps in a limited way with the Kanya-Kubja Brahmans, whom he had earlier studied, implying that this is an ideology that has wide currency, and in Nagda such views are commonly enunciated across a range of different castes.[91]

One important consequence of this conceptualization of the relationship between the evanescent body and the eternal soul is an attenuation of the link between visible and invisible qualities. Because the visible is not deemed to be anchored – in most cases – by an invisible realm of character (for there is usually a disjunction between the two), the external body is freed from the constraints with which it is shackled in the Western tradition of painted portraiture. What can be captured in a photographic studio is a person's general physiognomy rather than the face as a trace of an interior character. In Nagda, photography works at a second remove, with the physiognomy of, say, a deceased relative making possible the remembrance of an individual which then in turn permits the recollection of the behaviour and actions of that individual. In one Western tradition of portraiture[92] there is an attempt to do away with this relay mechanism whereby certain physiognomic inflections and nuances are perceived to directly transmit a highly compressed transcript of the sitter's individuality. In Nagda the mode of recognition demands a hieratic clarity – a full-face image with no shadow whose physical recognition is the starting point for the recollection of that individual's life.

Roland Barthes's celebrated search for epiphanal images of his deceased mother, recounted in *Camera Lucida*, which has served for some critics as paradigmatic of a Western fantasy about photography,[93] contrasts sharply with Nagda memorial photography. Barthes describes his quest as not simply for 'just an image,' but for a 'just image'[94] which revealed the 'truth of the face [he] had loved'.[95] The manner in which Barthes describes the image of his mother which finally achieved what he calls 'the impossible science of the unique being'[96] exemplifies in a hyperbolic form one strand of a Western portrait tradition with which Nagda practices have almost nothing in common. Barthes searches through images with a growing discontent:

I never recognized her except in fragments, which is to say that I missed her *being*, and that therefore I missed her altogether. It was not she, and yet it was no one else. I would have recognized her among thousands of other women, yet I did not 'find' her. I recognized her differently, not essentially. Photography thereby compelled me to perform a painful labour; straining toward the essence of her identity.[97]

Barthes finally finds a photograph of his mother as a child which 'collected all the possible predicates from which my mother's being was constituted'[98] and proceeds to unravel from the compressed cipher of her face her true 'being'.

One wonders how Barthes might have responded to a memorial image of his mother printed and painted by Nanda Kishor Joshi. Joshi is an itinerant Brahman artist from Beawar in Rajasthan who also travels through Gujarat and Rajasthan in search of work. He is a precise and appealing individual, always smartly turned out and with a quiet sense of humour. On the two occasions I met him he was spending a month in Nagda, lodging in a modest room in the Chandra Lok Lodge in the heart of Nagda's bazaar and had come to return completed portraits commissioned on his last visit, and to seek new orders. The occasion of our second meeting also coincided with the *Simhastha mela*, and Nanda Kishor was to punctuate his stay in Nagda with many trips to bathe in the River Kshipra.

A typical year's travels might take him twice to Nagda, where each time he would supply somewhere in the region of thirty to forty large framed portraits. Then he might spend two months in Beawar working on commissions with his family before journeying to Kota in Rajasthan, and then coming south along the Delhi–Bombay railway line, stopping at Ramgan Mandi, Jhalawar and Bhawani Mandi, before reaching Nagda. While in Nagda he also visited neighbouring towns and villages such as Khachraud and Unhel. After spending time in Nagda he would either travel west, into Gujarat, or east towards Bhopal, where his younger brother pursued a similar occupation.

Nanda Kishor Joshi's artistry is concerned with perfecting the past, rendering the transient flux recorded in photographic emulsion into more permanent, truer forms. I have tried to show how, in Nagda, little value is placed on photography's documentary ability to record the random and inconsequential. On the contrary, photography is prized for its ability to record idealized staged events characterized by a theatrical preparedness and symmetry. Nanda Kishor Joshi's economic niche is to be found precisely in the space between photography's indexical randomness and Nagda clients' demands for images constructed according to a significantly different aesthetic.

The framed images Nanda Kishor produces are designed to be the visible foci of relatives' memories and also to serve as icons for *shraddh* and *pitr paksh* commemorations. In theory, these memorial images will be displayed for seven *pirhi* or generations, the time during which propitiation aimed at settling the soul of the ancestor remains purposeful. Nanda Kishor described this process with the hybrid English/Hindi phrase *rotation jivan chakra* (rotating circle of life).

A photographic referent is the starting point of the whole process and these vary from very clear black and white images (which are Nanda Kishor's preferred form) or colour prints, to group photographs from which individuals have to be extracted, to degraded images from which it is very difficult to infer physiognomic features. In illus. 119 Nanda Kishor holds what is almost the ideal referent, a very clear black and white image from which an enlargement, which will form the basis of his overpainted image, can be made. By contrast, illus. 120 represents a more complex problem, for the task here is to extract the two figures in the middle right of the group. With such small images, immediately recognizable physiognomic detail is more fugitive and the degree of interpretive latitude on Nanda Kishor's part consequently greater.

When clients give him a photograph of the deceased he also completes a form of 'particulars' (illus. 121). The form is headed with Nanda Kishor's studio's name – 'Hemu Art Center' – and on it are recorded the desired colours of (in this order): hair, headdress, shirt, coat, jacket, sari, blouse, ornaments, eyes, *bindi* or *tilak*, trousers, petticoat. Following this there is a section for 'special instructions' and for the name which is to be written on the portrait and whether the dates of birth and death should be recorded. The form finally notes that these images are best seen from a distance of approximately 8 feet.

The original photograph – often extremely small – is scaled up by Nanda Kishor to the required size of the new portrait and the 'special instructions' are incorporated into the final work, which, once mounted and framed behind glass, costs in the region of 300–450 rupees.[99] Nanda Kishor[100] stresses the flexibility which his style of world-making offers:

Whatever a person wants can be put in the photo. . .make the clothes this colour, even put new clothes in – if no *kurta* is worn, no coat is worn, then a coat can be given, if they are wearing a turban and they want it removed then I can provide the hair, if there is no *topi* [a cap, in this context mostly worn by Jains], a *topi* can be provided, a *pagri* [turban] made – Marwari, Rajasthani, Panjabi, Gujarati, Haryani, Ratlami [styles of *pagri*] – whatever design a person wants can be provided.'

Nanda Kishor shows me his current commissions. He points out various additions in his coloured portraits – 'a Jodhpuri *pagri* . . . a Jain *topi*, a *kangressi topi* . . . a gold chain around a Jain's neck . . .', complete

119. Black and white photograph *c.* 1970, given by a client to the memorial portraitist Nanda Kishor Joshi.

120. Large group photograph from which Nanda Kishor Joshi has been asked to 'extract' two individuals for memorial portraits.

121. The form on which Nanda Kishor Joshi records clients' requests for memorial portraits.

transformations from *kurta* in the original photo to a Jodhpuri coat covering his throat. Or they might say, 'There's a *pagri*, give me a *kangressi topi* . . . give me a white shirt . . . give me a moustache.' Some asked for *tilaks*, while others asked for *tilaks* in the original photograph to be removed so that different *tilaks* could be applied on the glass.

Tejkaran Lunavat from Nagda had been killed by a train and his father wanted a photo but with more hair, the skin colour lightened and a blue Jodhpuri coat, rather than the white *kurta* he was wearing in the original photograph. That had been taken during a wedding and in it a balding Tejkaran, wearing a silk *kurta*, is framed by two coloured peacocks.

Nanda Kishor has a black and white print of a Jain from Sihor; his *kurta* was replaced with a Jodhpuri coat and he was given a gold chain. The original photo betrays a certain vulnerability, the subject's momentary glance at the photographer is quizzical, puzzled. There is no trace of this in Nanda Kishor's painted image. The quizzical has been transformed into the monumental, the face now betraying only a timeless and stern solemnity.

Sri— of Nagda had given him a coloured photo – 'He's alive (*zinda hai!!*), not deceased.' He wants his *pagri* the same colour as in the photo, but needs shaving and he wants a closed Jodhpuri coat. No. 867 a Porwal (middle-ranking trader caste). . . he was a teacher in one of the GRASIM schools and his *topi* is too high on his head, it will be lowered a little. The collar on his *kurta* is open a little too much . . . it will be closed a little.

The mother of one of Nagda's liquor barons has severe *khol* (vitiligo – lightening of the skin). The original photo, taken in the backyard of their house at Divali, shows a grandson touching her feet. Her face is disfigured by vitiligo, which extends across her brow and her chin. Nanda Kishor will restore her colour, straighten both her eyes – she's old and one eye is going over here, the other over there – and place a brass *bor* (ornament) in her hair.

The transformation of the past is perhaps starkest where Nanda Kishor has to rely on post-mortem photography. Photographs are often taken by relatives and studios after death, even when studies from life exist, but are given to Nanda Kishor only when they are the sole, or the best, image available. In such cases the physical manifestations of death can be turned back, mouths can be closed, and eyes opened as the *yadgar* (memento) takes shape. The relatives of Nandalalji Parmar of Alot gave Nanda Kishor a handcoloured black and white image of his body with a large *tilak* (illus. 122). Working from this, a large portrait was prepared in which Nandalalji's eyes were

122. Nanda Kishor Joshi, memorial portrait of Nandalalji Parmar, 1992, water-colour on photographic print. The original post-mortem photographic referent can be seen on the left.

opened, his mouth was given a more vital inflection and various facial marks were removed. In a transformation now becoming familiar, his *kurta* was abandoned in favour of a closed Jodhpuri coat.

Such portraiture practices have parallels elsewhere. In early-nineteenth-century America, painted mourning portraiture depicted the 'deceased subject, usually a child, as alive'.[101] Such images were engaged in denial of the death of the photographic subject through the appeal to 'sleep' as a temporary state from which the dearly loved would soon awake, and Dan Meinwald has suggested that 'in the rouging of cheeks, the role of the postmortem photographer comes intriguingly close to that of an undertaker. The photographer, like the undertaker, uses color to restore the appearance of life.'[102]

The contrasts with Barthes's search for the 'just image' of his mother are illuminating. Nanda Kishor's images lack the compressed epiphanal transcript that Barthes desperately searched for and his clients do not yearn for an 'impossible science of the unique being': their quest is for the 'merely analogical, provoking only . . . identity'.[103] This must in part be because of their function – they are public icons, often displayed in shop fronts and worshipped. But they also have to do the work of remembrance and will often be the only images of the deceased which are carefully kept. Similarly, Nanda Kishor Joshi's painted photographs suggest a striking answer to the question posed in the eighteenth century by Johann Caspar Lavater encountered earlier in this study: '. . . where is the art, where the dissimulation, that can make the blue eye brown, the grey one black, or if it be flat, give it rotundity?'[104]

Coomaraswamy would have described these images as 'effigies' rather than 'portraits'.[105] This is not merely because he argued that 'portraits' are 'likenesses of a person still living', but also because, as he perceptively noted, 'portraiture in the accepted sense is history'. This recalls LeGoff's characterization of the true subject of portraiture as an individual configured in a 'concrete spatial and temporal setting'.[106] The dominant tradition of Western portraiture in oils has given expression to such a chronotope framed by a perspectival window and much Western photography has in many ways reproduced the conventions established within this earlier tradition of painting. In Nagda, by contrast, the studio photographer rarely finds himself asked to picture a subject in the sense of a single being whose totality can be captured by a photograph. The choices that living subjects make before they face the camera are similar to the choices that relatives of the dead are able to record on Nanda Kishor Joshi's form. What the Nagda photographer is presented with is a series of bodies, a series

123. H. R. Raja, Chandra Shekhar Azad and Bhagat Singh, 1982, chromolithograph.

of surfaces, objects, planes and angles, which can be made to assume different qualities.

Ultimately, however, there is an ambivalence about contemporary Nagda portraiture. Earlier we saw how Govardhanlal Ravidas of Bhatisuda reproduced a gesture associated with the freedom fighter Chandra Shekhar Azad. In calendar images (illus. 123), Chandra Shekhar is almost always depicted together with Bhagat Singh, and these images have a very interesting characteristic. Chandra Shekhar Azad was a Brahman and Bhagat Singh was raised a Sikh. For many Britons in India, conditioned by those early anthropometric obessions that were examined in Chapter 1, this would have suggested a funda-mental difference, a separation that could be testified to by sartorial, physiognomic and physiological incompatibility. In popular Indian representations, however, they appear identical – Indian brothers dis-tinguished only by the presence of a hat or a wristwatch and sacred thread. Images of Singh and Azad became hugely popular in the 1930s and many proscribed images dating from this period can be seen in the Proscribed Indian Books collection in the India Office, London. Since the 1960s, most calendar images of the two have been painted by H. R. Raja, a Muslim artist based in Meerut who appears to have first developed this physiological similitude.

Raja's image suggests an oppositional practice, a political critique of the divisiveness of British policy and much of its imperial science. It also demonstrates how the face in contemporary Indian representa-tions can be erased of its physiognomy, its epiphanal qualities effaced in favour of more compelling arguments. In much post-Lavater Euro-pean practice, the exterior becomes a trace of the interior, but the originary privilege of the interior is never questioned. In H. R Raja's Chandra Shekhar Azad and Bhagat Singh images the body is not an inflexible sign of the interior, but is rather a fluid sign capable of suc-couring imaginary interiorities. It is this ambivalence which Nagda photographic subjects exploit as they seek to ensure that they 'come out better' in their photographs. Although strongly dualist discourses emerge in discussions about the problems of reading the face, the pre-occupation with posing and costume proposes (playfully and contin-gently) that internal signs may just, perhaps, be configured by subjecting the external body to particular visual regimes. But this is a very weak 'somaticity', and in the absence of the historically con-structed and visualizable self that figures in much Western portrai-ture, these external signs become infinite. It is this freedom from the need to conform to a particular order of signification, the absence of any burden of self-representation, that guarantees the creativity of Nagda photographic practice.

Epilogue

17/7/92: Chandni Chowk, Old Delhi: on the corner, where this busy road faces the Red Fort, are about eight photographers working with large home-made box cameras. Each photographer has a tressle stand consisting of photographs displayed behind glass panels. Some are predominantly passport images, their stock in trade. Those who quickly need them for a job application or visa can get them here for fifteen rupees for four. One frame is crammed full of dozens of these tiny likenesses, a mixture of the hopeful, the anxious, the suspicious, the quizzical (illus. 124). How many crucial moments in all these individual lives are collected here on public display – all those prospective loans, jobs in the Gulf, jobs nearer home, train season tickets that mark the possession of a job? These photographs are flickering across the desperate and uncertain space of contemporary urban India.

In other frames, the same people, or people very similar, inhabit a radically different world (illus. 125). Gone is the weary, deadened look on the face of the ex-student applying for his hundredth job, banished is the exhausted countenance of the rickshaw wallah seeking a loan to liberate himself from high rents charged by the syndicate that owns his vehicle. These same faces, fractured by the clumsy cutting of the photographers, now sit astride horses clutching guns. The film star Amir Khan puts a friendly arm around the shoulder of one of these interpolated heads, leather-clad starlets strain to press their bodies against the lithe torsos of their photographic partners. Some sit on Bombay's Marine Drive, deep in conversation with Bollywood tough-man Jackie Shroff; others are on intimate terms with Dilip Kumar and Dharmendra. One frame includes a small copy of a film poster, as if to establish the genre conventions of these disembodied heads.

Amar Jeet, whose family had come from Pakistan and who had been in the business for the last three generations, made a double composite portrait and then I asked him to do a marriage shot of myself with Madhuri Dixit, the leading Bombay star, whom I had just seen in the film *Beta*. A large crowd gathered and were entertained. The technique: a postcard of Madhuri is photographed upside-down, then I am. This gives two paper negatives which are carefully cut up with large scissors. These are then re-photographed to give a negative which comes out as a positive. This is the most potent magic I have ever seen, all accomplished on a street corner with a wooden camera and

124. Passport-style photographs displayed by street photographers in Chandni Chowk, Delhi in 1992.

125. Paper negative montages on display in Chandni Chowk, Delhi in 1992.

126. Photographs displayed in Chandni Chowk, Delhi in 1992.

127. *Vistas at Kishangarh, c. 1750.*

an old bucket, and I am left with a photographic trace of my intimate relationship with Madhuri.

Then, out of the corner of my eye, I see a remarkable composite print of a multiple-eyed sitter, poised between two different view-points (illus. 126). On either side of the combined print are the two original images, each respecting an eyewitness principle. I thought of Markandeya slipping in and out of the mouth of the god, but the wider setting of the image forced on me the awareness that this was not sim-ply the eruption of the past into this bustling Delhi thoroughfare. Above the image was a *videshi* (foreign) sitter, smiling genially. On either side of her were two montages with photographic heads inter-polated into postcard film stills in the manner of my Madhuri wed-ding images. Here was no mere traditionalism, but a metaphor for the complexity that living in post-colonial India demands. This image, and those around it in Chandni Chowk, epitomize the manner in which the 'concrete historical circulation'[1] of images reveals that 'the outcomes of liaisons with artifacts cannot be predicted'.[2] In Chandni Chowk the fall-out from enduring traditions of image-making, the engagement with and attempt to negate colonial encounters, and the bureaucratic needs of the state all seemed to jostle together in the same space.

But this Chandni Chowk Rodchenko was also the answer to a puzzle that had lain in my head for many years. This was the complex Indian who would be capable of comprehending an eighteenth-century Rajput view of the *Vistas at Kishangarh* (illus. 127) which had long fascinated me. This striking trace of the hybridization of schemata that occurs within colonialism was once described by Stuart Cary Welch as 'Versailles gone berserk'.[3] The imagination of a Chandni Chowk photographer captured the mobility and inventive-ness of many contemporary Indian identities, fragments of whose archaeology I have attempted to present in this book.

Glossary

The form used in the main text is given first. A transliteration with diacritics based on R. S. McGregor's *Oxford Hindi–English Dictionary* (Oxford, 1993) is given in square brackets.

achanak [acānak] suddenly, unexpectedly

acharya [ācārya] spiritual preceptor, leader of sect

adat [ādat] habit, custom, knack

adharma [adharm] unrighteousness, immorality

adhunik [ādhunik] modern

amavasya [amāvasyā] new moon

andar [andar] within, inside

atma [ātmā] soul, spirit, self, individual

bahar [bāhar] outside

barat [barāt] bridegroom's marriage party

bhakti [bhakti] religious devotion, adoration

bhatija [bhatījā] brother's son

bhautik [bhautik] material, corporeal

bhav [bhāv] emotion, sentiment

bhut pret [bhūt pret] ghosts and spirits of those dead not yet reincarnated

bidai samaroh [bidāī samāroh] departure ceremony

bindi [bindī] dot ornamenting the forehead

bor [bor] ornamental studs of gold, silver or brass

chakra [cakr] wheel, Vishnu's discus

charitra [caritr] character, behaviour, conduct, biography

chaukidar [caukīdār] local policeman, watchman

chehra [cehrā] face, features, expression

chhayachitra [chāyācitr] photograph (literally 'shadow-picture')

chitrakar [citrkār] painter, artist

darshan [darśan] seeing, having sight of a deity

dharma [dharm] duty, morality, virtue

dukan [dukān] shop

dukh [dukh] grief, distress

dusri shadi [dūsrī śādī] death (literally 'second marriage')

ekdam [ekdam] 'in a breath', immediately

ghi [ghī] clarified butter

gyan [gyān] knowledge

hat [hāṭ] market

havan [havan] sacrificial fire

itihas [itihās] history, tradition

jati [jāti] local endogamous group, community

jhujhar [jhūjhār, jūjhār] a warrior, decapitated in battle

jivan [jīvan] life, existence

jiyaji [jiyājī] sister's husband

kaccha [kaccā] built of mud

kachauri [kacaurī] deep-fried puri filled with lentils and vegetables

kalash [kalaś] water pot

kam [kām] work, occupation

karma [karm] deed, fate, the consequence of previous acts

khadi [khādi] coarse handspun cloth

khajur [khajūr] wild date tree

khushi [khuśi] happiness

kisan [kisān] farmer, cultivator

kurta [kurtā] collarless shirt

lota [loṭā] small brass pot

mahatma [mahātmā] saint

malmas [malmās] inauspicious intercalary month

mangalsutra [maṅgalsūtr] auspicious thread or necklace tied by the bridegroom around the bride's neck.

mantra [mantra] sacred verse or text, magical incantation

mastak [mastak] head, forehead

mataji [mātājī] lineage goddess

matka [maṭkā] large earthenware pot

maulvi [maulvī] person learned in Muslim law

mazdur [mazdūr] labourer, worker

mela [melā] fair

mohalla [mohallā] ward, neighbourhood

muhurt [muhūrt] auspicious moment

murti [mūrti] statue, figure

nazar [nazar] evil eye, glance, sight

nikalna [nikālnā] to take out, extract

nuqsan [nuqsān] loss, harm

paksh [pakṣ] light or dark half of lunar month

pagri [pagrī] turban

panchami [pañcamī] fifth day of lunar month

pandit [paṇḍit] learned Brahman

paramparik [pāramparik] traditional

phera [pherā] permabulation of the sacred fire by the bride and groom during wedding

pirhi [pīṛhī] generation

pitr [pitṛ] paternal ancestor

pitr lok [pitṛ lok] world inhabited by ancestors

pitr paksh [pitṛ pakṣ] fortnight when ancestors are worshipped

pran [prāṇ] vital breath, life

pranam [praṇām] bow, respectful greeting

pranpratishtha [prāṇpratiṣṭhā] installation or consecration of a deity

prasad [prasād] remnants of food offered to god

pret [pret] ghost, spirit of deceased

puja [pūjā] worship, adoration of deity

puri [pūrī] small deep-fried breads

qazi [qāzī] Muslim judge, officiating at weddings

rakshas [rākṣas] evil spirit, demon

riti rivaj [rīti rivāj] customary ritual

samadhi [samādhi] ascetic's cataleptic trance, place of entombment

samaj [samāj] community, caste

samosa [samosā] triangular savoury containing spiced vegetables or meat

sev [sev] spicy noodles

shakal [śakl] appearance, outward form

shakti [śakti] power, strength

sharir [śarīr] body

shauq [śauq] desire, yearning

shivling [śivliṅg] phallic emblem of Shiv

shraddh [śrāddh] ceremony honouring ancestors

shraddha [śraddhā] faith, belief

shubh [śubh] auspicious, lucky

sidha [sīdhā] straight, direct

suhag [suhāg] auspicious state of wife-hood

svarup [svarūp] 'own form' assumed by Krishna as Shrinathji

svastik [svastik] auspicious mark

svayambhu [svayambhū] self-willed form of a deity

tamasha [tamāśā] amusement, spectacle

tapasya [tapasyā] ascetic austerities

terha [ṭerhā] crooked, bent

tilak [tilak] religious mark on forehead

tithi [tithi] lunar day

toran [toraṇ] decorated gateway used in weddings

tufan [tūfān] storm, commotion

uttam [uttam] high caste (literally highest, best)

vastavik [vāstavik] real, realistic

vishvas [viśvās] belief, faith

vivah [vivāh] wedding

vyakti [vyakti] person, individual

vyaktitva [vyaktitva] 'person-ness', personality

yadgar [yādgār] memorial

yug [yug] era

zinda [zindā] alive

zyada [zyādā] more

References

Preface

1 Roland Barthes, *La Chambre Claire* (Paris, 1980); *Camera Lucida*, trans. Richard Howard (London, 1982).
2 Cited by Richard Brilliant, *Portraiture* (London, 1991), p. 21.
3 See Mahrukh Tarapor, 'John Lockwood Kipling and British Art Education in India', *Victorian Studies*, 24 (1980), and Patrick Brantlinger, 'A Postindustrial Prelude to Postcolonialism: John Ruskin, William Morris and Gandhism', *Critical Inquiry*, 22, 3 (1996), pp. 466–85.
4 Christopher B. Steiner, *African Art in Transit* (Cambridge, 1994), pp. 124–8.
5 Arjun Appadurai, 'Commodities and the Politics of Value' in *The Social Life of Things: Commodities in Cultural Perspective*, ed. Arjun Appadurai (Cambridge, 1986), p. 5.
6 John Tagg, 'Practicing Theories: An Interview with John Tagg' in *The Critical Image: Essays on Contemporary Photography*, ed. Carol Squiers (Seattle, 1990), p. 232.
7 See Nicholas Thomas, *Entangled Objects: Exchange, Material Culture, and Colonialism in the Pacific* (Cambridge, Mass., 1991), p. 207.

Prologue

1 Pierre Bourdieu, *Photography: A Middle Brow Art* (Cambridge, 1996), p. 6.
2 The connection is made clear by Rabindranath Tagore – 'Villages are like women . . . They are nearer to nature than towns and in closer touch with the fountain of life.' – and cited by S. Ghose, 'At the Heart of India', *Illustrated Weekly of India*, 20 April 1991, p. 9. See also Partha Chatterjee, *The Nation and Its Fragments: Colonial and Postcolonial Histories* (Delhi, 1993), and Lata Mani, 'Contentious Traditions: The Debate on *Sati* in Colonial India' in *Recasting Women: Essays in Colonial History*, ed. Kumkum Sangari and Sudesh Vaid (Delhi, 1989), pp. 88–126, for key insights.

1 'Stern Fidelity' and 'Penetrating Certainty'

1 John Tagg, *The Burden of Representation: Essays on Photographies and Histories* (Basingstoke, 1988), p. 63.
2 P. Pal and V. Dehejia, *From Merchants to Emperors: British Artists and India, 1757–1930* (Ithaca, 1986), p. 182.
3 Siddhartha Ghosh, 'Early Photography in Calcutta', *Marg*, XLI, 4 (n.d.), p. 35.
4 See Michel Foucault, *Discipline and Punish* (Harmondsworth, 1977); Martin Jay, *Downcast Eyes: The Denigration of Vision in Twentieth-Century French Thought* (Berkeley, 1993); Johannes Fabian, *Time and the Other* (New York, 1983); David Green, 'Classified Subjects – Photography and Anthropology', *Ten·8*, 14 (1984), pp. 30–37; C. Pinney, 'The Parallel Histories of Anthropology and Photography' in *Anthropology and Photography 1860–1920*, ed. Elizabeth Edwards (New Haven, 1992), pp. 74–95.
5 Simpson, p. i.
6 Grindlay, n.p.
7 *Journal of the Asiatic Society of Bengal* (1871), p. 393, cited in L. A. Wadell, *Among the Himalayas* (London, 1889), p. ix.
8 Harkness, p. 6.

9 R. L. Rooksby, 'W. H. Rivers and the Todas', *South Asia*, I (1971), p. 113.
10 Gordon Fyfe, 'Art and Its Objects: William Ivins and the Reproduction of Art' in *Picturing Power: Visual Depictions and Social Relations*, ed. G. Fyfe and J. Law (London, 1988), p. 79.
11 629 (23 April 1842).
12 I am concerned here only with contemporary evaluations and mythologies, not with an ontological consideration of the indexical truth claims of photography. Cf. W. J. T. Mitchell, *Iconology: Image, Text, Ideology* (Chicago, 1986).
13 *Journal of the Photographic Society of Bengal*, II (1857), cited by John Falconer, 'Photography in Nineteenth-Century India' in *The Raj: India and the British: 1600–1947*, ed. C. A. Bayly (London, 1990), p. 270.
14 Norman Chevers, *A Manual of Medical Jurisprudence for India including the Outline of a History of Crime against the Person in India* (Calcutta, 1870; first edition 1856), p. 75.
15 Ibid., p. 86.
16 William J. Herschel, *The Origin of Finger-Printing* (Oxford, 1916), p. 7.
17 Denzil Ibbeston, 'The Study of Anthropology in India', *Journal of the Anthropological Society of Bombay*, II (1890), p. 121.
18 See Pinney, 'Parallel Histories', p. 79.
19 He was later to become Principal of the Calcutta Medical College and President of the Bengal Social Science Association.
20 Chevers, *Manual*, p. 74.
21 Tagg, *The Burden of Representation*, p. 35.
22 G. Thomas, *History of Photography in India: 1840–1980* (1981), p. 14.
23 Veena Talwar Oldenburg, T*he Making of Colonial Lucknow, 1856–1877* (Princeton, 1984), p. 139.
24 Chevers, *Manual*, p. 74.
25 Samuel Bourne, 'Narrative of a Photographic Trip to Kashmir (Cashmere) and Adjacent Districts', *British Journal of Photography* (1863), p. 51, cited by Falconer, 'Photography in Nineteenth-Century India', p. 264.
26 Georges Didi-Huberman, 'Photography – Scientific and Pseudo-scientific' in *A History of Photography: Social and Cultural Perspectives*, ed. Jean-Claude Lemagny and André Rouille (Cambridge, 1987), p. 74.
27 Cited in John Falconer, 'Ethnographical Photography in India: 1850–1900', *Photographic Collector*, 5 (1984), p. 16, on which my summary of Mullins's talk also relies.
28 Memo from Colonel H. M. Durand, Officiating Secretary to the Government of India in the Foreign Department, Maharasthra Government Archives, XXVI, Comp. 457, cited by G. Thomas, 'The "Peccavi" Photographs', *History of Photography*, IV, 1 (1980), p. 49.
29 Asiatic Society Library, Bombay, '0.779.095473. Sin'.
30 J. M. Kaye, *The People of India* (London, 1872), VI, Plate 292. Houghton and Tanner had compiled detailed notes which were published by the Government of Bombay in printed lists (Thomas, 'Peccavi', p. 51) and *The People of India* letterpress may have drawn on these. The preface to the first volume lists various sources for the letterpress accounts (J. R. Melville, Meadows Taylor, J. M. Kay, J. Forbes Watson).
31 A well-known example of photographic 'environmental portraiture' is Robert Howlett's 1857 'Portrait of Isambard Kingdom Brunel Standing before the Launching Chains of the "Leviathan" (the "Great Eastern")'. Writing about this portrait, Richard Brilliant (*Portraiture* [London, 1991], p. 99) has argued that the backdrop is a 'part' – a 'permanent aspect of his being, of his identity, from which he cannot and, if properly portrayed, should not be parted'.

32 Kaye, *People of India*, VI, Plate 323.

33 J. Forbes Watson, *A Classified and Descriptive Catalogue of the Indian Department, The International Exhibition of 1862* (Calcutta, 1862), p. 200.

34 Scott was keen to keep in touch with photographic developments in England. A note in *The Photographic Journal* in 1859 records that he had sent in stereoscopic views of the Deccan and had written, 'I have about 200 negatives of most interesting subjects; they were taken with Bolton's collodion . . . I hope you will do me the kindness to offer to exchange with any member of the society for similar numbers of their pictures, so that I may see what progress photography is making in England' (7 May, p. 298).

35 On Tripe see Pal and Dehejia, *From Merchants to Emperors*, p. 196, and on Gill see Ray Desmond, *Victorian India in Focus* (London, 1982), pp. 3, 15.

36 It was originally announced that three volumes would be published, the first covering 'Gujarat, Kutch and Kathiawar', the second covering 'the Maratha country' and the third covering 'a miscellaneous collection', but only the first two appeared.

37 Gordon Baldwin, *Looking at Photographs: A Guide to Technical Terms* (Santa Monica, 1991), n.p.

38 John Falconer ('Ethnographical Photography', p. 19) notes that Dajee was a professional photographer and a council member of the Bombay Photographic Society.

39 Amit Ambalal, *Krishna as Shrinathji: Rajasthani Paintings from Nathdvara* (Ahmedabad, 1987), p. 70, and Rachel Dwyer (personal communication), to whom thanks.

40 Baldwin, *Photographs*.

41 *Report of the Nagpore Exhibition of Arts, Manufactures and Produce* (Nagpur, 1865), p. 97.

42 Tagg, *Burden of Representation*, p. 50. See also Roger Cardinal, 'Nadar and the Photographic Portrait in Nineteenth-Century France' in *The Portrait in Photography*, ed. G. Clarke (London, 1992), pp. 23–4, where he contrasts Nadar's 'moment of contact when a shaft of feeling lays bare human authenticity' with Disdéri's and Silvy's generation of 'redundant signals of social and financial prestige'.

43 Cited by Tagg, *Burden of Representation*, p. 53.

44 Ray Desmond, *History of the Indian Museum* (London, 1982), p. 119.

45 One consequence of this was a great concern with the actual state of each community in the 1860s: hence, for example, the observation in the first volume (Plate 11), 'Raj Bansis. Aboriginal. Now Hindoos'.

46 *People of India*, V, 'Afghan Frontier Tribes'.

47 *People of India*, VI, 'Note on the Frontier Tribes of Sind – Beloches'.

48 These remain hotly contested concepts and the divisions between them are extremely hard to define analytically. In the 1860s the categories were sometimes used interchangeably, but 'caste' was most commonly invoked where the community was recognizably part of mainstream Hinduism.

49 IV, Plate 193.

50 This was echoed in the text accompanying another Gujar image: '[they] have proved themselves impatient of restraint, breaking out into turbulent lawlessness whenever an opportunity occurs' (III, Plate 148).

51 'Orientalism is after all a system for citing works and authors' (Edward Said, *Orientalism* [Harmondsworth, 1985], p. 23).

52 Ibid., p. 6.

53 *British Association for the Advancement of Science, Report for 1913*, 83, p. 623. I thank Roslyn Poignant for drawing this to my attention.

54 Said, *Orientalism*, p. 7.

55 The left side is considered more polluted: hence a Hindu should

circumambulate a deity clockwise – with his right side closest to the god.

56 The phrase is Richard Vinograd's and is intended to draw attention to the negotiations which occur during the 'portait-making act', within which there is a 'framework of exchanges between sitter and portraitist' (*Boundaries of the Self: Chinese Portraits, 1600–1900* [Cambridge, 1992], p. 13).

57 Text to Plate 24, 'Khojahs'.

58 Roland Barthes, 'The Death of the Author' in his *Image Music Text*, trans. Stephen Heath (London, 1984), p. 148.

59 Bernard S. Cohn, 'The Past in the Present: India as a Museum of Mankind', paper delivered at Smithsonian symposium, 'The Poetics and Politics of Representation', 1988; forthcoming in *History and Anthropology*.

60 Cited by David Lelyveld, *Aligarh's First Generation: Muslim Solidarity in British India* (Princeton, 1978), p. 4.

61 *People of India*, III, Plate 139.

62 Lelyveld, *Aligarh*, p. 6.

63 G. F. I. Graham, *The Life and Work of Syed Ahmed Khan C.S.I.* (Edinburgh, 1885), pp. 188–9, part of which is cited in Cohn, 'The Past in the Present'.

64 Cited by Falconer, 'Photography in Nineteenth-Century India', p. 273.

65 Herbert Hope Risley, 'Address on the Progress of the Study of Indian Anthropology in Europe and Cognate Matters', *Journal of the Anthropological Society of Bombay*, II (1890), p. 253.

66 G. E. Dobson, 'On the Andamans and Andamanese', *Journal of the Anthropological Institute*, XXII (1875), pp. 457–67.

67 Roland Barthes, 'Rhetoric of the Image' in *Image Music Text*, p. 44.

68 Joseph Fayrer, *Proceedings of the Asiatic Society of Bengal* (1867), p. 90.

69 E. T. Dalton, *Descriptive Ethnology of Bengal* (Calcutta, 1872), p. i.

70 Ibid., p. ii.

71 Ibid., p. iii.

72 Ibid., caption to Plate XXXIII.

73 Ibid., p. 156. See also Emma Tarlo, *Clothing Matters: Dress and Identity in India* (London, 1996), pp. xvii–xx.

74 Herbert Hope Risley, *The People of India* (Calcutta, 1908), Plate XX.

75 J. W. Breeks, *An Account of the Primitive Tribes and Monuments of the Nilagiris* (London, 1873), p. iv.

76 Ibid., p. v.

77 Ibid., p. iii.

78 'No pains were spared to verify every statement, in cases where actual seeing or hearing at first hand was impossible' (Breeks's widow's preface to ibid., p. iii); 'I have actually witnessed most of the scenes described' (W. E. Marshall, *A Phrenologist Amongst the Todas* [London, 1873], p. vii).

79 Ibid., p. 29.

80 Ibid., p. 32.

81 Ibid., pp. 12–13.

82 Margaret Cowling, *The Artist as Anthropologist* (Cambridge, 1989), p. 19.

83 Michael Shortland, 'Skin Deep: Barthes, Lavater and the Legible Body', *Economy and Society*, XIV, 3 (1985), p. 284.

84 Entry on 'Physiognomics' in T. A. Sebeok (ed.), *Encyclopaedic Dictionary of Semiotics* (Berlin, 1986), 2, p. 725.

85 Johann Caspar Lavater, *Essays on Physiognomy, Designed to Promote Knowledge and Harmony among Mankind*, trans. Thomas Holcraft (London, n.d.), p. 171.

86 Ibid., p. 84.

87 'We no longer follow the logic of the deductions made, except, perhaps as regards those relating purely to expression. We no longer scrutinize the human face in this close manner, nor do we make any attempt to record

its features, in such detail, in life, in art, or in literature, still less do we attempt to deduce from those features specific information about the character of the person concerned' (Cowling, *Artist as Anthropologist*, p. 8).

88 'Compare a Negro and an Englishman, a native of Lapland and an Italian, a Frenchman and an inhabitant of Tierra del Fuego. Examine their forms, countenances, characters and minds. Their difference will be easily seen. . .' (Lavater, *Physiognomy*, p. 339).

89 Lavater gives this a theological explanation: 'as an individual's excellence of mind and physiognomy are the favour and gift of God, so are they equally the favour and the gift of God when bestowed upon nations, who, by residing in a more fortunate climate, have for that reason, greater excellence of understanding and of form' (ibid., p. 361).

90 Ibid., p. 33.

91 Ibid., p. 430.

92 Ibid., p. 243.

93 See Ronald B. Inden, 'Orientalist Constructions of India', *Modern Asian Studies*, XX, 3 (1986), pp. 401–46.

94 Ray McKenzie, '"The Laboratory of Mankind": John McCosh and the Beginnings of Photography in British India', *History of Photography*, XI, 2 (1987), pp. 113–14.

95 See Elizabeth Edwards, 'Photographic "Types": The Pursuit of Method', *Visual Anthropology*, III (1990), pp. 235–58.

96 Waddell, *Among the Himalayas*, p. ix.

97 This evokes a parallel with the continuing practice in modern social anthropology for personal narratives to be separated from the professional capital of formal ethnography (see Mary Louise Pratt, 'Fieldwork in Common Places' in *Writing Culture: The Poetics and Politics of Ethnography*, ed. James Clifford and George E. Marcus [Berkeley, 1986], pp. 31–2).

98 F. M. Coleman, *Typical Pictures of Indian Natives: Being Reproductions from Specially Prepared Hand-coloured Photographs* (Bombay, 1902, seventh edition). See also Brij Bhushan Sharma, 'Typical Pictures of Indian Natives', *History of Photography*, XII, 1 (1988), pp. 77–82.

99 Coleman, *Typical Pictures*, p. 30.

100 Ibid., p. 36.

101 Johannes Fabian, *Time and the Other*, p. 143.

102 D'Arcy Waters Collection, Centre of South Asian Studies, University of Cambridge.

103 Graham Clarke, 'Public Faces, Private Lives: August Sander and the Social Typology of the Portrait Photograph' in *The Portrait in Photography*, ed. Clarke, p. 73.

104 Jacques LeGoff, *Time, Work and Culture in the Middle Ages* (Chicago, 1980), p. 36.

105 William Crooke, *Tribes and Castes of the North-Western Provinces and Oudh* (Calcutta, 1896), I, p. cxxv.

106 For more on Crooke see C. Pinney, 'Underneath the Banyan Tree: William Crooke and Photographic Depictions of Caste' in *Anthropology and Photography*, ed. Edwards, pp. 165–73.

107 Herbert Hope Risley, *The Tribes and Castes of Bengal*, (Calcutta, 1891), I, p. xxxiv.

108 See Joseph Leo Koerner, 'Rembrandt and the Epiphany of the Face', *Res: Anthropology and Aesthetics*, 12 (1986), pp. 5–33, for a critique of Alois Riegl's view of Rembrandt as the culmination of Dutch painterly concern with 'the representation of the inner subjective life of individuals . . . particularly as it revealed itself obliquely, through suggestion or intimation, in the features of the represented face' (p. 10).

109 See Risley, *The People of India*, pp. lviii ff.

110 A. Lane Fox, 'Anthropometric Committee', *Journal of Anthropological Institute*, VII (1878), p. 392.

111 This image in the Royal Anthropological Institute Photographic Collection is undocumented but shares a similar format with a large number of images donated by Thurston.

112 Edgar Thurston, *Castes and Tribes of Southern India* (Madras, 1909), I, pp. xvi–xvii.

113 Cited by Carlo Ginzburg, 'Clues: Morelli, Freud, and Sherlock Holmes' in *The Sign of Three: Dupin, Holmes, Peirce*, ed. Umberto Eco and Thomas A. Sebeok (Bloomington, 1988), p. 117, fn. 65.

114 A. Conan Doyle, *The Sign of Four* (London, 1899), pp. 72–3.

115 'In last year's *Anthropological Journal* you will find two short monographs from my pen upon the subject' ('The Cardboard Box', cited by Ginzburg, 'Clues', p. 84).

116 In 1853 the Schlagintweit brothers were commissioned by the East India Company to survey the Himalayan region. During their travels they made a series of life casts which were later published as a series of metallic casts of 'Ethnographical Heads from India and High Asia'. In this series were 275 facial casts and thirty-seven pairs of hands and feet (see Christopher Pinney, 'Colonial Anthropology in the "Laboratory of Mankind"' in *The Raj: India and the British*, ed. Bayly, p. 279.

117 In the appendix on photography, the fourth edition of *Notes and Queries on Anthropology* (London, 1912) also recommends the taking of *squeezes*, 'copies of sculptured or engraved objects, made by pressing moist paper on the carved surface, of which the paper mould, when dry, retains the exact form and texture' (p. 271).

118 Ginzburg, 'Clues', p. 108. Ginzburg further notes that through dactylography 'what to the British administrators had seemed an indistinguishable mass of Bengali faces . . . now became a series of individuals each one marked by a biological specificity'. This of course also suggests a difference between photo- and dactylography: the photograph allowed the systematization of 'types' underpinned by various 'racial' classifications; dactylography (despite Galton's hope that 'monkey-like patterns' would be found among 'Indian tribes') threw this process into reverse, splintering types into individuals.

119 Herschel, *The Origin of Finger-Printing*, pp. 7–8.

120 Ibid., p. 9. Herschel wrote: 'The decisiveness of a finger-print is now one of the most powerful aids to Justice. Our possession of it derives from the impression of Konai's hand in 1858.'

121 Ginzburg ('Clues', pp. 109–10), in a characteristically brilliant argument, makes the claim that Herschel 'expropriated' an 'intuitive' Bengali knowledge and turned it against them. In his own account, Herschel lays more stress on the subliminal influence of Bewick's engravings of thumb impressions (used as colophons) half-remembered from childhood, and points to the difference between the Bengali *tep-sai*, an imprint made by the tip of the finger, and fingerprints (*Origin of Finger-Printing*, p. 37).

122 See H. M. Ramsay, *Anthropometry in Bengal, Or, Identification of Criminals by Anthropometric Measurement and Thumb Impressions* (London, 1895).

123 Herschel, *Origin of Finger-Printing*, dedication, n.p.

124 Tagg, *Burden of Representation*, p. 63.

125 *Emp.* v. *Sahdeo*, cited by K. J. Aiyer, *Law and Practice of Evidence in Criminal Cases in India and Pakistan* (Allahabad, 1949), p. 461.

2 Indian Eyes

1 L. K. Mitchell, *The Art of Photography with Special Reference to Its Practice in India* (Bombay, 1908), p. 69.

2 Judith Mara Gutman, *Through Indian Eyes: 19th and Early 20th Century Photography from India* (New York, 1982), pp. xi–xii.

3 Siddhartha Ghosh, 'Early Photography in Calcutta', *Marg*, XLI, 4 (n.d.), p. 45.

4 The volume was published by R. C. Lepage & Co. and may be the only extant copy is in the Asiatic Society Library, Calcutta. A catalogue at the end of the book lists another, presumably earlier, volume: *Cowley's Photography in India, Or, Practical Instructions in the Printing of Photogenic Pictures, and the Production of Calotype and Collodion Negatives.* Later volumes included John Blees's *Photography in Hindostan; Or, Reminiscences of a Travelling Photographer* (1877); George Ewing's *A Handbook of Photography for Amateurs in India* (1895); and H. M. Ibrahim's Urdu *Rahno-ma-il-photography-ya-usil-i-musawery* (1899). Cf. John Falconer, 'Photography in Nineteenth-Century India' in *The Raj: India and the British: 1600–1947*, ed. C. A. Bayly (London, 1990), p. 277.

5 This echoes the complaints made by Samuel Bourne in his famous 'Narrative of a Photographic Trip to Kashmir (Cashmere) and Adjacent Districts', *The British Journal of Photography* (25 January 1867), p. 39: 'The only difficulty I had generally to contend with was the obstinacy of the natives when I wanted to introduce them into my pictures. By no amount of talking and acting could I get them to stand or sit in an easy, natural attitude. Their idea of giving life to the picture was to stand bolt upright, with their arms down as stiff as pokers, their chin turned up as if they were standing to have their throats cut.'

6 F. Fisk Williams, *A Guide to the Indian Photographer* (Calcutta, 1860), pp. 41–2.

7 Andrew Wilton, *The Swagger Portrait: Grand Manner Portraiture in Britain from Van Dyck to Augustus John, 1630–1930* (London, 1992), n.p.

8 Ibid.

9 Sarah Kent, 'Portrait of an Ego', *Guardian*, 27 October 1992, p. 7.

10 Gutman suggests it was active *c.* 1896–1911 and notes a partnership with C. Laurie.

11 Exactly the same wording is to be found on cabinet cards produced by English studios.

12 *The Photographic Journal* (21 January 1859), p. 144.

13 These were *Harmonious Coloring as applied to Photographs*, *How to Colour a Photograph* and *Rintoul's Guide to Painting Photographic Portraits, Landscapes.*

14 Val Prinsep, *Imperial India: An Artist's Journals* (London, n.d.), p. 47.

15 Gutman, *Through Indian Eyes*, p. 108.

16 Ibid., pp. 108–15.

17 Ibid., p. 16.

18 Throughout his early career he transliterated his name as Lala Din Diyal; here I have used the more common later transliteration.

19 1881 Census figures cited by W. W. Hunter, *The Imperial Gazetteer of India* (London, 1886, second edition), VII, p. 9.

20 Ibid.

21 Rodney W. Jones, *Urban Politics in India: Area, Power, and Policy in a Penetrated System* (Berkeley, 1974), p. 50.

22 C. E. Luard, *Indore State Gazetteer* (Calcutta, 1908), II, p. 36. The quote continues: 'It had been the intention of the Government to mark distinctly on this occasion the difference of position between a nominee of the

Paramount Power and a Chief succeeding by hereditary right . . . this the precipitate action of the Resident had prevented.'

23 Lala Deen Dayal, 'Short Account of My Photographic Career', typescript of MS dated 18 July 1899, in possession of his descendant, Prabas Chand, Secunderabad.

24 Clark Worswick, *Princely India: Photographs by Raja Deen Dayal, 1884–1910* (London, 1980), p. 149.

25 Worswick (ibid., p. 149) cites *The Journal of the Photographic Society of India* (January 1892, p. 10): 'As this studio is for photographing native ladies only, special arrangements had to be made to protect them from the gaze of the profane and stern. So the place is surrounded by high walls and all day long within this charmed enclosure Mrs Kenny-Levick, aided by native female assistants, takes the photographs of the high-born native ladies of the Deccan.'

26 Drawing on accounts in *The Times of India* and *Bombay Gazette*, Judith Mara Gutman (*Through Indian Eyes*, p. 28) has described the opening of a new Deen Dayal studio in 1896 which comprised 'dressing rooms for ladies and gentlemen, a studio 45′ × 25′ . . . and a splendid showroom 60′ × 40′ [filled] with photographs of Viceroys, native chiefs, members of Council and well-known civil and military officers.'

27 Worswick, *Princely India*, p. 150.

28 *The Englishman* (15 March 1887).

29 On 20 March.

30 'A Short History of Our Business', typescript from Fotocrafts, Secunderabad.

31 G. Thomas, 'Maharaja Sawai Ram Singh II of Jaipur, Photographer-Prince', *History of Photography*, X, 3 (1986), p. 181.

32 Comprising several thousand glass negatives, held in the Sawai Man Singh II Museum, Jaipur.

33 Falconer, 'Photography in Nineteenth-Century India', p. 277, suggests that the photographer was Colin Murray, who was later to become a partner in Bourne and Shepherd.

34 Kalyan Kumar Chakravarty, *Nehru Centre, Lalbag, Indore* (Bhopal, n.d.), n.p.

35 Ibid.

36 The author possesses a photograph depicting four airborne ladies in a small monoplane to which the legend 'Souvenir de l'Exposition de Gand, 1913' is attached.

37 See Clark Worswick and Ainslee Embree, *The Last Empire: Photography in British India, 1855–1911* (London, 1976), p. 44.

38 Ashish Rajadhyaksha, 'The Phalke Era: Conflict of Traditional Form and Modern Technology', *Journal of Art and Ideas*, 14 and 15 (July–December 1987), p. 47.

39 Cf. Kajri Jain, 'Of the Everyday and the "National Pencil"', *Journal of Arts and Ideas*, XXVII–VIII (1995), pp. 57–90.

40 Isak Mujavar, *Dadasaheb Phalke* (Pune, 1970), pp. 9–12.

41 This account is summarized from S. N. Joshi, *Half-Tone Reprints of the Renowned Pictures of the late Raja Ravi Varma* (Pune, 1911), p. 55.

42 This image was purchased from a 'framing shop' in Ratlam in 1994.

43 Gutman, *Through Indian Eyes*, p. xiii.

44 Ibid., p. 5.

45 Peter Galassi, *Before Photography: Painting and the Invention of Photography* (New York, 1981).

46 Gutman, *Through Indian Eyes*, p. 4.

47 Gutman presumes the existence of a stable and culturally 'authentic' aesthetic. For an account of the historically complex construction of local

portrait aesthetics, see Jayasinhji Jhala, 'Power and the Portrait: The Influence of the Ruling Elite on the Visual Text in Western India', *Visual Anthropology*, VI (1993), pp. 171–98.

48 'Women at Sipi Fair', *c.* 1905, Gutman, *Through Indian Eyes*, p. 6.

49 Cited by Suresh Chabria, 'D. G. Phalke and the Méliès Tradition in Early Indian Cinema' in *Light of Asia: Indian Silent Cinema 1912–1934*, ed. Suresh Chabria and Paolo Cherchi Usai (New Delhi, 1994), p. 104.

50 Birdwood continues, with a fascinating and sly reference to a previous Viceroy: 'The strictly scientific fact is that Parsis are as unmixed an Aryan race as exists, having through their segregation in Western India preserved their archaic Iranian type almost as completely as the English aristocracy of "the Pale" have in Ireland so remarkably preserved in their original Norman physiognomy; of which the late Earl Mayo, and his brother, Lord Connemara, are notable proofs.'

51 Birdwood in Jehangir, *Representative Men of India*, p. v.

52 Arthur H. Nethercot, *The First Five Lives of Annie Besant* (London, 1961), p. 340.

53 *Who's Who in India, Burma and Ceylon* (Pune, 1938), p. 131. See Arthur H. Nethercot, *The Last Four Lives of Annie Besant* (London, 1963), pp. 259–64, for a detailed account.

54 Ibid., p. 319. For further, partial, details on Arundale see the anonymous *Personal Memories of G. S. Arundale, Third President of the Theosophical Society* (London, 1967).

55 Ronald Pearsall, *The Table-Rappers* (London, 1972), pp. 211–12.

56 Rules of the Theosophical Society, summarized in Anil Seal, *The Emergence of Indian Nationalism: Competition and Collaboration in the Later Nineteenth Century* (Cambridge, 1971), p. 250.

57 A reference to Koot Hoomi, one of the Tibetan Masters who directly communicated with Madame Blavatsky. See Nethercot, *First Five Lives*, p. 210.

58 Cited in Pearsall, *Table-Rappers*, p. 216.

59 Sumit Sarkar, *Modern India 1885–1947* (Basingstoke, 1989), p. 152.

60 Ibid., p. 151.

61 Moncure Daniel Conway, *My Pilgrimage to the Wise Men of the East* (London, 1906), pp. 201–2.

62 Ibid., p. 198. Conway, however, was denied this service: 'When I proposed to write a note, I was informed that only a few days before the Mahatmas had forbidden any further cabinet correspondence.'

63 C. Isherwood, *Ramakrishna and His Disciples* (New York, 1965), p. 339, cited by H. Daniel Smith, 'Hindu *Deśika* Figures: Some Notes on a Minor Iconographic Tradition', *Religion* 8, 1 (1978), p. 58.

64 *Report on the Administration of the Indore State During the Minority of his Highness Maharaja Raj Rajeshwar Sawai Shri Yeshwant Rao Holkar Bahadur (1926–30)* (Indore, 1930), pp. 114 ff.

65 The latter is now known as the Dr Bhau Daji Lad Museum. Gyan Prakash, 'Science "Gone Native" in Colonial India', *Representations*, 40 (1992), p. 175, fn. 23.

66 M. K. Gandhi, *An Autobiography: Or, the Story of My Experiments with Truth*, trans. Mahadev Desai (Ahmedabad, 1991), p. 70.

3 Chambers of Dreams

1 Rosalind Krauss, 'The Photographic Conditions of Surrealism' in her *The Originality of the Avant-garde and Other Modernist Myths* (Cambridge, Mass., 1985), p. 110.

2 From author's ethnographic notebook, 1991.

3 See Diana L. Eck, *Darśan: Seeing the Divine Image in India* (Chambersburg, 1981).

4 See Stephen Tyler, 'The Vision Quest in the West', *Journal of Anthropological Research*, XL, 1 (1984), pp. 23–40; and Richard Rorty, *Philosophy and the Mirror of Nature* (Oxford, 1980).

5 It was this image, now in a vast and elaborate temple structure, which fourteen years later was to be the chief ritual focus of one of its near neighbours, Vijay Vyas of Sagar Studio, who we will shortly encounter.

6 Amit Ambalal, *Krishna as Shrinathji: Rajasthani Paintings from Nathdvara* (Ahmedabad, 1987), p. 50.

7 Robert Skelton, *Rajasthani Temple Hangings of the Krishna Cult* (New York, 1973), p. 13.

8 Eck, *Darśan*, p. 40.

9 See A. Stewart Woodburne, 'The Evil Eye in South Indian Folklore', and D. F. Pocock, 'The Evil Eye – Envy and Greed Among the Patidar of Central Gujarat', both in *The Evil Eye: A Folklore Casebook*, ed. Alan Dundes (New York, 1981), pp. 55–65, 201–10; Clarence Maloney, 'Don't Say "Pretty Baby" Lest You Zap It With Your Eye – The Evil Eye in South Asia' in *The Evil Eye*, ed. C. Maloney (New York, 1976), pp. 102–48; and Lawrence A. Babb, 'Glancing: Visual Interaction in Hinduism', *Journal of Anthropological Research*, 37 (1981), pp. 387–401.

10 See H. Daniel Smith, 'Impact of "God Posters" on Hindus and their Devotional Traditions' in *Media and the Transformation of Religion in South Asia*, ed. L. A. Babb and S. Wadley (Philadelphia, 1995), pp. 24–50; and Chris Pinney, '"An Authentic Indian Kitsch": The Aesthetics, Discriminations and Hybridity of Popular Hindu Art', *Social Analysis*, 38 (1995), pp. 88–110.

11 John Tagg, 'The Burden of Representation', *Ten·8*, 14 (1984), p. 12.

12 This is termed, in Malwi, *paraba dena*. *Paraba* corresponds to the Hindi terms *visarjan* and *pravah*.

13 Cf. A. Appadurai and C. Breckenridge, 'Museums are Good to Think: Heritage on View in India' in *Museums and Communications: The Politics of Public Culture*, ed. Ivan Karp et al. (Washington, 1992), p. 52.

14 See Pierre Bourdieu, *Outline of a Theory of Practice* (Cambridge, 1977).

15 Maurice Godelier, '"Salt Money" and the Circulation of Commodities among the Baruya of New Guinea' in his *Perspectives in Marxist Anthropology* (Cambridge, 1977), p. 151.

16 '. . . the West is not so much a place, or even a culture, as an emblem of exotic decadent otherness, signified by whisky, bikinis and uncontrolled sexuality' (Rosie Thomas, 'Indian Cinema – Pleasures and Popularity', *Screen*, 26, 3–4 [1985], p. 126).

17 Siddhartha Ghosh, 'Early Photography in Calcutta', *Marg* 41, 4 (n.d.), p. 40, notes: 'From the very beginning, the acceptance of photographs – the ease with which photographs made their way into even very orthodox Hindu families – was rather unusual. No other product of . . . nineteenth-century Western technology was given such a welcome.'

18 The bulk of these are distributed by local businesses at the festival of Divali (see Smith, 'God Posters').

19 Laura Mulvey, 'Visual Pleasure and Narrative Cinema' in her *Visual and Other Pleasures* (Basingstoke, 1989), p. 29.

20 For a detailed account of wedding ceremonies in 1950s Malwa, see Adrian C. Mayer's excellent, *Caste and Kinship in Central India: A Village and Its Region* (London, 1960), pp. 227–35.

21 These are respectively a glossy channel broadcast by the state-owned

Doordarshan and aimed at metropolitan populations; a commercial Hindi channel showing numerous film quizzes, sitcoms and Hindi movies; and a music video channel, mostly in English, fronted by former employees of MTV's Hong Kong studio.

22 Christian Metz, 'Photography and Fetish', *October*, 34 (1985), p. 81.
23 Ibid., p. 88.
24 Ibid., p. 83.
25 Ibid., p. 84.
26 See, for example, Anil Sharma's *Faristhay* (1990), in which such a lens is used to replicate the disoriented vision of a drunken gangster.
27 Rosalind Krauss, 'Photography in the Service of Surrealism' in her *L'Amour Fou: Photography and Surrealism* (London, 1985), pp. 25–6.
28 Cited by Ian Jarvie, *The Philosophy of Film* (London, 1987), p. 147.
29 Vijay Vyas noted a local variant in his natal town of Khachraud (near Nagda). Here only women have their photograph taken on the day after Divali, men choosing to have theirs taken at Dashahara, twenty days earlier.
30 A *muhurt* is technically a period of forty-eight minutes but is commonly used to invoke an auspicious moment, pregnant with future possibilities.
31 Vijay here refers both to the opening of new workshops and to rituals held within established units (such as the commissioning of new machines).
32 This text is printed on the back of the folios.
33 See Jonathan Parry, *Death in Banaras* (Cambridge, 1994), pp. 172–8, for an exceptional account of mortuary ritual.
34 Nelson Goodman, *Languages of Art: An Approach to a Theory of Symbols* (Indianapolis, 1976), p. 38.
35 Because his son died on a Tuesday, Manaklal always fasts on this day. Both he and his youngest surviving son, Prakash, also fast on *panchami*, the fifth *tithi*, which is associated with Tejaji.
36 The Sanskrit equivalent of this is *akal mrityu*, 'untimely death'.
37 Pierre Bourdieu, *Photography: A Middle-Brow Art* (Cambridge, 1996), p. 34.
38 Alan Trachtenberg, 'Albums of War: On Reading Civil War Photographs', *Representations*, 9 (Winter 1985), p. 1.
39 Ibid., p. 7.
40 Umberto Eco, 'Critique of the Image' in *Thinking Photography*, ed. Victor Burgin (Basingstoke, 1982), p. 38.
41 Pannalal spoke in mixed Hindi-Malwi, but here he used the English word 'original'.
42 Bourdieu, *Outline*, p. 23.
43 A *bigha* is approximately three-fifths of an acre.
44 C. J. Fuller, *The Camphor Flame: Popular Hinduism and Society in India* (Delhi, 1992), p. 57.
45 Bourdieu, *Photography*, p. 24.
46 Kobena Mercer, 'Home from Home: Portraits from Places in Between' in *Self Evident*, exhibition catalogue, Ikon Gallery (Birmingham, 1995), n.p.
47 David MacDougall, 'Photo Hierarchicus: Signs and Mirrors in Indian Photography', *Visual Anthropology*, V (1992), p. 104.
48 Michael O'Hanlon, 'Unstable Images and Second Skins: Artefacts, Exegesis and Assessments in the New Guinea Highlands', *Man*, 27 (1992), pp. 587–608.
49 Mikhail Bakhtin, 'Forms of Time and Chronotope in the Novel' in *The Dialogic Imagination: Four Essays by M. M. Bakhtin*, ed. Michael Holquist (Austin, Texas, 1981), p. 246.
50 Perhaps the best example of this is in the film *Deewar* (Yash Chopra, 1975).
51 Mercer, 'Home from Home', 1995.
52 Sumita S. Chakravarty, *National Identity in Indian Popular Cinema:*

1947–1987 (Delhi, 1996), p. 4.

53 MacDougall, 'Photo Hicrarchicus', p. 104.

54 A. Appadurai, 'How to Make a National Cuisine', *Comparative Studies in Society and History*, 30 (1988), pp. 3–24.

55 Chakravarty, *National Identity*, p. 4.

56 These translations are taken from Rimli Bhattacharya's exceptionally stimulating 'Actress-Stories and the "Female" Confessional Voice in Bengali Theatre Magazines (1910–1925)', *Seagull Theatre Quarterly*, 5 (May 1995), pp. 3–21. Thanks to Raminder Kaur for this reference.

57 Ibid., p. 18.

58 Pitt Rivers Museum, Underwood and Underwood Collection, (49)–3507.

59 Oliver Wendell Holmes, *Soundings from the Atlantic* (London, 1864), p. 148 and *passim*.

60 Krauss, 'Photography in the Service of Surrealism', p. 28.

61 Krauss, 'Photographic Conditions of Surrealism', p. 113.

62 James Clifford and George E. Marcus, eds, *Writing Culture: The Poetics and Politics of Ethnography* (Berkeley, 1986).

63 Krauss, 'Photographic Conditions', p. 107.

64 Ibid., p. 112.

65 Cited by Peter Brunnette in *Roberto Rossellini* (New York, 1987), p. 53.

66 Gerald Mast, 'Kracauer's Two Tendencies and the Early History of Film Narrative' in *The Language of Images*, ed. W. J. T. Mitchell (Chicago, 1980), p. 130.

67 Ibid., p. 150.

68 Phalke's earlier films included *Raja Harischandra* (1913).

69 Suresh Chabria, 'D. G. Phalke and the Méliès Tradition in Early Indian Cinema' in *Light of Asia: Indian Silent Cinema 1912–1934*, ed. Suresh Chabria and Paolo Cherchi Usai (New Delhi, 1994), p. 105.

70 Ibid., p. 106.

71 For a fuller account, see P. K. Nair, 'Looking at a Mythological', *Cinema India* (April, 1992), pp. 32–7.

72 Religious behaviour was commonly observed in cinemas screening *Jai Santoshi Ma*, and these sequences were read by much of the audience as proof of the goddess's power.

73 'Tolerance of overt phantasy has always been high in Hindi cinema, with little need to anchor the material in what Western conventions might recognize as a discourse of "realism", and slippage between registers does not have to be marked or rationalized' (Thomas, 'Indian Cinema', p. 127).

74 Nelson Goodman, *Ways of Worldmaking* (Indianapolis, 1978), p. 94.

75 Wendy Doniger O'Flaherty, *Dreams, Illusions and Other Realities* (Chicago, 1984), p. 317.

76 Norman W. Brown, *Man in the Universe: Some Continuities in Indian Thought* (Berkeley, 1970), p. 42.

77 *Bhagavata Purana*, cited by O'Flaherty, *Dreams*, p. 111.

78 *Matsya Purana*, cited ibid.

79 S. Kakar, 'The Ties That Bind: Family Relationships in the Mythology of Hindi Cinema', *India International Centre Quarterly*, VIII, 1 (1981), p. 17.

80 Jacques LeGoff, *Time, Work and Culture in the Middle Ages* (Chicago, 1980), p. 36.

81 M. Marriott, 'Interpreting Indian Society: A Monistic Alternative to Dumont's Dualism', *Journal of Asian Studies* 36, 3 (1976), p. 194.

82 Mattison Mines, *Public Faces, Private Voices: Community and Individuality in South India* (Berkeley, 1994).

83 Ronald B. Inden, 'Orientalist Constructions of India', *Modern Asian Studies*, XX, 3 (1986).

84 L. Dumont, 'The Functional Equivalents of the Individual in Caste Society', *Contributions to Indian Sociology*, 7 (1965), p. 99. For critiques see M. Mines, 'Conceptualizing the Person: Hierarchical Society and Individual Autonomy in India', *American Anthropologist*, 90, 3 (1988), pp. 568–79; and E. L. McHugh, 'Concepts of the Person among the Gurungs of Nepal', *American Anthropologist*, 16 (1989), pp. 75–86.

85 Joseph S. Alter, 'The Body of One Color: Indian Wrestling, the Indian State, and Utopian Somatics', *Cultural Anthropology*, 8, 1 (1993), p. 49.

86 Parry, *Death in Banaras*, pp. 170, 171. He continues: 'A Brahman who has black teeth, bad nails or is excessively corpulent should be excluded from the feast for Brahmans held on the thirteenth day after death; and nobody with an open wound should act as chief mourner.'

87 This is indeed a service offered by some astrologers who advertise in national newspapers. J. M. Karmakar of Calcutta, the author of *Earology: The Secret Language of the Ears* (Calcutta, 1981), is also able to read external signs, in this case the outer ear.

88 In the English language, 'personality' is used to invoke both an external aura (as in 'she has a vibrant personality' or 'he is completely lacking in personality') and what the *Shorter OED* terms 'distinctive individual character'. In Nagda, *vyaktitva* is used in the former but not the latter sense.

89 These features may also be indicative of social and professional status.

90 R. S. Khare, *The Untouchable as Himself: Ideology, Identity, and Pragmatism among the Lucknow Chamars* (Cambridge, 1984), p. 53.

91 One might expect also to encounter a preoccupation with 'gross' and 'subtle' bodies, but in Nagda this was never raised in relation to photography. See Anthony T. Carter, 'Hierarchy and the Concept of the Person in Western India' in *Concept of the Person: Kinship, Caste and Marriage in India*, ed. A. Oster, L. Fruzzetti and S. Barnett (Cambridge, Mass., 1982), pp. 118–42.

92 I refer here to the dominant tradition that presents the face as a transcendent sign (cf. J. Koerner, 'Rembrandt and the Epiphany of the Face', *Res: Anthropology and Aesthetics*, 12 (1986), pp. 5–32. We have already encountered radically different Western traditions, such as the 'swagger' portrait, which have greater similarities with the twentieth-century central Indian images discussed here.

93 For example, John Tagg, *The Burden of Representation: Essays on Photographies and Histories* (Basingstoke, 1988), pp. 1–3.

94 R. Barthes, *Camera Lucida* (London, 1984), p. 70.

95 Ibid., p. 67.

96 Ibid., p. 71.

97 Ibid., pp. 65–6.

98 Ibid., p. 70.

99 Approximately £6–8 at 1997 exchange rates. Though a small sum for many prosperous Nagda traders, it might be contrasted with agricultural labour rates of between twenty-five and thirty rupees per day.

100 The following are based in my translations of extensive taped interviews in 1991 and 1992.

101 Dan Meinwald, 'Memento Mori: Death in Nineteenth Century Photography', *California Museum of Photography Bulletin*, 9, 4 (1990), p. 8. See also Jay Ruby, *Secure the Shadow: Death and Photography in America* (Cambridge, Mass., 1995).

102 Meinwald, ibid.

103 Barthes, *Camera Lucida*, pp. 70–71.

104 Johann Casper Lavater, *Essays on Physiognomy, Designed to Promote Knowledge and Harmony among Mankind*, trans. Thomas Holcraft (London, n.d.), p. 84.

105 A. Coomaraswamy, 'The Part of Art in Indian Life' in *Coomaraswamy, Selected Papers*, ed. R. Lipsey (Princeton, 1977), I, p. 89.
106 LeGoff, *Time, Work and Culture*, p. 36.

Epilogue

1 Arjun Appadurai, ed., *The Social Life of Things: Commodities in Cultural Perspective* (Cambridge, 1986), p. 36.
2 Nicholas Thomas, *Entangled Objects: Exchange, Material Culture, and Colonialism in the Pacific* (Cambridge, Mass., 1991), p. 208.
3 Stuart Cary Welch, *Room for Wonder: Indian Painting during the British Period, 1760–1880* (New York, 1978), p. 130.

Select Bibliography

Arjun Appadurai, 'The Colonial Backdrop', *Afterimage*, March/April 1997, pp. 4–7.

Roland Barthes, *Camera Lucida*, trans. Richard Howard, London, 1982.

Jean M. Borgatti and Richard Brilliant, *Likeness and Beyond: Portraits from Africa and the World*, New York, 1990.

G. Clarke, ed., *The Portrait in Photography*, London, 1992.

Ray Desmond, *Victorian India in Focus: A Selection of Early Photographs from the Collection in the India Office Library and Records*, London, 1982.

Elizabeth Edwards, ed., *Anthropology and Photography, 1860–1920*, New Haven, 1992.

Wendy Ewald, *I Dreamed I Had a Girl in My Pocket*, New York, 1996.

John Falconer, 'Ethnographical Photography in India: 1850–1900', *Photographic Collector*, V, 1984.

– 'Photography in Nineteenth-Century India' in *The Raj: India and the British: 1600–1947*, ed. C. A. Bayly, London, 1990.

Carlo Ginzburg, 'Morelli, Freud, and Sherlock Holmes: Clues and the Scientific Method', in *The Sign of Three: Dupin, Holmes, Peirce*, ed. Umberto Eco and Thomas A. Sebeok, Bloomington, 1988.

Judith Mara Gutman, *Through Indian Eyes: 19th and Early 20th Century Photography from India*, New York, 1982.

David MacDougall, 'Photo Hierarchicus: Signs and Mirrors in Indian Photography', *Visual Anthropology*, V, 1992.

Christopher Pinney, 'Colonial Anthropology in the "Laboratory of Mankind"' in *The Raj: India and the British: 1600–1947*, ed. C. A. Bayly, London , 1990.

– 'Photographic Portraiture in Central India in the 1980s and 1990s', in *Portraiture: Facing the Subject*, ed. Joanna Woodall, Manchester, 1997.

Stephen Sprague, 'Yoruba Photography: How the Yoruba See Themselves', *African Arts*, III, 1 (1978), pp. 52–60.

John Tagg, *The Burden of Representation: Essays on Photographies and Histories*, Basingstoke, 1988.

Val Williams and Anna Fox, eds, *Street Dreams*, London, 1997.

Clark Worswick, *Princely India: Photographs by Raja Deen Dayal, 1884–1910*, London, 1990.

List of Illustrations

Where known the name of the photographer or artist is given first.

1   Colour publicity photograph issued by Midas Color Studio.
2   Composite print by Suhag Studio, c. 1980. Suresh Panjabi.
3   Composite print by Suhag Studio, c. 1980. Suresh Panjabi.
4   'A Toda Family'. Frontispiece to *A Description of a Singular Aboriginal Race Inhabiting the Summit of the Neilgherry Hills* by Henry Harkness, 1832. Balfour Library, Pitt Rivers Museum, University of Oxford.
5   'A Tudar family in the Neilgherries'. Woodcut in *The Saturday Magazine*, 23 April, 1842. Private Collection.
6   Albumen print labelled 'mufsalman' (Muslim), and leaf skeletons pasted on same sheet, c. 1860s. British Museum.
7   'Photograph by means of which the victim of the "Amherst Street Murder" was identified', from *A Manual of Medical Jurisprudence for India* (2nd edition) by Norman Chevers, 1870. Tipped-in albumen print. School of Oriental and African Studies, University of London.
8   'Kadir Buksh, Khosa. Mussalman landowner. Sind.' W. R. Houghton and H. C. B. Tanner, 1861-2, albumen print. Asiatic Society Library, Bombay.
9   'Amils of Sind. Lohanas in Government employ. Hindoos.' W. R. Houghton and H. C. B. Tanner, 1861-2, albumen print. Asiatic Society Library, Bombay.
10 'Vallabhacharya Maharajas', c. 1863, albumen print. Original portrait image by Narrain Dajee, montage by William Johnson. Plate IV in *The Oriental Races and Tribes, Residents and Visitors of Bombay*, vol. I, 1863. Dr Bhau Daji Lad Museum, Bombay.
11 Narain Dajie, Vallabhacharyas, c. 1862, albumen print. Private Collection.
12 'Nagar Brahmin Women', c. 1863. Original portrait by William Johnson and W. Henderson, c.1857, montage by William Johnson, 1863. Plate III in *The Oriental Races and Tribes, Residents and Visitors of Bombay*, vol. I, 1863. Dr Bhau Daji Lad Museum, Bombay.
13 G. Western, 'A Sannyasi', c. 1860, albumen print. Museum of Archaeology and Anthropology, University of Cambridge (Haddon Collection).
14 G. Western, 'A Fakir', c. 1860, albumen print. Museum of Archaeology and Anthropology, University of Cambridge (Haddon Collection).
15 'A Zemindar. Goojur Landholder. Saharunpoor', albumen print. From *The People of India*, vol. III, 1868. Syndics of Cambridge University Library.
16 'Hindu hookahs illustrating the use of the cocoa-nut and the same copied in other materials', late 19th-century albumen print of museum display. Museum of Archaeology and Anthropology, University of Cambridge (Haddon Collection).
17 'Brinjara and Wife. Itinerant Merchants. Saharunpoor', albumen print. From *The People of India*, vol. III, 1868. Syndics of Cambridge University Library.
18 'Bunnea. Hindoo Tradesman. Delhi', albumen print. From *The People of India*, vol IV, 1869. Syndics of Cambridge University Library.
19 'Khojas' (including Nansi Parpia), montage by William Johnson, 1863. Plate III in *The Oriental Races and Tribes, Residents and Visitors of Bombay*, vol. I, 1863. Dr Bhau Daji Lad Museum, Bombay.
20 G.E. Dobson, 'Group of five young Andamanese women', 1872, albumen print. Royal Anthropological Institute Photographic Collection.
21 Tosco Peppé, 'Juang Girls', 1872 lithograph after Peppé's earlier photograph.

From Edward Tuite Dalton's *Descriptive Ethnology of Bengal*. School of Oriental and African Studies, University of London.

22 'Kota Man's Head', *c.* 1872, albumen print. From J. W. Breeks, *An Account of the Primitive Tribes and Monuments of the Nilgiris*, 1873. School of Oriental and African Studies, University of London.

23 Wiele and Klein, profile and full-face portrait of Toda man, autotype. From W. E. Marshall, *A Phrenologist Amongst the Todas . . .*, 1873. School of Oriental and African Studies, University of London.

24 Johnston and Hoffman, 'Rong – the "Lepcha" of the Nepalese and Indians . . .' from an album commissioned by L. A. Waddell, Royal Anthropological Institute 194.

25 Johnston and Hoffman, 'Khambu or Jimdar of Eastern Nepal – not so typical as No. 30' from an album commissioned by L. A. Waddell. Royal Anthropological Institute 252.

26 'Mehtar (Sweeper)', *c.*1910, postcard. Published by Moorli Dhur & Sons, Ambala Cantt. Private Collection.

27 Page from photograph album *c.* 1925-6, photographs, postcards and newspaper clipping. From the D'Arcy Waters Collection, in the Cambridge South Asian Archive, University of Cambridge, Centre of South Asian Studies.

28 Sergeant Wallace, two Chamars, *c.* 1896, albumen print. Royal Anthropological Institute 2722.

29 Sergeant Wallace, Mallah, *c.* 1896, albumen print. Royal Anthropological Institute 2726.

30 Display of glass eyes, late 19th century, glass set into plaster. Government Museum, Madras. Photo: Christopher Pinney.

31 'Colour Types of M. Broca', 1874, colour photo-lithograph. From *Notes and Queries in Anthropology*, 1874. British Museum.

32 Quantifying the face: collecting anthropometric measurements, late 19th century. Royal Anthropological Institute.

33 Salvador Dalí, *Le Phenomène de l'extase*, 1933. © DEMART PRO ARTE BV/DACS 1997.

34 'Measurement Roll Card', from Colonel H.M. Ramsay, *Anthropometry in Bengal, Or, Identification of Criminals by Anthropometric Measurement and Thumb Impressions*, 1895. British Museum.

35 Maurice Vidal Portman and W. Molesworth, tracings of Andamanese hands and feet, 1894, pencil on paper. British Museum.

36 'Konai's hand, Bengal 1858'. From W.J. Herschel, *The Origin of Fingerprinting*, 1916. Syndics of Cambridge University Press.

37 The Bengal Photographers, cabinet card, late 19th century. Private Collection.

38 Pompeo Girolamo Batoni, *Portrait of a Gentleman*, 1760s, oil on canvas. National Gallery, London.

39 EOS Photographic Company, cabinet card, late 19th century. Private Collection.

40 Obverse of EOS Photographic Company cabinet card. Private Collection.

41 Printed advertisement for Vanguard Studios, Bombay. *c.*1931. From Mahatma Gandhi, *India's Case for Swaraj* (Bombay), n.d. Private Collection.

42 Obverse of Lala Deen Dayal cabinet card, *c.* late 1870s-80s. Museum of Archaeology and Anthropology, University of Cambridge (Haddon Collection).

43 Painted *carte-de-visite*, late 19th century, watercolour on albumen print. Private Collection.

44 Narottam Narayan Sharma, portrait of Mewar prince, *c.* 1930, watercolour on albumen print. Anandalalji Narottam.

45 Lala Deen Dayal, portrait study, modern print from original (broken) negative, late 19th century. Private Collection.

46 Maharaja Sawai Ram Singh II, sadhu, modern print from original negative,

c. 1870s. Sawai Man Singh Museum, Jaipur.

47 Maharaja Sawai Ram Singh II and T. Murray, portrait of Ram Singh, modern print from original negative c.1870s. Sawai Man Singh Museum, Jaipur.

48 Ramchandra Rao and Pratap Rao, woman with photograph album, c. 1900, albumen print on cabinet card. Private Collection.

49 Ramchandra Rao and Pratap Rao, Shivaji Rao flying, c. 1890s, photographic print. Nehru Centre, Lalbag Palace, Indore.

50 Ramchandra Rao and Pratap Rao, Shivaji Rao rowing, c. 1890s, photographic print. Nehru Centre, Lalbag Palace, Indore.

51 Krishna killing Kaliya (film still from D.G. Phalke, *Kaliya Mardan*, 1919). National Film Archive of India, Pune.

52 Ravi Varma, 'Usha and Chitralekha', c.1890, later half-tone from original oil. From S.N. Joshi, *Half-Tone Reprints of the Renowned Pictures of the Late Raja Ravi Varma*, 1911. School of Oriental and African Studies, University of London.

53 Portrait of four unknown males by unknown Ratlam studio, c. 1900, albumen print. Private Collection.

54 'Dadabhai Naoroji, Esq.', 1889, from Sorabji Jehangir, *Representative Men of India: A Collection of Memoirs, With Portraits, Of Indian Princes, Nobles, Statesmen, Philanthropists, Officials, and Eminent Citizens*. School of Oriental and African Studies, University of London.

55 B.P. Wadia, Annie Besant, and G.S. Arundale during internment in 1917. Nehru Memorial Museum and Library, Delhi.

56 Portraits in the Nara Ratna Mandir. Photograph from a brochure published in 1923.

57 Photolithograph showing Ramakrishna, Vivekananda and The Mother with the Dakshineshvar Temple Kali image. Calcutta, 1960s. Private Collection.

58 The late Manohar Singh's driving licence, 1986. Nanda Kishor Joshi. Photo: Christopher Pinney.

59 Manoj Jha, proprietor of Venus Studio, Nagda. Photo: Christopher Pinney.

60 Painter unknown, *Shiv, Parvati, Ganesh and Kumar*, c. 1980, chromolithograph. Associated Calendars.

61 Calendar depicting Shiv and Parvati within the form of a shivling, 1983. Like most calendars this is overprinted with an advertisment by a local company (in this case an Indore spice manufacturer). Private Collection.

62 Composite print by Suhag Studio, c. 1980. Suresh Panjabi.

63 Colour print of village wedding party in the Venus Studio, c. 1988. Ramchandra Suttar, Bhatisuda.

64 Composite print of Pritibala from her wedding album, by Suhag Studio, 1983. Pukhraj Bohra.

65 Composite print of Pritibala and Pukhraj from their wedding album, by Suhag Studio, 1983. Pukhraj Bohra.

66 Composite print from wedding album, by Suhag Studio, c. late 1970s. Dinesh Khandelwal.

67 Colour double exposure by Sagar Studio, c. 1993. Vijay Vyas.

68 Colour print made with a 'multiple image' lens by Sagar Studio, c. 1995. Vijay Vyas.

69 Suresh Panjabi holding a 'Ring Ceremony' card template of the sort used in 1970s and 1980s black and white composite prints. Photo: Christopher Pinney.

70 Khubiram, *Netaji ka Jivan* (The Life of Netaji [Subhash Chandra Bose]), c. 1946, chromolithograph. Bose's biography is pictured within the frame of the Hindi slogan, *Jay Hind* (Victory to India). Private Collection.

71 Composite print from Pritibala's and Pukhraj's wedding album by Suhag Studio, 1983. Pukhraj Bohra.

72 Colour composite print produced by an Indore colour lab for Sagar Studio,

1996. Vijay Vyas.

73 Colour composite print produced by an Indore colour lab for Sagar Studio, 1996. Vijay Vyas.

74 Vijay Vyas, colour collage, 1996, photographs, watercolour and ink.

75 Hand-painted photograph by Suhag Studio, 1991. Private Collection.

76 Bina and Pushpa, c. 1980. Babulal Bohra.

77 Post-mortem photograph, c. 1975. Manoj Khandelwal.

78 Painted memorial image by Sagar Studio, 1996, and original photographic referent, c.1975. Vijay Vyas.

79 Painted memorial image by Sagar Studio, 1996, and original photographic referent, c.1985. Vijay Vyas.

80 Painted photograph of the author, in the style of memorial image, by Sagar Studio, 1993, watercolour on photographic print. Private Collection.

81 Presentation of a photographic portrait of Bhairav Bharatiya to the author in 1983. Photo: Suhag Studio.

82 Studio portrait of Khubchand, former Zamindar of Bhatisuda village, c. 1940. Photo: Christopher Pinney.

83 Manoharlal Bharatiya worshipping a photograph of his father, 1991. Photo: Christopher Pinney.

84 Composite print by Bombay Photo Studio, Ujjain, of Manaklal's son, c. 1965.

85 Pukhraj Bohra displays his earliest photograph album. Photo: Christopher Pinney.

86 Pukhraj, Manoharlal and Rajendra on Juhu Beach, Bombay, c. 1975. Babulal Bohra.

87 Kachru's son's only photograph of his father. Bherulal Kachrulal Ravidas. Photo: Christopher Pinney.

88 Framed colour photograph of Kanvaralal Ravidas touching the feet of his Guru, c. 1990. Kanvarlal Ravidas.

89 Large frame containing black and white and colour photographs belonging to Kanvarlal Ravidas, c. 1985–92. Kanvarlal Ravidas.

90 Photograph of Pannalal Nai's work group in the Engineering Section, GRASIM, c. 1970. Pannalal is standing on the far right. Pannalal Nai.

91 Photograph of Pannalal Nai's son seated in front of painted backdrop of the Taj Mahal, c. 1980. Pannalal Nai.

92 Colour photograph of Pannalal Nai's son holding two bulls on the day of Govardhan puja, c. 1990. Pannalal Nai.

93 Lakshman Motilal's son holding a frame containing photographs collected by his father. Photo: Christopher Pinney.

94 Colour-printed photographic mount of the sort sometimes used in Nagda and Bhatisuda.

95 Bihari's framed colour photo of Pannalal, an ascetic formerly resident in Bhatisuda. Bihari Banjara.

96 Bihari's framed photograph of the talking bull of Aslod. Bihari Banjara.

97 Ramesh Suttar holding a framed colour image of Shri Paramhansji. Photo: Christopher Pinney.

98 Interior of Kesarbai's house, showing chromolithographs and framed images of her husband Ganpat and son Hira. Photo: Christopher Pinney.

99 Hira holding a framed photograph of his late father, Ganpat. Photo: Christopher Pinney.

100 Ramlal holding a framed print of the image that appears here as illus. 99. Photo: Christopher Pinney.

101 Colour print of Hira, c. 1991, overpainted and re-photographed by Sagar Studio. Kesarbai Ravidas.

102 Framed black and white photograph of members of Nagu Ravidas' family taken in travelling studio in Nagda, c. 1980. Nagu Ravidas.

103 Framed black and white photograph of Sitabai's son posing in front of painted studio backdrop. Sitabai Banjara. Photo: Christopher Pinney.

104 Black and white photograph of Kalu Singh posing in front of painted studio backdrop of the Taj Mahal.

105 A Jain couple posing in front of the Taj Mahal. Babulal Bohra.

106 Framed photographs belonging to Govardhanlal Mangilal, *c.* 1965–80. Govardhanlal Mangilal. Photo: Christopher Pinney.

107 Early photographic copy of a chromolithograph of Chandra Shekhar Azad, possibly by Rup Kishor Kapur, *c.* 1931. Nehru Memorial Library and Museum, Delhi.

108 Studio photograph of Chandra Shekhar Azad on which illus. 107 was based, late 1920s. Nehru Memorial Library and Museum, Delhi.

109 Studio photograph of Orissan tribal woman wearing wristwatches, *c.* 1990. Satish Sharma.

110 A female sitter dons Sagar Studio's all-purpose Rajasthani costume, 1996. Vijay Vyas.

111 Two photographs juxtaposed in a Nagda album, *c.* 1985. Babulal Bohra.

112 Guman Singh astride a travelling studio's Royal Enfield Bullet, *c.* 1983. Guman Singh.

113 Sunil Chhajed astride a motorcycle outside a temple. Photographic montage made by cutting two paper negatives, *c.* 1985. Unknown Delhi photographer.

114 Girish Chandra Ghosh giving form to various *bhav*, or emotions. From *Natya-Mandir* (Bengali), ed. Amandenranath Dutta and Munnilal Bannerjee, December 1910. R.P. Gupta, Calcutta.

115 D. G. Phalke's daughter transmogrified into Krishna in *Kaliya Mardan*, 1919. National Film Archive of India, Pune.

116 Black and white montage made by cutting two paper negatives showing Sunil Chhajed and friends inside the mouth of a mythical beast, *c.* 1985. Unknown Delhi photographer.

117 Triple portrait by Suhag Studio, composite print, *c.* 1980. Suresh Panjabi.

118 Over-painted black and white photograph by Venus Studio, 1991, watercolour on photographic print. Private Collection.

119 Black and white photograph, *c.* 1970, given by a client to the memorial portraitist Nanda Kishor Joshi. Nanda Kishor Joshi.

120 Large group photograph from which Nanda Kishor Joshi has been asked to 'extract' two individuals for memorial portraits. Nanda Kishor Joshi.

121 The form on which Nanda Kishor Joshi records clients' requests for memorial portraits. Photo: Christopher Pinney.

122 Nanda Kishor Joshi, memorial portrait of Nandalalji Parmar, 1992, watercolour on photographic print. The original post-mortem photographic referent can be seen on the left. Photo: Chris Pinney.

123 H. R. Raja, Chandra Shekhar Azad and Bhagat Singh, 1982, chromolithograph. Private Collection.

124 Passport-style photographs displayed by street photographers in Chandni Chowk, Delhi in 1992. Photo: Christopher Pinney.

125 Paper negative montages on display in Chandni Chowk, Delhi in 1992. Photo: Christopher Pinney.

126 Photographs displayed in Chandni Chowk, Delhi in 1992. Photo: Christopher Pinney.

127 Vistas at Kishangarh, *c.* 1750. Private Collection.

Index